D0942678

# CULTURE SHOCK!

## San Francisco
### At your Door

Frances Gendlin

**Graphic Arts Center Publishing Company**
Portland, Oregon

Illustrations by TRIGG

This book is published by special
arrangement with Times Media Private Limited
Times Centre, 1 New Industrial Road, Singapore 536196
International Standard Book Number: 1-55868-593-6
Library of Congress Control Number: 2001087503

Graphic Arts Center Publishing Company
P.O. Box 10306 • Portland, Oregon 97296-0306 • (503) 226-2402

Printed in Singapore

# CONTENTS

# ACKNOWLEDGMENTS AND NOTES

San Franciscans, as you will come to understand, are an opinionated lot. My friends and colleagues, many of whom have lived in the city as long as I have, gave me helpful suggestions for material to be included in this book, and they will no doubt either be gratified or disappointed upon reading it. Nonetheless, I thank them all, for I truly did appreciate their comments, their willingness to try new restaurants with me, to drive around neighborhoods in the far reaches of the city, to participate with me in my musings about what makes San Francisco tick, and to read early versions of chapters that I hoped would interest them. In these regards, thanks especially to Fred Allardyce, Eleanor Burke, Helen Cohn, Jean Coyner, Robert Domush, Connie Easterly, Jaem Heath-O'Ryan, Allan Jacobs, Edith Jenkins, Faye Jones, James Keough, Sarah Keough, Andy Leakakos, Peter Linenthal, Ann Magennis, Ronda Nasuti, Les Plack, Candida Quinn, Ken Rosselot, Newby Schweitzer, Linda Sparrowe, Patricia Unterman, Al Williams, and John Zaugg.

Regardless of all our efforts, there may be a mistake here and there concerning a business that might no longer exist, or perhaps a neighborhood that has changed almost overnight. If there are any such errors, they are, of course, mine alone. Some things are sure, however. There is an old joke among chauvinistic San Franciscans, that "one of these days there will be a big earthquake here, and the rest of the country will fall into the sea." But as of the book's publication, at least, the city was intact: the "big one" had not hit and San Francisco and the rest of the continent were still firmly attached. In addition, all the establishments mentioned in the book were going concerns as of this writing, but since San Francisco thrives on change, don't be surprised when looking for a particular address if something newer, more trendy, more crowded, and even more expensive has replaced what once was.

In terms of format, note that important places, organizations, and other entities are shown in **bold face** where they are first described. The few foreign words are in *italics*, but not those that have entered the standard American vocabulary — sushi, for instance. Readers may be surprised to find some spelling inconsistencies and should understand that this has more to do with the current American psyche than a malfunction of the word processor. Although our American ancestors rebelled against the British and forged their own language and spelling of certain words — theater and center, for example — some current Americans seem to find British spelling more elegant. Thus there will appear here a shopping *centre* or two and a *theatre* or two amid the centers and theaters, but no matter how spelled, they are American in every important regard. The same holds true for the word cafe, which is American, but which may variously be spelled *caffè* or *café*, depending on the nationality or whim of the owner of the establishment.

Note that where services or shops will be sought out owing to their location (*e.g.* bakeries), they are listed by the neighborhood closest to them; where the services might be needed no matter where they happen to be (*e.g.* churches), they are listed alphabetically or by category. Also, Internet addresses have been included for information that readers might reasonably want to access online — such as housing options, visa formalities, business advice — but not for every Internet address in this totally cyber-friendly city.

Last, the area code for all telephone numbers in this book is 415 unless indicated otherwise.

# INTRODUCTION

*I have always been rather better treated in San Francisco than I actually deserved.*

— *Mark Twain*

## THE CITY

Welcome to San Francisco, certainly the most open city in the United States, and probably the most tolerant. Here is a city where you can not only openly *be* who you are, you can also try out whatever it is you *want* to be. Just about anything goes, whether you've come to make a fortune or to squander one, whether you've decided to join the established culture or any one of the myriad counter-cultures that call San Francisco home. Some nicknames this freewheeling city has acquired over its two-century history can begin to provide some clues: "The Barbary Coast" during the 1850s, when the rowdy behavior of gold miners recalled the old-time Barbary pirates, to the current, exotic "Baghdad by the Bay." Yet the city for its residents is much more than these appellations would indicate, and other nicknames demonstrate their pride: "The City That Knows How," "The City by the Bay," or as some residents sometimes call it, just "The City," as though it were the only one—as for many residents it is. One nickname it does not ever have—at least for locals—is Frisco. Don't call the city Frisco.

About 16 million visitors a year come to "everyone's favorite city." You might think the reasons obvious: San Francisco is the most beautiful—ravishing—cosmopolitan city in the United States, with clean air, sparkling water on three sides, steep hills rising in the middle of the city, and breathtaking views. Quaint cable cars clang up and down the hills, and exotic aromas waft through the streets. People are outgoing and friendly. And when the sun shines and the sky is bright blue, it feels as though there is no other city in the world where you would want to be. But although beauty and charm stretch far, they do not tell the entire story. The deeper story unfolds as you come to understand the city and its residents, as time goes on.

Some of San Francisco's substance, of course, is in plain view. Perched on the Pacific Rim, the city is home to some of the most important banks and trade institutions in the country. It is the northern focus of Silicon Valley—an area that may not appear on any map, but which nonetheless commands most of the world's high technology development and trade. It is a major port for passenger cruises. It has an outstanding opera company, symphony orchestra, and ballet, plus impressive art museums and galleries. It has excellent universities, hospitals, and research institutions. It has a glorious climate and beautiful parks and promenades from which to enjoy it. And it has some of the best restaurants in the country.

*Photo: San Francisco Convention & Visitors Bureau*

*The Golden Gate, discovered in 1769 by Spanish soldiers, now spanned by the famous Golden Gate Bridge.*

You will find all this in a tourist guide book, and you should keep one handy at first. Such guides describe the city and its unique attractions in detail, review restaurants, and suggest hotels of all categories. Each tries to present the material in an eye-catching manner, and each has its own approach to capturing the spirit of this enchanting city by the sea. All, however, have one thing in common: they are designed for people visiting for a short while — those visitors who think that what they see in a week is what the city is all about.

The truth is that you need to dig a little deeper to see what makes this city hum and to understand why *Money* magazine in 1999 rated San Francisco as the best city in the country to live in. Certainly, many of the things you've heard about Baghdad by the Bay do ring somewhat true. Definitely it is charming at its core, and it is also always vibrant, ever pushing toward the future. And its beauty goes far. That Tony Bennett has sung to the world "I left my heart in San Francisco" is no mistake. But it is also odd, offbeat, perhaps even outrageous in some ways, and its outright iconoclasm contributes a great deal to its delicious mystique. When you begin to understand the city's acceptance of the unusual and its constant search for any next frontier, you'll realize that it wholeheartedly embraces the new, which should be important to you as you settle in.

## GETTING SETTLED

First, you need to get to know your new home. This book, thus, starts where tourism ends and is designed to offer advice and assistance in understanding daily life in San Francisco. Whether your stay is for a month or two or a year or two, the type of information you need for a successful stay is different—deeper and more detailed than that found in tourist guides. How to choose a neighborhood that suits you, how to cope with the difficulties of finding affordable housing or the right school for your children, how best to get up and down the hills or commute in from other towns, how to find out what's going on, and where to find the most interesting markets and shops are just a few examples of basic information that should help you move comfortably onto the San Francisco scene.

With the basics out of the way, you can then meet your neighbors, not as a tourist but as someone who has settled in. Tourists compare San Francisco with their own city and others they have seen, saying, "San Francisco is so European," or "so Asian," or "it's not like home at all." All those things are partly true, yet it *is* like home, because it *is* home to 750,000 San Franciscans—of all ethnic backgrounds, religions, political persuasions, and sexual preferences—who have created a city in their image. San Franciscans, whoever they have decided to be, are in

11

love with their city, adore its views (visual, political, and social), appreciate its eclectic population, and in general are convinced they live in the best, most exotic city in the United States, if not the world. And, sometimes tediously, they never stop telling everybody so.

## A CLOSER LOOK

One way to look at San Francisco is to understand that it is a city of minorities, for no ethnic, religious, or societal group represents more than 50% of the population. Of the 750,000 people who live in the city, there are some 185,000 Asians, 60,000 Latinos, sizeable populations of Russians, Italians, and African Americans, and throughout all these ethnic groups, some 175,000 gays and lesbians. This leads tourist guides to devote separate sections to Chinatown, Japantown, the Mission, or the Castro, describing them to people passing through. But in a guide designed for people moving to San Francisco, no such delineation would help you understand how the city works, for these areas and their peoples are each just a part of the overall scene. Part of what makes San Francisco so interesting is that each separate community is open enough that anyone can feel welcome, but closed enough not to lose its sense of place.

San Francisco, with all its idiosyncrasies, remains a town to take seriously, and people coming for the lifestyle soon find out that "everyday life" rules: if San Franciscans are known for playing hard, they work hard, too. In the soaring office buildings of the Financial District and in the funky warehouses of Multimedia Gulch, workers earn salaries that, on average, are among the highest in the country; more than half of the city's residents hold college or professional degrees. Locals spend their dollars in almost 13,000 retail businesses and eat out in more than 3,500 restaurants, all of which must appeal to a population that demands creativity and excellence—and something ever new to tickle its changing fancy. Even the municipality itself has done its best to make its urban life attractive and rewarding. Where other cities have seen their downtowns collapse as people fled to the suburbs, San Francisco has conscientiously upgraded its own with the Moscone Convention Center, Yerba Buena Gardens, Museum of Modern Art, the light rail system, the refurbished waterfront, and the downtown baseball park.

Businesses that manage to capture the changing, eclectic tastes of San Franciscans tend to succeed. Yet those that do not often see failure as an opportunity to start again, to reinvent themselves with a different—even more novel—approach. The city has always been known for its creative energy, and, since Gold Rush times, for risk taking. If San Francisco is on the cutting edge of technology and finance now, think back to 1853 when Levi Strauss came to San Francisco to work with his brother-in-law. By 1871, they had received a patent for securing the seams of their duck twill work pants with copper saddlebag rivets. Now the headquarters of the multi-million dollar Levi Strauss & Company sits in its own lovely green park along the Embarcadero, and the company provides some 2,000 people with work.

On the other hand, there is a lot not to take seriously in The City by the Bay: the attitude that makes living here downright fun. This book also describes the area's myriad sporting opportunities, the varying Chinese cuisines, and some cultural—and decidedly non-cultural—events. What it cannot impart in detail—but you'll soon find out for yourself—is how the lighthearted and mischievous nature of the city's population contributes to the whole. If Americans have found that it's easier to get along together by avoiding talk of politics, sex, and religion—San Francisco doesn't agree.

Where else would you find the citizens of a city irreverently twitting their rather imperial mayor Willie Brown by referring to him as "His Williness?" Where else would you find a group of gay men forming an "order" of nuns, "The Sisters of Perpetual Indulgence," with one of those men — Sister Boom Boom — running for the Board of Supervisors, as "nun of the above?" (Some 23,000 voted for him, but not enough for him to win.) And where else would the electorate, countermanding the police department's prohibition, vote to allow a friendly policeman to carry a ventriloquist's dummy wearing a little police uniform on his beat? Stories like these abound and quickly go into the city's legends and lore.

## POKING FUN

If some of the humor is not to your taste, just roll your eyes and shake your head, for San Francisco's enjoyment of the outrageous goes far back and it has encompassed all strata of the city's society. Take the case of one Joshua Abraham Norton. Having left San Francisco in the mid-1850s a financial failure, he returned just a few months later styling himself as "Emperor of the United States and Protector of Mexico." His proclamations were published in the newspapers, and he became the "darling of everybody in town." For twenty years Emperor Norton sported regal finery, was fed for free at various establishments around the city, and pontificated at corporation board meetings, and when he died in 1880, he was given a fittingly royal funeral, to which ten thousand of his "subjects" came.

More recently, when Tom Ammiano, a gay politician, was sworn in as President of the Board of Supervisors in 1999, his predecessor gave him a tiara and feathered scepter she had received at the beginning of her term, and declared him "queen of the realm." Acknowledging the change in the city's leadership and in societal tolerance, Ammiano responded by quoting from *The Wizard of Oz*, a movie favorite, "We're not in Kansas anymore."

# GAYS IN THE CITY

In fact, San Francisco from its beginnings was a town of men: the priests and soldiers who adventured north to Alta California to settle the area two centuries ago, the Chinese fleeing famine who sailed the Pacific, and the adventurers who flocked to the California frontier in 1849 seeking gold. That the miners also sought booze and bawdy women convinced some moralists that the city should be punished, and after the 1906 earthquake they thought it had been. But a port city it was and it remained, welcoming more sailors after the opening of the Panama Canal in 1914 and ship workers through World War II. During the war, San Francisco was a military port of embarkation, where eagle-eyed officers mustered out men who were homosexual, many of whom then decided to stay. By the 1960s, when it was said that the 70,000 gays who lived here frequented "decadent" gay bars, national newspapers stereotyped the city as a haven for sexual deviates. Far from having the desired effect, the news spread throughout the country that this was a place for gays and other iconoclasts to feel at home.

Unfortunately, there's still occasional "gay bashing," despite the city's official stance on affording equal rights to domestic partners of any persuasion. Although other "hate crimes" occur from time to time, they are rare, for San Franciscans tend to get along together. That you can find a beautifully dressed society matron at the opera sitting just one row away from a Rastafarian sporting dreadlocks and wearing blue jeans isn't a paradox. That you can find a middle-aged straight couple eating dinner at Asia SF, a transvestite "gender illusion" bar, isn't unusual. That you can find the best martini in town at a bar in the seedy Inner Mission doesn't keep anyone away. And that a distinguished looking gentleman driving a Mercedes can order take-out ribs from a shack called Brother-in-Law's #2, in the problematical Western Addition, means only that he has good taste. (And no one cares that there is no Brother-in-Law's #1.) Since its beginnings, San Francisco has carried the country's vision of the "melting pot" where differing societal cultures and attitudes enrich the whole. What is different about San Francisco is that each mini-society in its own way embraces this vision and is—at least for the most part and on most days—proud of it.

## FAMILIAR PROBLEMS

San Francisco, of course, has its problems. Although the city is often rated near the top of "quality of life" surveys, and its workers earn above the national average, the cost of living in the Bay Area also ranks among the highest in the country and is the highest in the state. This is owing to a lack of affordable housing, brought about by a shortage of housing in general and the willingness of newly wealthy cyberspace professionals to pay high rents and purchase prices. Housing in the Bay Area costs three to four times more than in most areas of the country, and rents run about double the national average. If this trend continues, some people are concerned that San Francisco may in the future become a city dominated by the interests of the rich.

Other top problems are a public transport system that too often does not transport very well and, as in other major urban areas, too many homeless people on the streets. A succession of mayoral candidates has used homelessness as a campaign issue, and those elected come into office with big plans, only to find that, without being able to address the causes of homelessness, few "Band-Aid" solutions work. Mayors also set out to address the problems of transportation and parking, housing, and more serious crime, and occasionally it seems—at least temporarily—that some progress is being made.

San Francisco also has its true undesirable elements, its occasional robberies and muggings. Yet women need take only the usual precautions of staying on well-traveled streets and jogging in the parks with friends on designated paths and in daylight hours. And there should be no reason at all for anyone to enter the Tenderloin alone at night—that area between Union Square and the Civic Center that might in other cities be termed "skid row"— or Hunters Point to the south. Some other neighborhoods that are trendy in some spots—the Mission, Western Addition, Lower Haight—also have their pockets of disagreeable streets and attitudes.

Unlike some other cities, however, San Francisco copes— even triumphs—in its own unique way. The intensity San Franciscans bring to their lives translates into a civic activism that cuts through all levels of society. As Mayor Brown has said, "Here in San Francisco, you have 750,000 people, and each and every one of them is informed, interested, and has an opinion on everything." It is true. Residents volunteer at food banks that feed the homeless, at non-profit cultural institutions, for environmental and political causes, and at organizations for needy kids. They form groups to protest injustice and to call for reform. They insist volubly on better transport, more parking, and more affordable housing. They vote in higher percentages than in most other major cities, and if it appears that San Francisco is to the far side of "liberal," look at the issues and see that residents vote for the very things that make their city work: good social programs, preservation of cultural institutions, improvement of the downtown areas, and equality and tolerance for all.

Where else would all levels of society flock to an elegant restaurant on the Embarcadero (Delancey Street) that is staffed entirely by former drug addicts and felons who now are on their way back up? And where else would a Methodist church in the gritty Tenderloin (Glide Memorial) that feeds hundreds each day at its soup kitchen, also draw San Franciscans of all strata and religious beliefs on Sunday mornings to its rafter-raising, rocking, gospel message? This is San Francisco at its best.

All in all, as you will shortly discover, San Francisco is — and isn't — just like any other city. This book should help you find that out as you begin to settle in. Scout out the neighborhoods it describes, stroll the outdoor markets, experiment with unfamiliar dishes in offbeat Asian eateries. Get to know your neighbors and your colleagues at work, for San Franciscans are welcoming folk. Volunteer in your community. Spend Sundays in one of the city's beautiful parks, go whale watching not far offshore, and find the view that best makes your own heart soar. San Francisco's Convention & Visitors Bureau says that the three commandments when visiting San Francisco are to "explore, experience, and enjoy." When you join long-time San Franciscans in following these "commandments," soon you too will understand what led the city's beloved writer Alice Adams to term San Francisco "the last lovely city." Welcome home.

# CHAPTER ONE

# THE CITY BY THE BAY

## THEN ...

When the founding fathers of the United States were signing the Declaration of Independence in 1776, what is now San Francisco had only recently been discovered and was still wild lands and sand dunes as far as the eye could see. That people date this "discovery" to 1769 by Spanish soldiers looking for Monterey Bay of course doesn't take into account the thousand years the area had already been inhabited by the Miwok, Ohlones, and Wintuns, hunters and gatherers who were quickly subjugated by the intruders and then overcome by their diseases. The soldiers and missionaries coming to control and convert these native peoples very shortly did them in.

One wonders whether those Spanish soldiers were as awed by the beauty of their find as we are today. The sandy shoreline they took over was backed by soaring cliffs. Rocky hills were covered with live oaks and sweet-smelling grasses, and the ever-shifting sand dunes reached toward little inland marshes and streams, borne by the constant ocean breeze. But, as with the native peoples, even the bay we currently see, spectacular as it is, is not as the Spaniards found it, for some 40 percent has been filled in. Bay waters originally came as far as what is now Montgomery Street, lapping at Kearny Street, and the Marina was dredged only for the 1915 Panama-Pacific Exposition. By Francisco and Taylor Streets there once was a protected sandy cove called North Beach, but now all that remains is the name.

The Spanish named the area Yerba Buena, after those herbal grasses on the hills. By 1776, Juan Bautista de Anza and his contingent of 200 Spanish soldiers had established the Presidio, a military fort that commanded a strategic overlook of both ocean and bay, and it remained a base until just the last decade. By 1776, too, the priest Junipero Serra had founded the sixth of the Franciscan missions that stretched up the 600-mile Alta California coast, several years later dedicating what is now known as Mission Dolores, an adobe building which still stands.

Although the areas that are now the Mission District and the Presidio were the first to be settled, the original village of Yerba Buena was founded along the city's easternmost waterfront. Yerba Buena Plaza, now Portsmouth Square in Chinatown, was the heart of the village, which was first Spanish, then Mexican, and finally, in 1846, American. The town also rolled down the hill to the waterfront and today the old brick buildings on streets with names such as Balance Street and Gold Street still attest to their role during the Gold Rush, a century and a half ago.

It may be that only a few buildings remain, but the spirit of a city determined by the 1849 discovery of gold persists today. While thousands of adventurers seeking quick fortunes came to the Sierra foothills, clever merchants of all sorts readied their wares to take some of that fortune for themselves. Restaurants, bordellos, hotels and rooming houses, groceries, baths, and laundries almost exploded overnight around the Barbary Coast. Banks and financial services set themselves up toward Montgomery Street. Levi Strauss started producing his trousers. And a sleepy town that a short while before had counted only 500 residents, one newspaper, and one school became a city of 35,000 on the country's western edge. By the end of the century the city held ten times that number, and today, with the population having doubled once again, the frontier spirit holds—in the soaring steel and glass downtown office buildings, with this century's financial adventurers looking out, this time over the Pacific Rim.

San Francisco's colorful history may not be long—just over 200 years—and earthquakes and fires have taken their toll. But the city's background is still visible in some of its streets, and it is also evident in its residents' continuingly iconoclastic attitudes towards life, focusing on opportunities seen and grasped. Learn how these diverse factors have shaped, and continue to influence, the development of the city: for an excellent history of San Francisco, neighborhood by neighborhood and street by street, look for *San Francisco: The Ultimate Guide* by Randolph Delahanty, and for a detailed overall tourist guide, *Time Out: San Francisco*.

### And Now ...

Today, the City of San Francisco makes up the entire San Francisco County, the most important of the nine counties comprising the Bay Area (see Chapter Two). Yet it is the smallest of the nine, and almost half of it is water, most of it San Francisco Bay. In fact, it is the smallest county in the state. Situated on about the same latitude as Tokyo and Washington D.C., the beautiful, hilly, wind-swept city sits at the top of a peninsula, and it encompasses 46.6 square miles, just seven miles across. Only since 1937 has the city been connected to the north and east by its two famous bridges, and ferries that have long brought people to the city still traverse the sparkling bay. The city itself swells like the ocean tides: each day it accommodates 200,000 workers who commute in from around the Bay, plus, over the course of a year, 16 million visitors—tourists and conventioneers—who filter through.

## CLIMATE

Climate may be a general factor when choosing a place to live, but in San Francisco, and indeed in the extended Bay Area, there are so many microclimates that if weather is important to you you'll find what you want somewhere in the area, from warm and sunny to cool, windy, fog. As to San Francisco itself, surrounded on three sides by cold water and buffeted by strong ocean winds, its bracing, changeable climate makes some people joke that the city does have four seasons—they just take place in a single day.

To be simple about what is truly complex, the city's climate is determined by the ocean, by the 40 or so hills that break or conduct the ever-present wind, and by the long Central Valley that cuts down the middle of the state. When the Central Valley swelters in the summer and the hills are golden and dry, the hot air rises, as it must. This forces cold ocean air to whip through the natural opening of the Golden Gate and across the bay to cool the valley, but bringing to the city foggy days and brisk winds that move bitingly through the streets. Sometimes the fog burns off by late morning and early afternoons can be clear and warm. Other times, however, the fog hovers and doesn't move for days, leaving visitors surprised that they need a jacket in mid-summer and residents amused by the tourists in their shorts and tee shirts, hunched against the wind. Conversely, when the Central Valley cools off in September and October, San Francisco can have its sunniest summer days, perhaps even reaching about 90°F for a day or two. This is when diehard San Franciscans complain the most, bemoaning the absence of their beloved fog.

Winter itself is cool and damp, but not really cold. Although climate is changeable in San Francisco, as it seems to be everywhere, there has traditionally been a winter "rainy season" and a summer "dry season," but there is never a season of snow. Rains can be gentle or hard, but there are rarely thunderstorms, and usually part of each day is clear. With the city rarely seeing temperatures below freezing, flowers bloom outdoors in the winter, athletes play tennis in shorts and sweatshirts, office workers eat their sandwiches at outdoor tables, and people walk to work wearing light wool jackets — perhaps carrying an umbrella, just in case. On those rare occasions when a flake or two of snow does appear, so do the amazed telephone calls: "Did you see the snow?" People love snow, though, as long as it is in the Sierra, so they can head past the vivid green hills, up to the mountains to ski.

Within the city are about a half-dozen separate microclimates, depending on which side of which hill or valley you are looking at and the patterns of the winds. No matter where, however, the climate is bracing and the average annual temperature is about 55°F. Generally, the areas near the ocean are the foggiest and cool, as are the summits of the highest hills. Areas away from the ocean and on the lee sides of hills — the Mission, Noe Valley, and the Castro, for instance — are often sunny when other parts of the city are socked in, and in fact, these are the warmest parts of town, occasionally called "the banana belt." But if having four distinct seasons is important to you, or if you hate wind and fog — or earthquakes — perhaps one of the other counties around the Bay would be your best bet.

## EARTHQUAKES

It's a fact one has to admit: San Francisco sits directly above the intersection of several of the earth's tectonic plates. Earthquakes regularly assault the entire Bay Area, owing to adjustments in the rifts of those tectonic plates: the famous San Andreas and Hayward faults, as well as the San Gregorio, Greenville, and Calaveras faults.

Two major tremblers, two "big ones," are still remembered with awe: the 1906 quake, registering 8.2 on the Richter scale, whose aftermath all but destroyed the city, and the lesser one in 1989, registering 6.9, which caused great damage and a restructuring of the downtown waterfront.

No matter how long people have lived here, everyone talks about the minor occasional quakes, and few people get used to the even rarer large seismic jolts. Despite nervous jokes about "waiting for the big one," the dangers earthquakes present do not seem to drive people away. All recently constructed apartment and office buildings in the city must be "earthquake-proof," which means they should sway during a quake, but not collapse. Nonetheless, earthquakes remain dangerous, and if they worry you, you might consider living away from the faults in one of the other counties of the Bay Area where the risk is perhaps somewhat less. Scientists are now saying there is a 70 percent chance of a major quake within the next 30 years, and although no one knows exactly when the next "big one" will come, everyone knows that it will.

But earthquakes, for better or worse, bring new beginnings. After the 1906 "big one" destroyed some 25,000 buildings in the eastern part of the city, a modern, well-planned city rose from the ashes, today's downtown districts. And after the 1989 Loma Prieta quake damaged the freeway that hid the city's waterfront, San Franciscans—who had always grumbled about tearing the eyesore down—voted to demolish it and to refurbish the five-mile strip, reclaiming it beautifully for their own. Now the Ferry Building and clock tower that withstood both "big ones" are visible at the foot of Market Street and can once again be a symbol of city pride.

## THE CABLE CAR

Although an omnibus system of horse-drawn carriages was in operation in the city by 1851, the heavily laden horses could not climb the steep hills, whose summits remained out of reach as residences. Thus, the availability of efficient, mechanized public transportation—especially the cable car that tourists find so charming today—affected the development of the modern city as much as its climate and geology. In their heyday at the end of the 19th century, some 600 cable cars traversed more than 100 miles of tracks, bringing what had been distant or inaccessible areas of the city into easy commuting distance, transforming those daunting rocky summits—Nob Hill, Russian Hill—into areas of prime real estate. Although the poor had long trudged partway up those and other hills to their small cottages (enjoying the best views in town), the advent of the cable cars opened up the city in a way that nothing else had. The Castro, Diamond Heights, the Mission—all seen as distant from the city's commerce—were suddenly vital neighborhoods of their own. If these working class neighborhoods were not as fashionable as Nob Hill, Pacific Heights, or the then aristocratic residential Van Ness Boulevard, one hundred years later that is certainly no longer the case.

## THINKING ABOUT PLACE

San Francisco is, by and large, a residential city. Its major businesses and largest banks cluster in the eastern portion that became the city's financial hub during the Gold Rush, and the rest—extremely diverse residential areas—maintain the local services and shops that residents of each area would expect. The city calls its widespread areas *districts*, and their names often reflect their history, such as the Mission or Cow Hollow. Yet the hills and their microclimates, and the lifestyle each area has molded, have created myriad little neighborhoods with names of their own, and it shouldn't be surprising that in such an individualistic city each area has its own character, often fiercely defended. Some of these neighborhoods may take more understanding than others, and some may display distinctly different characteristics even just from block to block, such as in the Mission or Western Addition. Many are charming and welcoming. Some are warm, sunny, and relaxed, some foggy, wind-swept, and brisk. Some are known for their social activism, some clearly defined by their ethnicity. Some are slightly more reasonably priced than others, but in any neighborhood worth considering, this will not last. And a very few are not worth considering at all.

Some San Franciscans regard the eastern part of the city as urbanized and progressive and the western parts as more suburban and conservative. It is true that although neighborhoods overlap and populations change as prices rise and older districts become gentrified, people still tend to be characterized by the districts they call home. This, however, is beginning to change. In fact, the ethnic and social population is diffuse, and the city's balanced cultural diversity constitutes a great part of its cosmopolitan charm. While Pacific Heights is known to be predominately wealthy Caucasian, the Castro gay, Chinatown Chinese, the Mission Latino, and the Western Addition African-American, in general there is a pleasing—and sometimes surprising—ethnic distribution throughout the city. Asians are now predominant in the area around Clement Street, and a diverse mix of San Franciscans is moving into the Mission, Bernal Heights, Potrero Hill, and the Haight—all areas where people have been taking advantage of the remaining reasonably priced housing—of course then driving prices up. In fact, young professionals with an abundance of discretionary dollars to spend on housing are moving into all the different neighborhoods, bringing life and color to those areas that were once uninspired, or, conversely, that were once considered only private enclaves of the rich.

As in any city, some districts are more open, beautiful, or well-kept than others. No matter where you live, however, you will have access to open space, whether it is the sandy strips that form the miles of ocean beaches or the beautiful concrete promenade that runs alongside the bay. If the eastern half of the city, destroyed in the 1906 earthquake, does not see as many leafy streets as its western counterpart, green squares and large landscaped plazas nonetheless pleasantly dot the area, allowing spectacular views of the nearby mountains and the often bright blue, almost iridescent, sky. Away from downtown, large parks, both sculpted and wild—Buena Vista, Glen Canyon, McClaren, and Harding—offer as many attractions, in their own ways, as the city's most famous, the Presidio and Golden Gate.

Each district, naturally, abuts at least one other. Sometimes there is a dividing boulevard or street or a hill, but sometimes just a subtle sense of change. In some areas, just one small street will mean the difference between an area you might consider for housing and one you would not. Although all the districts are given a broad look here, some mini-neighborhoods may not be mentioned, only partly for lack of space. Some are too small to describe and, given the overwhelming need for housing, some are in the process of change or rebirth; these may lose their longtime flavor to gentrification, or they may not, if residents of those areas have their way. In any case, change is what San Francisco is all about.

# THE DISTRICTS

### North of Market
Named after the pro-Union rallies held here during the Civil War, **Union Square** is San Francisco's downtown shopping and theater district. Although there are some pleasant rental apartments north of Geary and on the southern foothill of Nob Hill as it heads toward Polk, others may be shabby, and some may be too close to the seedy Tenderloin, which stretches out toward Polk Street. Nonetheless, reasonable rents are drawing a younger, student population that finds access to public transportation convenient.

A century ago this area that nestles around the 2.8 acre park was wealthy residential, but when the cable car made the steep hills more accessible, the wealthy moved up or out toward the new elegant residential district along Van Ness. Yet the high-quality shops and artisans that had served the residents stayed on when the neighborhood changed, and after the 1906 fire,

27

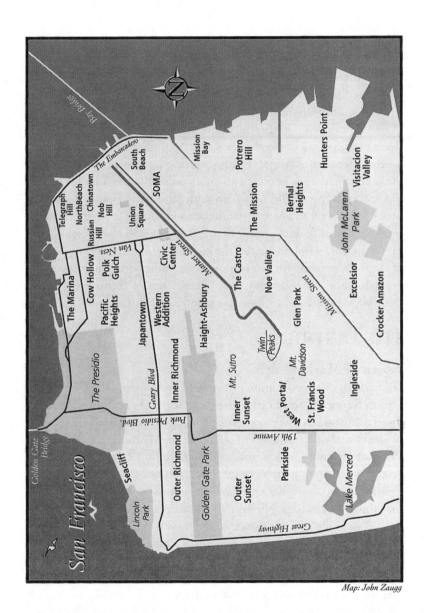

Map: John Zaugg

commerce moved back as soon as it could.

Today the pleasantly landscaped green square is ringed by luxury hotels and modern department stores; although most of the original shops are long gone, a few—such as Shreve's Jewelers—still exist. Hotels and theaters cluster near Geary, and chic restaurants that cater to both tourists and locals nestle in the side streets, along with small, interesting boutiques.

Until recently this vibrant downtown district stopped abruptly on the south at Market Street, but now it heads well across to what is known as SOMA (South of Market Area), embracing the Museum of Modern Art, the spectacular Yerba Buena Gardens entertainment complex, and the Moscone Convention Center. Restaurants and hotels are opening up, and this area is becoming more exciting day by day. To the west, however, Union Square is bordered by the Tenderloin, a seedy area of low rents and transient residents. New Asian immigrants, especially the Vietnamese, are bringing businesses and ethnic restaurants to this grubby area that stretches out toward the **Civic Center,** but improvement is slow.

Straddling Van Ness Boulevard, the Civic Center, with its beautiful Beaux Arts buildings, is the city's center for government and culture. It is interesting that almost a century after the 1906 fire destroyed it, the Van Ness corridor is once again becoming an upscale residential area, with its new condominiums, supermarket, multi-screen theater, and chic restaurants in all directions.

Stretching east to the Bay from Union Square is the **Financial District**, the "Wall Street of the West." As people hurry down the windy corridors of Montgomery and Sansome Streets, they probably don't think about the early days of San Francisco, when everything east of Kearny was mud flats, and the waters of the bay came up to what is now Montgomery Street. Having solidified its hold on the city's commerce during the Gold Rush, the Financial District (along with Los Angeles) is now the Western capital of the Pacific Rim, and some 300,000 people work here in about 50 million square feet of office space. The Financial District—with just a few steel-shell buildings remaining from before the 1906 earthquake—is home to almost all of the city's modern high-rise office buildings.

Here, however, the wind can whip through the concrete canyons, and here quite often is a "neighborhood" deserted when the corporate types go home after work. Some restaurants thrive on lunchtime customers and close early in the evenings (except in upbeat Belden Street), and a few close on weekends. But because so many people work in this area, it is filled with little treasures of restaurants and shops; the closer to Union Square, the more expensive they become. There are one or two mixed-use high-rise buildings—offices below, apartments above—but true residential districts are within easy walking distance in any direction except east.

To the west, **Nob Hill** is closest. Perhaps the best known of the city's hills, Nob Hill still houses some of San Francisco's wealth, but not in any of the palaces ostentatiously constructed at the end of the last century by San Francisco's "Mother Lode" and railroad tycoons. The opulent lifestyle that allowed for 50-room homes came to an end in 1906, and today only one old mansion remains, a private club whose facade allows us a glimpse at what once was.

Today, residents at the summit live in elegant apartment buildings, sharing the impressive views with Grace Cathedral and upmarket hotels. The little park in the middle holds a playground for the area's children, but except for this slight nod to residents of this expensive aerie, conveniences for daily living are found down the hill.

Until the end of the 19th century, Nob Hill was too steep for horse-drawn carriages, and it was workers who built little cottages along the lower slopes. But although cable cars allowed the tycoons to claim the summit, after the 1906 earthquake most rebuilt on safer terrain. Small frame apartment buildings began to appear, and these buildings—refurbished and modernized—remain

*The summit of Nob Hill.*

convenient today for people working in the Financial District or Chinatown. High-rises appeared at the summit in the fifties, but here, as in other areas, height limits were instituted, limiting the amount of skyline that could be blocked. Now there is a six-story limit on new construction, but that doesn't affect those fortunate few who are already there, enjoying the view.

The 1-California bus has made this steep hill convenient for Asians, as Chinatown expands up Clay and Sacramento from the east. On the west, low-rise apartment buildings line the narrow streets heading down to the Polk Gulch corridor. You probably won't find housing on the top of Nob Hill itself, although on its slopes apartments do come available.

Down Nob Hill to the north is **Chinatown**. You may not want to live here, but no discussion of San Francisco would be complete without a bow to this colorful, iconoclastic area that — the Mission and military Presidio aside — formed the original

31

Photo: San Francisco Convention and Visitors Bureau

*The Chinatown Gate.*

settlement of Yerba Buena and that in its own way dominates much of the spirit of the modern city.

Chinatown, until recently contained from Bush to Broadway, and from Kearny to Powell, now crosses over Broadway into North Beach and up Russian and Nob hills. The Chinese community has also expanded out to Clement Street and into the Sunset, but Chinatown remains home base, and no matter where people live, many come back on a Sunday for shopping and a family lunch. Although residents complain that their traditional area is becoming too homogeneous in its commercial effort to lure tourists, Chinatown is still a crowded warren of streets and alleys, of small Chinese-speaking shops and apartments above them, perhaps with an open window and laundry waving in the breeze. In fact, behind some of the shabby, unmarked doors in the little alleyways is where the most interesting—and quietly private—business of this sometimes secretive community takes place. The tantalizing aromas from the restaurants and the inexpensive markets crowded with elderly women carrying their grandchildren on their backs in cloth sacks also conspire to give Chinatown an air of other-worldliness.

Although only about half of the city's 150,000-strong Chinese population lives here, this 24-block area is one of the city's most densely populated districts. Its constant bustle is perhaps at least slightly reminiscent of the original Chinese quarter founded in the 1850s, when Cantonese immigrants flocked to these shores. During the Gold Rush they were cooks, launderers, and shop-keepers, even brothel keepers, and then workers on the railroad. By 1881, some 25,000 Chinese were resident in the city, and so many were coming to the United States that the Chinese Exclusion Act of 1882 was passed to stop the influx, meaning that until its repeal in 1943 the Chinese population became older—and poorer. Only in the post-World War II period did immigration begin once again and did the Chinese come again to Chinatown.

The main local shopping streets are to the north, on Stockton and Powell, which leaves Grant to the tourists looking for gifts. But the spiritual heart of the community is Portsmouth Square, which as Yerba Buena Plaza was originally only one street away from the shoreline. Until commerce moved south to Montgomery Street, this was the center of town, and it was at Yerba Buena Plaza that the discovery of gold was announced.

Rents in Chinatown are reasonable, but conditions may not be particularly agreeable. This is not the cleanest part of the city by any means, nor is there anything leafy green. Many of the area's renters are poor and elderly, speaking no English, and they often live in substandard housing without knowing the recourse to city agencies that could help them, exploited by landlords who have little incentive to make improvements to their holdings. Yet this is certainly the most exotic part of the city, and although you might

33

easily enjoy living nearby—along the Embarcadero, up Russian Hill, or in North Beach—think carefully if Chinatown appeals. Chinatown is another planet, deep in the heart of San Francisco.

Down along the bay, as the working piers along the eastern edge of the city head north toward Pier 39 and Fisherman's Wharf, which draw 10 million tourists each year, the refurbished **North Embarcadero** becomes more pleasantly residential on its inland side. Long in decline, the area took on a new life in the 1960s, when an old produce market was demolished and warehouses were spruced up to hold offices, television studios, and art galleries. At Jackson Street, the Golden Gateway Center added more than one thousand apartments and townhouses, creating an instant neighborhood. Expensive though it is, the Golden Gateway is convenient to the massive four-building office, shopping, and restaurant complex of the Embarcadero Center—an extension of the nearby Financial District—which is almost a city in itself.

This flat land-filled area was once the Barbary Coast, its dance halls, boarding houses, and bawdy night life catering to the boisterous goldminers down from the hills. Now the surviving red brick buildings dating from the 1860s have been turned into antique shops and art galleries in an area called the Jackson Square Historic District, and with restaurants, cinemas, and theaters open late, the area is once again offering somewhat more sedate succor to those looking for fun.

There are several open plazas in this sunny area, in addition to the splendid promenade that runs along the bay. Sidney Walton Park, with its sculptures and fountain, brings office workers to its grassy knolls at lunchtime. Overlooking the park are the Golden Gateway Commons, spacious red brick condominiums built around private landscaped walkways. These town homes are sometimes rented out by their owners; when they come up for sale, the prices are extremely high.

Farther along, nestled below the eastern granite outcropping of Telegraph Hill, several condominium complexes bring quiet residentiality to an area that was enhanced by the construction of Levi Strauss Plaza, with its fountains, streams, and grassy lawns. Some of these condominiums along Lombard or Montgomery are rented out by owners and some come up for sale, and the prices are what one would expect. Unfortunately, as yet, there are few commercial services, and residents must head over to Bay Street or back toward Jackson for supermarkets and pharmacies. Up Telegraph Hill — on the sheer eastern side that no car can traverse — are the Filbert Street Steps, a landscaped walkway with charming clapboard cottages along lanes and terraces that might seem precarious, but that (at least so far) have survived earthquakes, rains, and whatever else the San Francisco climate (or politicians) might inflict.

## Two Hills and a Valley

Over the top of the hill is **North Beach**, a sunny valley nestled between the western slope of **Telegraph Hill** and the eastern edges of **Russian Hill**. One hundred and fifty years ago there were a few docks and a little beach along the northern waterfront. Fishermen lived close by, some Basque and Portuguese, but primarily it was the Italians in what came to be called Little Italy who gave the area its flavor, one that still remains. Italian restaurants, coffee houses, bakeries, and delis draw the crowds, and old Italian-American gentlemen sit in the sun at Washington Square, the heart of the community, watching the passers-by. That this working class area of cheap rents was also home to the "beat" poets in the fifties brought a rather bohemian feel to the area, but prices today are no longer cheap. And the atmosphere has also changed: Chinese restaurants and groceries have crossed their erstwhile boundary at Broadway, and now along Stockton they compete noisily for attention, while in the early morning Washington Square is filled with Chinese practicing tai chi. The result is an agreeable mix, one that tourists and San Franciscans appreciate to their full. North Beach is one of the most treasured areas of the city.

35

As a residence, North Beach is popular with people who work in the Financial District, as it is only a 15-minute walk away. Reasonably priced low-rise apartments hover above interesting shops and restaurants. On the east, the quiet residential neighborhood of Telegraph Hill rises slowly, and as it does, many of the three- and four-story apartment buildings command excellent views. Long-term residents live in cottages or in old buildings that new arrivals would love to get their hands on to refurbish. Some do become available from time to time, and the prices vary, according to the view and the work needed. Not all of these buildings have garages, and finding parking on North Beach streets is always a challenge.

Heading up the winding road to Coit Tower, private homes of all sizes and apartment buildings command prices that are as steep as the hill; the hill is on bedrock and its buildings less liable to damage during earthquakes, and the views can be grand. The old beach itself may be gone, but beach town it remains: keep your windows open at night and you'll hear the sea lions barking at Pier 39 and the foghorn piercing through.

This holds true, too, for parts of steep Russian Hill, which climbs up from North Beach to the west. Its location couldn't be better. With trendy Polk Street on the west, North Beach to the east, Cow Hollow down past the western slope, and Chinatown to the south, Russian Hill is ringed by every convenience one could want. If the area took its name from the Russian seal hunters who 150 years ago were said to have buried their dead up here, the area is now very much alive.

People don't talk much about Russian Hill, and few tour buses labor up the hill—which suits the residents very well. The businesses here cater to locals, and in general this is a rather peaceful district with many enchanting pockets of almost-hidden charm. On Russian Hill, with its varied residential opportunities, you can probably find something you want. What everybody finds is a well-kept residential community with an active community

*Photo: San Francisco Convention and Visitors Bureau*

*The eastern side of Telegraph Hill is too steep for roads and cars.*

37

association to keep it so. People may live in small apartments above neighborhood shops, in large buildings that push up against the fog, in luxurious condominiums on little landscaped lanes, or even in single-family homes—small, large, or enormous—that persist despite the desire of development to encroach. Some streets have Mediterranean villas or simple redwood homes, and some cul de sacs even have houses with gardens in front. Russian Hill seems to have it all.

## West of Van Ness

Past North Beach and the commercial **Fisherman's Wharf** area, the exquisite, residential **Marina** sits on marshland dredged for the 1915 Panama Pacific Exposition celebrating the opening of the Panama Canal. If the Exposition was designed to show the world that the city was once again on its feet after the 1906 earthquake, the quake of 1989 that damaged so much of this landfill district showed how fragile that footing actually was. Nonetheless, defying nature's whims, most Marina residents decided to stay, rebuilt their homes and are today enjoying spectacular views of the Bay, the Golden Gate Bridge, and the distant hills—at least until the next "big one" hits.

Looking majestically out over the broad, grassy strip of Marina Green, a line of elegant Mediterranean-style private homes stands as entry to the peaceful, often fog-shrouded neighborhood within. Grand stucco houses, smaller homes, and gracious Art Deco apartment buildings that impose on broad, winding, windy streets are home to a smart set of young professionals—many singles but also some families—who enjoy the proximity to the Marina Green, the eucalyptus-fragrant Presidio, and also to Chestnut Street, the Marina's vibrant commercial and nightlife scene. The area here may be flat, but the rents are quite steep.

Across Chestnut and the broad, commercial Lombard Street, **Cow Hollow** bridges the Marina below to aristocratic Pacific Heights above. An area of tranquil dairy farms 150 years ago, the restaurants and nightspots of Union Street—from Franklin to Divisadero—are today a playground for the upscale singles crowd. Interesting apartments and homes line just about every street, and climbing the steep hill up to Pacific Heights, the houses along Green and Vallejo are generally Victorian. On Union Street itself, the old Victorians have been converted into offices and trendy shops.

Combined, the Marina and Cow Hollow are great areas for living and hanging out. It's hard to park in these areas, so if you're interested in living here, make sure of a garage for your car. Yet services, supermarkets, and shops are all within walking distance, and public transportation to the Financial District is so convenient that you may not need a car.

Just up the hill, **Pacific Heights** is the most expensive residential district in the city. In Pacific Heights, luxurious apartment buildings near Broadway and Fillmore quickly give way to beautiful single-family homes, and even these give way—as the broad streets head west toward Divisadero and Presidio—to the exquisite mansions of the truly rich. The tranquil, empty streets climb hills and dip into valleys, making the outer part of Pacific Heights a rather removed enclave, with little to disturb its serenity. Once seen as almost a suburb of San Francisco, in places the area does feel remote. Properties occasionally come on the market here, and the prices soar above the unbelievable.

Yet streets to the sides of Fillmore, although still decidedly Pacific Heights in character, see rental apartments nestled among large private homes. This area is less removed, more in touch, as residents are seen with their children at Alta Plaza or Lafayette Park, or walking dogs. Upper Fillmore Street itself, from Washington to Pine, is becoming trendier by the day, with restaurants, chic boutiques, an international cinema, a high-quality supermarket, and crowds of people strolling and browsing the shops.

An extension to the west, **Presidio Heights**, is perhaps slightly less aristocratic in demeanor than Pacific Heights, but the grand, well-landscaped houses lining Clay, Washington, and Jackson nonetheless offer extremely gracious living in the heart of the city, with tree-lined streets, few passers-by, and the security that a rather suburban lifestyle might provide. Proximity to shopping in Laurel Village and to the Sacramento/Presidio intersection make the area feel connected to city life, while the leafy Presidio and its edge of Mountain Lake Park make it feel less so. Apartment buildings ring the edges, but vacancies are rare and prices are high. The beautiful houses do come up for sale from time to time; they sell quickly and well.

Out beyond Arguello (technically the dividing line into the Inner Richmond) the atmosphere of wealthy tranquility continues on the avenues east of Lake, with large single-family homes, some of which are divided into flats. Certainly **Presidio Terrace** is one of the most exclusive and beautiful enclaves in the city.

Starting at California and reaching to Geary are the almost hidden, overlapping communities of **Laurel Heights** and **Jordan Park**, whose broad, clean streets are often swept by fog and wind. Quiet neighborhoods of apartments and private homes, they are rather underrated, except by those fortunate enough to live there.

## Moving South

The **Western Addition** is one of the districts you should know well before you consider making it home. Although parts of it — near the Panhandle (a green belt leading to Golden Gate Park) or upcoming Hayes Valley, Alamo Square, or the Lower Haight — may offer pleasant homes and welcoming communities, the entire area is in transition and has always been so, in one way or another. Its image and population makeup change, but the area starting south of Geary, extending to the Panhandle, and centering between Fillmore and Divisadero has long been controversial, riddled by problems and perhaps only now on the way to some solution.

Originally **Japantown** (to the east of that great concrete swath called Geary Boulevard) was considered a part of this district, but now it has a character of its own. By the end of the 19th century, while the Chinese population was diminishing, the Japanese population increased. Many Japanese immigrants lived south of Market, but others moved out to the Western Addition, buying small houses and settling in the area they called *Nihon-jimachi*, or "Japanese people's town." After the Chinese Exclusion Act, the Japanese bore the brunt of racism, setting the atmosphere for Order 9066, during that infamous period of World War II, when Japanese Americans were sent to "relocation centers," forcing them to abandon their homes.

By 1942, ship workers—many African Americans—found empty buildings and low rents. Ultimately the Western Addition became known as a "black neighborhood," and when the Japanese came back, most settled in the Richmond and the Sunset. Only a small percentage of the city's 12,000 Japanese lives in Japantown now, separated from the rest of the Western Addition by Geary's concrete. But the area is once again the central focus of the community: the 5-acre Japan Center shopping, cinema, and restaurant complex at Post and Fillmore draws people from all over, but *Nihonjimachi* remains firmly and locally Japanese.

Across Geary, the Western Addition was an area that had long been poised to go downhill. Fillmore Street near McAllister, the commercial center of town after the 1906 devastation, was more or less abandoned by 1912, when commerce moved back downtown. The lovely 1890s Victorians on Alamo Square—and just about all the others—went to seed. Eventually the area became known only for its shabby housing projects, dilapidated homes that lined the once-tranquil streets, and for crime and drugs, which it still has in some small pockets.

Finally, urban renewal stepped in, as did people looking for affordable homes. The Victorians on the once again chic (but not always tranquil) Alamo Square have been restored to their brightly colored glory. The development of a shopping center and several large modern apartment complexes just south of Geary are bringing more stability to the area, and people throughout are sprucing up apartments and single-family homes. Restaurants of all levels are becoming popular, and more services are moving in.

Some streets remain rough, but others are cleaning themselves up. On the eastern edge of the district, **Hayes Valley,** which was formerly known for crime-ridden housing projects and drugs, is a neighborhood that blossomed almost overnight after the demolition of the freeway that loomed over it. Now, stretching out to Octavia Street, it is home to little restaurants, boutiques, art galleries, and apartments that are being refurbished, and it is becoming both an extension of the Civic Center and a lively neighborhood in itself.

## South of Market

**South Beach**, as the eastern edge South of Market is coming to be known, is an important area to watch. After the "big one" of 1906 destroyed what had been a wealthy residential district, South of Market was left to wither, becoming a seedy area of industry, shipyards, and cheap rooming houses; this atmosphere only increased during World War II with the influx of men who came to work in the yards. Now, however, modern entrepreneurs have found this frontier—starting at Mission Street and moving south past the old dockyard areas of Mission Rock and China Basin— and San Franciscans are once again moving back into the sun. The demolition of the freeway that obscured the view of the waterfront allowed the development of a spectacular promenade along the Bay, and this plus a new light-rail transportation network has made apartment living in this area both convenient and fun, a chic neighborhood that will soon take on a new life of its own.

Old warehouses are being converted into residential lofts or artisans' studios, and scruffy empty lots are being developed. Rental and condominium complexes now line the waterfront, with more to come. Prices vary wildly. The Rincon Center, once the main post office, has long been a moderately priced rental residential and commercial complex, but just a few streets away, the expensive condominium in the old Hills Brothers coffee factory sets a different tone, and new residential complexes—both rental and condominium—are not cheap. Although the new baseball stadium has brought trendy businesses in, currently there are few services for a residential population—no supermarket-pharmacy complex, for example—and some areas remain deserted at night. There is no doubt that this will change, as people increasingly flock to South Beach. Fueled by the influx of a new set of professionals to the area, those who have caused the area just a few streets inland around **South Park** to be referred to as Multimedia Gulch, this entire area is on the way up.

More is yet to come at **Mission Bay**, past China Basin and Pacific Bell Park, at a new development that is already beginning to retake a wasted industrial area between Potrero Hill and the bay. This sunny area that was long ago the hunting grounds for the native peoples will eventually hold some 6,000 homes, schools, parks, and stores, all anchored by a 43-acre campus of the University of California, San Francisco. It encompasses an area called **Central Waterfront** and is just beyond the Mission Creek community of houseboats, whose residents are fiercely protective of their neighborhood and have successfully sought legal protection so that they may stay.

Between Third and Fifth streets, in a reclaimed area now called **SOMA,** the huge Moscone Convention Center, the beautiful Yerba Buena Gardens, the Sony Metreon entertainment complex, and the Museum of Modern Art have become a southern extension of Union Square. Although these streets are always full of people, Fifth Street is currently a kind of boundary, as trendy South of Market disappears, and streets moving west toward South Van Ness are solidly commercial. Repair shops, wholesalers, light industry, and automobile garages line the uninspired streets, still solidly entrenched despite the steady encroachment of modern life. Factory outlet stores come and go, and several enormous

43

discount chains—Costco, Office Max, Bed Bath and Beyond—have established their large centers here. Although there are popular nightspots here, some of the streets are unwelcoming after dark.

This holds true of the neighboring **Mission District**, where in several sections crime rates are high. This is one of the sections of town that you should understand well before choosing: some pockets of the Mission are charming and some will be charming soon, but others are not charming at all.

Yet this is where it all started, and where, after more than 200 years, it seems to be starting once again. Since the Spanish priests established their mission here in 1769 the area has maintained a Latin tone, and despite waves of other nationalities that have left their mark on the Mission, Latino it remains. Some 60,000 people currently live in the Mission, in a melting pot of races and nationalities, yet it is the 60 percent Latino population that gives the area its colorful, uninhibited flavor.

Mission Street, which centuries ago linked Mission Dolores to the port at Yerba Buena, is the city's longest; as it cuts to the southwest, it takes on the character of each surrounding neighborhood. Here it is a Latino main street, with businesses displaying their wares on the sidewalk, *taquerias* offering inexpensive meals, and neighborhood folk volubly carrying on an outdoor life. The 24th Street intersection is the heart of the *barrio*. Many of the side streets are uninspired, with three-story, bay-windowed flats and other low-rise apartments perched over the neighborhood stores. Although now in the process of a great change, this has long been—and still is—a poor, working class area. Some streets are noisier and dirtier than others, and occasionally there are turf battles between gangs of differing nationalities.

This wasn't always a poor neighborhood: toward the end of the 19th century, it was solidly middle class. Yet this was one area that did not benefit from the advent of the cable car, for when the hills became accessible, many people moved up. As industry developed near the waterfront, Irish, German, and Italian workers flocked to this sunny area from which they could walk to work. Although the area had been international for decades, what solidified it as Latino was the establishment of international fruit and coffee companies that dealt with Latin America. Many people think of the district as solely Mexican, yet from the early 20th century it has had a mix of Latin cultures. Unfortunately, despite the bilingual ballots and campaign materials, this neighborhood has traditionally voted less than many others, and its political clout has been low.

Now, however, the Mission has been rediscovered by San Franciscans, especially by cyberspace entrepreneurs, who see an area ripe for investment and for refurbishment of old, decaying houses. The Mission is a booming town.

Drive around the district and you will be convinced. Hundreds of restored large Victorians and small bungalows line side streets between Valencia and Guerrero. See well-maintained grassy Dolores with its Canary Palms, Fair Oaks with its Chinese elms, and streets such as Capp Street or Hill Street with Italianate Victorians on one side and Stick Victorians on the other. Here a few are already brightly restored, others no doubt soon will be. Chula Lane to Abbey Street is a cul-de-sac of Victorians as well. Crossing over Cesar Chavez, the Precita Park area that backs up on Bernal Heights Park is a community of small homes on short streets that is suburban in feel. These are all areas new home buyers are finding, and when you look around you'll see beautifully restored homes perching majestically over some that look as though they would fall over in the next breeze, and new apartment complexes rising in any inch of space.

Rents and purchase prices in the Mission may still be low in comparison to other parts of town, but they are quickly climbing. Chic non-Latin restaurants, hip bars, galleries, and charming boutiques are following the money, raising prices even more, especially around Inner Valencia, which in its current trendiness is

45

now sometimes called Valencia Gulch. Some traditional businesses are being forced out by the rise in rents. In addition, the rent for a two-bedroom apartment may now approach $1,800, and this may ultimately mean a displacement of low-income families. But not yet, and the Mission remains a mixture of cultures like nothing else in the city, for better and for worse. Again, if this area appeals to you, make sure you understand it well.

East of the Mission, sunny **Potrero Hill** has traditionally been a working class district, removed from San Francisco's downtown more in spirit than in distance. Few early tourists braved the hill and the wind, and in fact, there was little to explore in what was a rather sedate, residential quarter settled by Scottish and Irish shipbuilders. Yet a few decades ago, as prices around the city escalated, this area became ripe for gentrification. Now artists and professionals, straight and gay couples, and young families are mixing pleasantly with old-timers in a neighborhood that is viewed as an easy commute to the Financial District and Multimedia Gulch. Houses here are in demand, especially those "fixer-uppers" that then increase in value, although people who come to live on Potrero Hill tend to stay. A rather iconoclastic ambience persists, but for how long?

Although industrial sites, furniture shops, and offbeat businesses dominate the northern flats, local commerce is clustered up and down the 18th Street hill. Residential areas that follow the hill's contours seem quiet, and lining the leafy streets are small clapboard houses, large spaces converted into lofts, multi-story Victorians, attached single-family homes, and apartment buildings—a pleasant mix that looks sunnily out over other parts of the city that may already be enveloped in fog. Potrero Hill is bordered on the east by several public housing projects, and their proximity to the hill has contributed over the years to robberies and auto break-ins. Yet, a new condominium complex is transforming the southern section near 24th and Wisconsin, and ongoing building and restorations are making this area increasingly attractive. Potrero Hill is the kind of neighborhood for which its residents swear they would never live anywhere else.

There are no supermarkets or banks on the hill, but the Potrero Center down on the flat at Potrero Boulevard is becoming a neighborhood hangout. Multimedia Gulch is quickly expanding out here, and its proximity to the Mission makes some people call it Baja Mission; but except for the hilly Utah Street with its little houses, this area is not residential—yet. What much of it is, at least today, is a superficially arid stretch of warehouses and old buildings—that inside house some of the city's newest restaurants and breweries, avant-garde theaters, and multimedia businesses. It will be interesting over the years to see which of the districts claims it as its own.

## The Castro and Noe Valley

Certainly no discussion of San Francisco would be complete without some understanding of the **Castro.** In San Francisco geography it is actually Eureka Valley, although no one calls it that any more. Originally part of a large ranch owned by José de Jesùs Noe, whose name remains on the next valley over, this colorful district that begins around Market and 16th Street, and climbs up the steep hill to its south, is known simply as the Castro, although little of the Castro is simple at all.

Until the end of the 19th century, this was one of those hilly areas that was seen as remote by San Francisco's elite, and so it remained rural and agricultural longer than its neighbors closer in. But when the cable car made the hill with its 18.4 percent grade habitable, real estate speculators laid out a grid of streets, built Victorian houses and peak-roofed cottages and sold them to the working class Irish, Scandinavians, and Germans, who created a traditional Catholic neighborhood—or so they thought.

Look at the Castro today. To outsiders it may look like the city's "gay ghetto," but to most San Franciscans it is much more than that. It truly is a small town with its own set of urban pleasures

47

and problems, its local services and shops, its particular sense of what a community should be. Look at the bright, rainbow-colored flags waving from windows, and you will understand this community's pride. Both light-hearted and serious, this is a community that will no longer be anything but bold.

Some of the Irish population still lives in the warm, sunny Castro, but most moved away as the neighborhood changed, leaving the then-shabby Victorians their families had inhabited for almost a century. And the white-collar workers and professionals stepped in, refurbishing the houses, setting up shops. This is what gregarious Harvey Milk did in the seventies, and his subsequent rise in city politics and tragic assassination drew together what had been a rather disparate community, one that has stood its ground ever since. Do not underestimate its political clout; politicians now understand that, like everyone else, gays need public transportation, affordable housing, and reasonable zoning laws. Unlike everyone else, however, they often get out to vote as a bloc. Now, although gays—like all San Franciscans—live anywhere they can afford, the Castro is the community's spiritual and political home. Castro Street is bustling with men doing their daily shopping and errands, cruising, frequenting the late-night clubs, or going to the Castro Theater, along with other San Franciscans who come for the film festivals and for the trendy restaurants nearby.

As a residential area, the center of the Castro is a sunny valley. Steep hills shelter the small houses, and flowers bloom in backyard gardens or in pots on the sunny decks. As the streets rise steeply toward Twin Peaks, the homes become larger—Victorians and Queen Anne cottages—and these, when they come up for sale, are snapped up in the blink of an eye, no matter the cost. Rentals are also climbing; one-bedroom apartments in the center may rent for as much as $1,200, a two-bedroom for $2,500.

Across Market, up toward Corona Heights and Buena Vista Parks, the Castro's suburbs have large, well-landscaped homes on winding, hilly streets. This is a more traditional, less noticeable area, agreeable and calm, and prices are rising considerably here. And farther in is the Duboce Triangle, less wealthy but always in demand.

Just to the south, **Noe Valley** takes and gives to both the Castro and the Mission, but is in fact a village unto itself. Some old German and Irish still live here, as they do in the Castro, but it is now one of the most sought-after areas of town by young couples, by lesbians and gays spilling over from the Castro, and by artists and others with a bohemian outlook. Protected from the fog by three steep hills, this sunny valley is one of the city's most popular areas for young families; mothers pushing their children in strollers do their shopping on 24th Street or sit with their friends at outdoor tables in front of any of the area's charming little cafes. Twenty-fourth and Church is the main shopping intersection, but the shopping district really stretches from Diamond to Dolores. Since the J-Church streetcar line comes here, it is as convenient to downtown as any other district.

The entire area is relaxed in feel, less frenetic than the Castro, more solidly comfortable. Streets are fairly wide, and the small houses that line them are painted in light colors. The streets leading up to Diamond Heights are steep and the large Victorians have exceptional views, although the higher the climb, of course, the denser the fog. The residents of Noe Valley value their village and are trying to keep out the big businesses and chains, successfully so far.

Just a few years ago you wouldn't have paid much attention to Noe Valley's eastern neighbor, a rather placid, uninspired — sometimes rundown — area of small private homes nestled on low-rising hills. Now, however, sunny **Bernal Heights** is on the way up. The area's excellent location — with borders also on Diamond Heights and the Mission — meant that it was a logical expansion for those neighborhoods, as well as for men and women who might also have thought of the lively Castro or Inner Mission as their home. Pleasantly winding streets heading up low-rising hills, several welcoming green parks, gentle breezes, and lovely views from Bernal Hill drew a new generation of San Franciscans, ready to spruce up the Victorian bungalows and Queen Anne cottages, many of which were suffering from neglect. Bernal Heights is now an area with its own cachet.

Fortunately, the area has not lost its traditional multiracial, multi-ethnic character, but it took the work of community activists opposed to excessive gentrification to bring about a moratorium on "certain types of development." It is true that new businesses and restaurants are moving in, but so far the neighborhood ambience persists, even on Cortland Avenue, the district's main commercial street, which offers to residents all the conveniences and services that a small town would want.

Bernal Heights thus remains a mixed area, one of agreeable proportions. Old-timers still inhabit their homes, young professionals and artists are fixing up cottages throughout, and Latino families are finding their way out from the crowded Mission to homes that are still within financial reach, both for rental and purchase. But the good prices here will not last long. Home prices increased nearly 18 percent in just one recent year, to the point that now the median price for a two-bedroom, one-bath house has reached $320,000. Rent control means that a long-term renter might be paying $650 per month, but a young professional who is just moving in might pay $1,800. Clearly, this is a neighborhood still in transition, and fortunate is the person who can seize an opportunity here.

### The Mountainous Center

To the south and west of Noe Valley the highest hills in the city impose themselves over a dozen interesting communities. Wind-swept and foggy for the most part, Twin Peaks, Mount Davidson, and Mount Sutro command the city's geographical center; many of their neighborhoods are blessed with exquisite views and park-like settings, some a bit sheltered from the cold ocean wind. Despite the winding and dead-end streets, each area is convenient to—or overlaps—another of interest, and all are in proximity to the city's major universities, making them attractive to faculty and students. There are pockets of mansions and grand private homes, small cottages, and well-maintained apartments, but what you'll find depends on where you look, for each area has its own character.

**Diamond Heights**, which is the major district on the eastern slopes of Twin Peaks, was developed in the 1960s, and its modernity shows in its large apartment complexes and well-designed, single-family homes. Its proximity to its eastern neighbors makes it ever more desirable, as prices in Noe Valley and the Castro soar. Being "discovered" also is the attractive hilly **Glen Park** district to the southeast, with its many rental apartments, Victorians, and almost reasonably priced homes, although it had long been a sedate, well-kept neighborhood. And the Glen Park BART Station makes the Financial District even more quickly accessible than some areas closer in. Nearby, the steep Glen Canyon Park offers a wilderness park, although playgrounds, tennis courts, and a baseball field have tamed it somewhat.

Mount Davidson's summit is foggy and wild, but on its western downslopes some incredibly beautiful neighborhoods are almost a surprise in this outer part of the city. That they are near the universities and Stonestown makes them very much in demand. Drive around **Sherwood Forest** and **St. Francis Wood**, for example, to see the lovely homes on impeccably landscaped grounds. Houses occasionally come up for sale here, but as in Pacific Heights, the prices are astronomical. The pleasant homes of **West Portal** bridge toward the more ordinary **Miraloma Park**, **Westwood Highlands**, and **Westwood Park**, where some areas and streets are more appealing than others.

Just above the UC Medical Center, Mount Sutro and its fragrant eucalyptus forest may be the city's best-kept secret. On the hill's eastern edge, within walking distance of the hospital, the

51

charming enclave of **Sutro Heights** backs on the forest, and here are several of the most beautiful and flowery streets in the city, especially Edgewood Avenue, which is paved in red brick. Circling the hill, wild, foggy Sutro Forest sees private homes and apartments in addition to institutional housing for medical students. And around the hill to the west is **Forest Knolls,** a grouping of more than one hundred small, uniform homes on winding streets, each facing the forest itself.

## The Haight and 9th Avenue

Just to the east is the **Haight**, which for some is still identified by its most famous moment—the flower children's 1967 "Summer of Love." Yet time has moved on, and funky shops and eateries are coexisting with the upmarket boutiques and restaurants that are gentrifying an area that had become extremely seedy. Haight Street itself doesn't seem to have changed, a colorful street with cluttered storefronts and this generation's anti-establishment youth lounging the sidewalks. These street people mix with—or more likely ignore—the new home owners who are refurbishing the Victorians that line the side streets and the Panhandle.

In fact, the district has a rather surprising appeal. The neighborhoods that abut—**Upper Haight, Cole Valley, Parnassus Heights, Buena Vista**—offer an extremely appealing mix of large and small private homes on tree-lined, sometimes winding, streets. These are still inhabited by long-term residents, by young couples who value the backyards for their children, and by faculty and researchers at the UC Medical Center, for whom this area is prime. Rentals are available throughout the district. In terms of purchase, although this is not one of the city's most expensive areas, the homes are often large and thus prices can be steep. Nonetheless, some houses that need refurbishment do come available and sell very quickly. This is also true for **Lower Haight**, east of Masonic, which is just beginning to come up.

The Haight's attraction for the flower children is not hard to understand. This area along the Panhandle was once quite fashionable, as the Victorians attest. But during the economic depression of the 1930s, it was hard to maintain the large homes, and during the war, some were split into apartments with cheap rents. When North Beach became too popular and expensive, many Beat Generation poets and "beatniks" moved here, and by 1962, the entire area was rather bohemian. By 1967, very hippie. But years of decline took their toll. Finally the City stepped in to subsidize the refurbishing of buildings and to limit the building of new units, which encouraged people sensing bargains to buy and restore the lovely old homes.

All these areas—and indeed some of those in the previous section—are near Golden Gate Park and the hilly Buena Vista Park, with its cypress, pines, and redwoods. They are also near commercial but charming Cole Street, and residents also head down the hill to the west, toward 9th Avenue and Irving.

Years ago, the sleepy intersection at 9th and Irving (which is actually in the **Inner Sunset**) held a few shops, restaurants, and local services, but not much else. Now, despite the fog that whips in early, it is one of the city's liveliest scenes. As with many other areas that have been discovered, however, small businesses are being forced out as rents are raised, allowing chain eateries and cafes to move in. Yet residents of this area—students, faculty, artists, and young Asian families who live in low-rise apartments or two-story stucco homes—are fighting back, trying to force businesses to keep the scale and size of stores appropriate to their sites. Several large chains were rejected, and at present the area is invitingly trendy, but with its community ambience intact.

## The Avenues

To the west of Arguello are "the avenues," grid-like streets that start at 2nd Avenue and go west until they can go no more. They stretch on both sides of Golden Gate Park, and it is the park that

53

divides its two adjacent districts, the **Richmond** and the **Sunset**, which have much in common, although slightly less as time goes on. In terms of climate, these are the foggiest districts in the city, and on some days when downtown areas are still basking in the sun, the Outer Richmond and the Outer Sunset are shrouded in mist, buffeted by wind. Both these large residential areas were developed only in the 1920s and 1930s; pleasantly culturally diverse, they are solidly middle class, known for their two-story, stucco, pastel-colored homes, sitting side by side, street after street. In each district, however, there are pockets of luxury, of magnificent views, of exquisite homes — to be had at a price. These roomy communities — safe, comfortable, and well-kept — are seen by some as far from the city life, and some residents rarely feel the need to go downtown.

As mentioned, Richmond's eastern edges remind one of Pacific Heights, from Arguello all the way out to Seacliff, with its mansions standing stately in the fog. Just across California Street, however, the Richmond is increasingly Asian: some 35 percent of the Chinese community has settled here, making Clement Street the focus of a "new Chinatown." Geary, its neighbor to the south and one of the city's longest commercial thoroughfares, has long been the stronghold of the Russian community, marked by the impressive gold-domed Cathedral of the Holy Virgin; all along Geary there are Russian delicatessens, bakeries, and stores, firmly ensconced in the increasingly Asian strip.

South of Geary begin the alphabetically consecutive streets, starting at Anza. Residentially, there are low-rise homes and apartments on wide, straight, rather bland streets. As the area heads out toward the ocean, however, it begins to feel like the wild beach town it is. At the very edge of the continent, past the tourist attractions at Cliff House, the condominiums of **Ocean Beach** sit along the Great Highway, behind the sandy dunes.

South of Golden Gate Park, in the Sunset, the alphabetical streets start again at Lincoln and end far to the south at Wawona.

The trendy area around 9th and Irving begins to fade, and the straight wide streets carry on as far as they can to the west and into the chilling fog. Despite seemingly endless rows of small, undistinguished single-family bungalows and semidetached homes, the Outer Sunset has some attractions, including Asian commercial districts on Irving and Noriega, especially around 19th Avenue. With access to beaches and several large parks, and close to the major Stonestown Galleria and San Francisco State, the residents seem content. All along the westernmost stretches, past 19th Avenue and surrounding the long Sunset Avenue greensward, a few of the discreet, pleasantly residential communities — **Parkside, Pine Lake Park** — seem part of a more tranquil world. Prices here are reasonable in relation to the rest of the city.

## The Southwest

Just south of the "avenues" and still in proximity to the university and Stonestown sits the **Oceanview Merced Ingleside (OMI)** set of communities. These green, fragrant areas are often totally socked in by fog, but their residents enjoy the coastal winds and the smell of the sea. Revolving around Ocean Avenue and 19th Avenue, these are three middle class neighborhoods trying to form a cohesive whole. In general, they are known for pleasant, single-family homes with neatly kept yards. Some apartment areas exist around Stonestown, inhabited by both long-term local residents and students who come and go. Park Merced, adjacent to the university, is an extensive apartment and townhouse complex.

To the west, near the university in its wooded and garden-like setting, near large Harding Park, near Lake Merced, and close to the ocean with its crashing waves, the area begins to take on the aspect of the coastal town it is. Lining the western side of the lake, along John Muir Drive, a large complex of rental units can be seen in a community known as **Lakeshore.**

Ocean Avenue, the northern border of the district, is gently residential to the west of 19th Avenue, but commercial to the east.

This is one of the commercial areas that service Ingleside Terrace, known for the looping residential Urbano Drive that follows the course of the long-gone Ingleside Race Track. The comfortable, well-kept houses here give off the atmosphere of suburban living, and, fortunately, one may occasionally come up for rent.

Yet Ingleside and Oceanview themselves are in transition, and in fact have long been so. Fifty years ago, when the decaying Fillmore districts were being redeveloped, African American families were evicted with a promise they could return to new housing. Instead, many families migrated outward to the OMI and affordable homes, as the traditional White communities bought automobiles and moved to suburban living. Decades later, centralized shopping centers and large cinema complexes forced small local businesses to close, and the area declined. Recently, however, although some parts still remain rough, an active citizens' effort is striving to bring the area back to its residents, with rebuilt and expanded public facilities and an overall sense of renewal.

### The Southeast

Also at the south, but on the city's eastern edge, are several districts that seem not to fit into the vibrant San Francisco mold. Separated from Bernal Heights by Interstate 280, **Portola** is a generally lower-middle class melting pot. Originally an Italian neighborhood, then Jewish, it is now truly multicultural, as evidenced along San Bruno Avenue, with its Latin American establishments, Italian butchers, and Asian restaurants of all kinds. People buying their first homes often settled here, but now prices are rising as everywhere else, and especially in this area so near Bernal Heights.

Surrounding the large John McLaren Park are several neighborhoods — **Excelsior**, **Visitacion Valley**, and **Crocker Amazon** — that are generally characterized by middle-income and working class families living in bland single-family homes. Originally Italian, these areas now see more Latinos and Asians. The foggy, rather uninspired streets with their rows of little houses are convenient to Daly City, to San Francisco State, and to the city by BART. In this area there are also some apartments, flats, and duplexes, many needing refurbishment, and these present opportunities for neighborhoods to come back, which they will eventually do. Crocker Amazon has some slightly newer homes on more interesting streets such as Chicago Way.

But just across the Highway 101 corridor are **Hunters Point,** an area of city-wide concern, and **Bayview,** which seems now to be on the upturn. During World War II military shipyards here bustled with some 35,000 workers. Now, however, with much of the city's public housing—some of it still in use since the war—these are the areas most beset by poverty and crime. Yet, a few artists have their studios at the old naval base, and the city is perhaps beginning to address the problems.

This broad look at the city should help you get a feel for it as you explore it on your own. As you do, you will discover that it still has its little mysteries which no doubt will eventually be resolved. Will the charming enclave of private homes around the University of San Francisco continue to be considered part of the nearby Western Addition, which currently has so little charm? Will the industrial South of Market become gentrified to match its eastern edge at the upcoming South Beach? Will the enormous mixed-use development planned for China Bay succeed? Is Corona Heights a suburb of the Castro? And will the formerly commercial Van Ness corridor, now sparkling with new condominiums, supermarkets, and theaters, coin a name for itself? The answers to these puzzles will certainly unfold. In any case, the architect Frank Lloyd Wright summed up his own understanding: "What I like best about San Francisco is … San Francisco," he said. For overall, as San Franciscans believe, the city is unique.

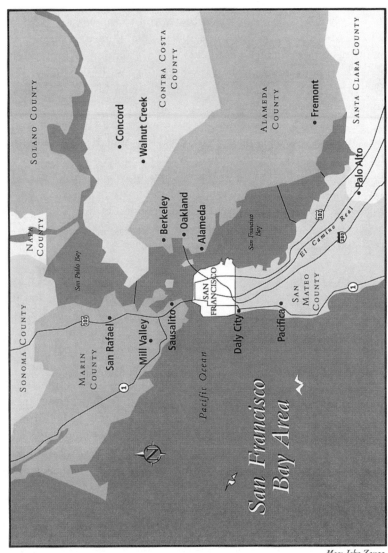

Map: John Zaugg

San Francisco Bay Area

SOLANO COUNTY

CONTRA COSTA COUNTY

• Concord

• Walnut Creek

NAPA COUNTY

ALAMEDA COUNTY

• Fremont

SANTA CLARA COUNTY

• Berkeley

• Oakland

• Alameda

San Pablo Bay

San Francisco Bay

• Palo Alto

El Camino Real

SONOMA COUNTY

MARIN COUNTY

SAN FRANCISCO

SAN MATEO COUNTY

• San Rafael

• Mill Valley

• Sausalito

• Daly City

• Pacifica

Pacific Ocean

San Francisco Bay Area

N

# Chapter Two

# AROUND THE BAY

## SUBURBAN LIVING

The eight outlying counties of the Bay Area stretch about fifty miles south toward the major metroplis of San Jose, east past the industrial port of Oakland, and north to Sonoma, up toward what is known as the Delta. Bay Area counties are generally referred to by their position in relation to the Bay: the North Bay (Marin, Sonoma, Napa, and Solano counties), the South Bay whose farther reaches are called the Peninsula (San Mateo and Santa Clara counties), and the East Bay (Alameda and Contra Costa counties). Thousands of people commute to the city from the nearer portions of these counties, and now even some of the farther reaches are beginning to be seen as within commuting distance. People choose to live in the greater Bay Area rather than in San Francisco for a variety of reasons: a tranquil suburban or even rural lifestyle, lower housing costs (in some places), good public and private schools, low crime rates, fewer earthquakes, or perhaps even a more "normal" climate. Although the details of the towns and villages of the Bay Area are beyond the province of this book, they are well worth considering in terms of residence.

Unlike San Francisco, the rest of the Bay Area sees four distinct seasons. While San Francisco is enjoying its natural summer air conditioning, it is warmest inland, away from the bay. Temperatures in the rest of the Bay Area can soar in the summer, but even in these areas, winter climes are mild, with perhaps a touch of snow in Sonoma, on the peaks of Mount Diablo, or on Mount Tamalpais.

All these counties are dotted with delicious little towns, gentle and leafy green, linked by country roads and, for the most part, touched by major highways. Living here, thus, requires keeping a car, perhaps more if two people in a household are working, or if a child needs to be taken to school. If living outside the city appeals to you, think about living along the BART line, which goes from San Francisco under the bay to the east, and somewhat toward the south (see Chapter Ten). Commuting by car during rush hours is slow and tedious, but BART is reliable and fast. From the North Bay, commuting is most often by car, crowding the lanes of the Golden Gate Bridge; there too, however, the public commuter buses and even ferries are reliable and practical. And from the south also come the buses and BART (from Colma), and, unfortunately, long lines of cars.

Rents and purchase prices vary from the merely expensive to the outrageous, depending on the home's size and its views of the Bay, and the town's amenities. Some of the communities have new subdivisions with planned developments of single-family and multi-family homes, some clustered around golf courses. Whereas the towns close to San Francisco were considered an easy commute to the City, now communities as far north as Petaluma or Novato, or as far east as Concord are being developed and considered within commuting distance. Whatever the price range, the beauty and lifestyles of these more relaxed areas are considered by many — especially young families — to be essential for a well-balanced life. Towns around the Bay Area are never called suburbs, but the life is truly suburban.

## EAST BAY

Across the $8^1/2$-mile Bay Bridge is the East Bay, known for its warm climate and beautiful grassy, rolling hills rising toward Mount Diablo, the highest peak in the region. It is home to **Oakland**, the Bay Area's major shipping port, and its contiguous neighbor, **Berkeley**, with its prestigious University of California campus. Both are in **Alameda County**, which has the highest population of the Bay Area. Yet there are many almost rural towns to consider, both in Alameda County and, farther east, in **Contra Costa County**. Formerly seen as less desirable than the upscale counties to the north or south of San Francisco, the East Bay — although recently "discovered" by young, upcoming professionals — is still characterized by lower rents, and a more traditional lifestyle. This won't last long. Providing its own cultural attractions, modern shopping and extensive services, good schools, and lovely parks and outdoor recreation areas, the East Bay is even known for its efficient public transit, including access to BART, and the Oakland International Airport, increasingly used by travelers trying to avoid SFO.

In the mid-1960s, Oakland, which had refitted its waterfront to handle the new container ships, became the the area's major international shipping port, when San Francisco decided to spend its public funds to draw tourists instead. Unfortunately, Oakland's new industries did little to make the sprawling city into a desired residential locale, and it became known for drugs, crime, and poverty, a situation that is finally being addressed. Currently, the

61

city is in the process of an exciting renewal. New construction is changing the skyline, neighborhoods are being spruced up, businesses are moving in, and Oakland is striving to show itself as on the move.

The new spirit of Oakland—and its still reasonable rents and purchase prices—is drawing people from across the Bay and from Silicon Valley. Prices are beginning to climb, and as in San Francisco, long-term residents are concerned about the gentrification of the city and about being forced out as prices increase. The market is definitely heating up. Yet construction of rental units is part of the overall renewal plan, and you can look for graceful apartments near trendy, waterfront Jack London Square and around the large Lake Merritt, a man-made, saltwater, tidal lake which serves as a recreational haven for the area's residents.

Towns close by which heretofore appealed to those looking for lower rents—**Alameda** and **San Leandro**, for example, and down to **Fremont**—are also experiencing a surge in housing costs, but none of these as yet approach the prices in San Francisco. Some areas have always been expensive and will remain so: in **Piedmont**, an exclusive enclave of large homes and an understated yet elegant atmosphere, there is little to rent, and purchase prices are high. This is also true of the Oakland hills, a prestigious, wealthy aerie between Oakland and Berkeley that was all but destroyed by a massive fire a decade ago, but which was quickly and splendidly rebuilt.

Berkeley, Oakland's neighbor to the north, may no longer be called "berserkeley" for its once-strident mixture of radical politics and New Age sensibilities, but this is still a city on the cutting edge of the nation's intellectual and political life. You can find whatever you want in Berkeley, whether it is a beautiful home in the secluded hills or a moderately priced room near the university and the student life along Telegraph Avenue. Whether student or faculty, or neither, the residents are activists in all senses, and this is a lively, well-kept community that never hesitates to make its opinions known. There is a lot to be said for Berkeley: a generally sunny climate, the university atmosphere, the beautiful Tilden Park, excellent theater and concerts, some of the best restaurants in the Bay Area, and good schools.

Inland and through the Caldecott Tunnel are the small communities of **Contra Costa County**: **Orinda** and **Lafayette**, and the charming, comfortable city of **Walnut Creek**. Continuing along the line are **Pleasant Hill** and then **Concord**. Some 880,000 people live in these "bedroom" communities of Contra Costa County, but nestled among the green rolling hills or under Mount Diablo, some of it feels almost bucolic. Check out towns such as **Martinez, Antioch, El Cerrito**, or **Clayton**, which are still affordable and which have good access to public transportation and BART for commutes into the City or Oakland.

## NORTH BAY

Like San Francisco, **Marin County** is fairly surrounded by water. More than 100 miles of its borders are ocean, lagoons, or bays. Marin is two counties in one. East of the coastal mountains are trendy towns with lovely homes and elegant, peaceful living. To the west is the rugged coastline with its cliffs and surf. The weather to the east is sheltered, warm, and sunny, and the towns and their services and conveniences easily available to all. On the coast, however, are foggy, tiny villages that draw hearty lovers of wild beauty. One winding, narrow road links them. A quarter million people live in Marin, from corporation executives who commute to San Francisco from their $4 million homes, to solitary artists and writers who leave their cottages to brave the winds and stroll the beaches, but who rarely want to come out "over the hill."

Just over the Golden Gate Bridge, picturesque **Sausalito** was once a sleepy fishing village. Now, however, tourists dominate the spectacular waterfront with its restaurants and boutiques. But the dramatic hills, steep and green, with their winding narrow lanes, are held by residents, many of whom commute into the city, escaping San Francisco in evening traffic back to their beautifully landscaped homes with striking views of the city they just left. Sausalito's quaint Mediterranean atmosphere is drawing young professionals who are bidding against each other for the few available properties and who are driving prices up from the merely expensive to the outrageous.

Farther out along Highway 101 are the charming towns of **Mill Valley**, **Larkspur**, **San Rafael**, **Corte Madera**, and **San Anselmo**. In these family towns, the pace is slower, the tourists at a distance. There is a mixed blue- and white-collar population that mingles easily with the corporate or artsy set. Small homes may approach the affordable, but hillside houses appeal to those who want the lifestyle no matter the cost, a situation that is increasing throughout the North Bay. Charming San Rafael, one of the oldest cities in California yet one of the most well-maintained in terms of schools, services, and atmosphere, is convenient either to a commute to the East Bay over the Richmond Bridge, or to the city by ferry, bus, or car.

San Rafael is the area's largest town, but it is Mill Valley, stretching from the flat up to the tip of Mount Tamalpais, that provides in gentle microcosm much of what Berkeley is known for: artists, writers, an annual film festival, lovely little galleries and boutiques. All these towns are accessible to San Francisco by commuter bus, but the ferries at Sausalito, **Larkspur**, and **Tiburon** make commuting even somewhat pleasant.

Tiburon and **Belvedere**, at the end of a causeway heading east from Highway 101 toward the bay, are almost hidden communities of astronomically expensive, lovely houses. Close to the natural harbor and to the local commerce are modern upscale condominium apartments, which sometimes come up for sale. Quiet, remote Belvedere is home to the truly rich.

Yet Marin has its pockets of affordable rental housing, in any of the towns mentioned above. Where you live here will depend also on whether you will commute daily into the city. The western and northern portions of Marin, heretofore seen as too remote, are currently enjoying an upswing for people who telecommute, for those who work in the North Bay, and for those who will put up with the commute for the lifestyle — and almost reasonable housing costs — these towns allow. Look at towns such as **Fairfax,** or **San Geronimo** and **Nicasio**, where new housing developments are under way.

## SOUTH BAY

Mirroring Marin, **San Mateo County**, which stretches from **Daly City** to **Menlo Park**, has two distinct climates and lifestyles, and as would be expected, the stretch that is oceanside of the coastal mountains is often socked in by fog. Unlike Marin, however, the beach town of **Pacifica** is close to Interstate 280, making a commute into the city feasible for those who want to live in the fresh ocean air. This is less true of **Half Moon Bay**, about 20 minutes farther south, for winter mud slides sometimes make the commute difficult. Yet these charming coastal fishing communities are populated by families and singles who live in small, comfortable houses or in affordable apartments, often with a view of the waves.

Inland, past the southern edge of the city but still well within its fog belt, are the working class Daly City and **South San Francisco**. Here people commute into the city on BART, but they also work in the industries that line the Highway 101 corridor, at the airport, at the huge shopping complexes in **Serramonte** or **Colma**, or at San Francisco State. Colma is the southern terminus for BART, making for an easy commute into the city. These are areas of small, square, stucco homes, apartments, duplexes, townhouses, and condominiums. This part of the South Bay may not be the most exciting place to live in, but its price and convenience may be appealing to some.

But this is not all there is. Just beyond the fog belt, **San Mateo**, **Belmont**, and **Burlingame** offer pleasant ranch houses on wide, tree-lined streets. Here the residential areas are varied and prices may be quite reasonable. Yet here, too, they are rising, for at the end of the century, the median price of a single-family detached home in San Mateo County was $461,000; **East Palo Alto** had the most affordably priced homes, and in general condominiums are reasonably priced. Along the long north-south artery of El Camino Real, an Asian business community makes itself known, and to the east of "the Camino" interesting, well-priced homes become available from time to time. At about 15 minutes south of the airport, **Foster City,** between 101 and the bay, is a lovely, sprawling town of upscale rental and condominium apartments, plus well-landscaped streets of private homes. Sheltered by the hills from the fog and wind, its climate is moderate, its parks pleasant, and its proximity to the highway makes it convenient both to San Francisco in the north and Silicon Valley in the south. If you look for housing close to the airport, inquire about flight patterns and noise.

# THE PENINSULA

**Santa Clara County** accounts for more than one million of the six million people living in the Bay Area. The geography of the area is beautifully varied: flat areas along the 101 corridor, green rolling hills, wooded retreats, agricultural lands, horse farms farther east toward Highway 280, and charming towns. The county starts around **Menlo Park** on the north, encompasses the major highways of Route 101 and Interstate 280, flanks El Camino Real, and heads south to the edge of **San Jose,** a bustling, forward-looking city with a population larger than its more celebrated neighbor to the north.

Santa Clara County is now famous as "Silicon Valley," headquarters for most of the country's high-tech industries that have brought some 800,000 well-paid jobs to the area and a younger set of entrepreneurs looking for housing they can easily afford. What is sometimes called "dot.com" money has caused a doubling of housing prices in just the past few years, in an area that was already quite dear. That housing prices range from the merely upscale to the astronomical shouldn't be surprising in an area in which the median family income is currently $82,000, the highest in the United States. Yet condominiums do come available, temporary rentals come up from time to time in the homes of faculty members at Stanford University who are off on sabbaticals, and in some flat pockets near commercial areas, almost affordable homes can still be found.

The leafy campus of Stanford is nestled in the charming town of **Palo Alto**, which is known for its Craftsman-style bungalows, although in recent years houses have become larger and prices have climbed considerably. Palo Alto is home to the Stanford Shopping Center, an extensive and popular mall that serves this part of the Peninsula.

Nearby, the exquisite towns of **Hillsborough** and **Atherton**, with median home prices hovering in the $2 million range, are becoming home to those who commute into San Francisco, work in Silicon Valley, or head down to San Jose. These and the elegant **Los Altos** and **Los Altos Hills** are gentle towns with high-quality services and impressive homes hidden on large, well-landscaped grounds. Farther into the rolling hills to the west, the horse farms and estates of **Woodside** off Interstate 280 are remote and rarefied in atmosphere—and price.

Yet, the sections of any of the towns that are on the flats closer to the industrial 101 corridor than to the less developed Interstate 280 are for the most part pleasant, middle class "bedroom communities." Here, rents for the smaller houses and apartments— as well as more affordable purchase prices—give access to worlds in all directions. Check them out.

# Chapter Three

# HOUSING: PROBLEMS & SOLUTIONS

## THE SITUATION

As small and compact as it is, San Francisco offers a wide range of housing, from elegant mansions and single-family homes with gardens to semidetached row houses, from high-rise complexes to low-rise apartments over neighborhood stores, to flats in two-story homes. Thousands of charming Victorian houses and small homes coexist peaceably with the few tall modern structures, and each of the almost thirty distinct neighborhoods has its own eclectic blend. In general, San Franciscans are apartment dwellers. Of the more than 330,000 residences in the city, some 229,000 are multi-units, and only about 105,000 are single or semidetached one-family homes.

Fortunately, San Francisco is a city of renters. Some two-thirds of the population rent their homes, while only slightly more than one-third own theirs. Unfortunately, San Francisco is a city whose boundaries are fixed by water, and its expanding commercial areas have reduced residential possibilities just as an influx of affluent newcomers is demanding more space. This has pushed prices up to the point where the city is rated as one of the least affordable housing markets in the United States. That the city has decided to keep its residential ambience and put height restrictions on new building construction has also created a low inventory of available apartments, and increasing demand has fueled a difficult price situation. This holds true for both purchase and rental units.

In fact, San Franciscans themselves consistently rate the lack of affordable housing and the city's high rents as the city's most pressing problems. Rental vacancies hover around 1 percent, and apartments listed for sale may well be snapped up after a bidding war with the winner paying hundreds of thousands of dollars *above* the asking price. In the last four years of the 20th century, the number of transactions doubled, but price per sale also doubled.

The problem began with the construction boom after World War II. Just about all the high-rent commercial skyscrapers in the city were built during what critics called the "Manhattanization of San Francisco," which stopped only because there was no more space downtown. Small businesses were driven to the outer reaches, some lower-end apartments were demolished to build hotels or upscale apartments, and some former rental units themselves converted to expensive condominiums.

Yet, the most important part of why housing costs are so high is that the economic boom of the nineties brought new high-tech and multimedia entrepreneurs into the city, people who were willing to pay even more than the asking price for a place they liked. Despite a commute to Silicon Valley, many of the "dot.com" entrepreneurs prefer to live in San Francisco; sometimes San

Francisco itself seems a bedroom community as cars create a new, southbound morning rush hour. These people work hard, have little time for private life, and they want to be where the surroundings are vibrant. Thus, they are willing to pay whatever it takes for the finest location and most spectacular view, ignoring traditional purchase procedures, forcing the market to become even more competitive.

It is beginning to hold true, as some people say, that in San Francisco nothing worth living in is inexpensive. Don't be shocked, don't be upset, it's just the way it is. Finding the right home at the right price is not an easy matter, but eventually you will, especially if you understand that you will have to compromise. But do not expect to arrive in San Francisco and stay in a hotel for two or three days before moving into the "just right" inexpensive apartment with a spectacular view. San Francisco doesn't work that way. Expect instead to find a short-term apartment or residence hotel (see below), and to spend several months in search of a home.

Yet the news is not all bad. Although the cost of living in San Francisco is higher than the United States average, income levels in the Bay Area are generally commensurate. Costs other than housing are not particularly high: the mild climate allows customers to spend less on household utilities than in some other cities, for instance, and San Franciscans are always happy to say how little they paid for something, whether clothing bought at a discount or a delicious meal in an Asian restaurant.

## RENT CONTROL

Another plus is that renters do have some protection under San Francisco law. Apartments in San Francisco have been rent controlled since 1979, meaning that rents for tenants with leases may only be raised a certain percentage each year, determined by a formula tied to the Cost of Living Index. Currently, the rate of increase is $2^1/_2$ percent. Rents may be raised to "market levels," however, when a tenant leaves and before a new tenant moves in;

this sometimes encourages landlords to force tenants out under one pretext or another, or to insist on month-to-month contracts, rather than leases.

In some apartment complexes, tenants who have held leases for twenty years are paying only a fraction of what a new tenant pays. This may seem unfair, but without some regulation to protect tenants, rents in San Francisco would be even higher than they are. Although some people claim that rent control is forcing the higher rents and that a free market would bring rents down, the unregulated commercial market has not shown this to be true.

Some landlords are taking advantage of a law that allows them to evict tenants if they themselves, or their families, are planning to move in. Such evictions rose some 200 percent in the last years of the nineties, and not all landlords actually moved in; new tenants did, paying higher rents. In addition, the controversial Ellis Act allows landlords to take their properties off the market, evicting existing tenants. In just six months in 1998, some seventy buildings were taken off the market — sometimes just temporarily. These are issues that the Board of Supervisors are constantly struggling with, to be fair both to the renters and landlords in the city.

## THINKING ABOUT RENT

Rental units are strewn throughout the city; the areas to the north and east have more apartments, and to the west and south, more private homes. Their price, of course, depends on the neighborhood and the view; the more central or trendy the neighborhood, the higher the price. Even areas that were once seen as lower-priced are no longer so, and this at least benefits the long-term tenants who are protected under rent control. It is said that less than one-third of the people who moved to an apartment in the Mission a decade ago could afford to move in today; even in this formerly low-rent area, the current median rent for a two-bedroom apartment is approaching $1,600. In terms of luxury housing, the

71

1,000 apartments of the Golden Gateway Center that were offered as moderate-income housing in the sixties are now charging up to $2,950 per month for a studio and up to $3,995 for a two-bedroom apartment. In fact, the median price for an available apartment in the city is now $1,500, having risen from $860 just six years ago. Nonetheless, you should be able to find housing in your price range, but it might take some time and compromise.

It is hard to predict the type of rentals in any given area. Older apartments may be found in newly trendy areas, and some recent construction may be found in areas thought of as traditional. And some reasonably priced rentals may be just on the edge of higher-priced districts, in areas called the Outer Mission, Lower Haight, or Upper Market. Except for a few areas near the Tenderloin and down by Hunters Point, there are practically no areas of the city that are not appropriate for the apartment search, although some—the Mission and the Western Addition—require some caution.

## STARTING THE SEARCH

You can begin to understand the San Francisco rental market in advance of arrival by looking online. Some listing services charge a small access fee, usually good for three months; these services, however, allow search by location or by housing requirements (number of rooms, elevator, etc), and they often offer advice on moving and landlord requirements. See also Roommates below.

- San Francisco daily newspapers: classified ads (www.sfgate.com) provide links to Spring Street, Metro Rent and Rent Tech, listed below
- *Renter's Digest*: advertisements for large complexes that have a fair amount of tenant turnover, as well as some short-term options (www.aptguides.com)
- *Bay Area Rental Guide*: Advertisements for housing in the Bay Area (www.rentalguide.com)

- **Spring Street**: $75 for rental listings; $65 for roommate listings. Nationwide service; one of the most extensive (www.springstreet.com).
- **e-Housing**: Covers East Bay. $60 for rental listings; $25 for roommate listings (www.e-housing.com).
- **Metro Rent**: Rental and roommate listings from San Francisco to San Jose; $85–95 for two months of access; $65 for 90 days for roommate listings (www.metrorent.com)
- **Rent Tech**: San Francisco and East Bay rental listings; $85 for access to rentals; prices vary for roommate services (www.renttech.com)

Once in San Francisco, you can read the local publications and walk around the neighborhoods you are interested in to spot the "for rent" signs in apartment windows, which give a telephone number to call. Some people also rent bicycles for leisurely explorations of neighborhoods that interest them (see Chapter Fifteen). If you can afford it, however, work with a real estate agent, who knows what is available in the various neighborhoods. You will have to pay a commission, but it may be worth it to streamline the search. Although most real estate agents and roommate services handle rentals (see below), **Hill & Co**, at 2107 Union, is especially known for its rental properties (rental tel: 921-3040).

Daily newspapers are excellent sources for rentals, but if you see something you like, act immediately. Fast-spreading news of the availability of a good apartment may mean that by the time an ad appears in the paper, the apartment might well have been taken. Nonetheless, both the *San Francisco Chronicle* and *The San Francisco Examiner* are important resources. The *San Francisco Weekly* has apartments at the lower end of the scale, and shares (www.sfweekly.com). For apartments and shares throughout the Bay Area, try the *Bay Guardian* (www.sfbg.com); in the East Bay, look for the *Oakland Tribune* and *The Express*, but for housing farther out—in Walnut Creek and Concord—try the *Contra Costa County*

*Times*. The best resources in the South Bay are the *San Mateo Times* and, farther south, the *San Jose Mercury News*. In the North Bay, look for the *Marin Independent*.

# THE APARTMENT

San Francisco real estate makes a distinction between an apartment and a flat. A flat is an entire floor of a small apartment building or two-story house, and it has its own entrance. Thus, you might walk up an outdoor flight of stairs to your door, and inside, the entire floor is your own. An apartment, however, is one of several— or many—on a floor. Foreigners should understand that, in the United States, the first floor is the ground floor, and the second floor is the next floor up.

If you are bringing a car, pay attention to the parking situation. Although new buildings must include off-street parking, older dwellings may have no garages, and parking in San Francisco is a problem in all but the western neighborhoods. Some areas have public garages that rent spaces by the month; in addition to price, which varies from district to district, inquire about hours of access. If you intend to park your car on the street, you may need a city-issued parking permit (see Chapter Ten).

On the other hand, you should also determine the closest access to public transportation. Even people with cars often take public transport or walk to work, to avoid congested traffic and expensive parking.

Landlords generally ask for an application fee, which covers the cost of a credit check, plus the first and last months' rent, and/or a security deposit when the application is approved. Be prepared to provide a credit reference and the names of your past and current employers and landlords. Identification might include your driver's license, bank account numbers, and Social Security number. Many places don't allow pets, but it is illegal for a landlord to prohibit children.

74

A lease must specify a beginning date and termination date (not when you are required to move out, but when the lease must be renewed). If there is no termination date, the contract is not a "lease," but an "agreement," which will run month to month indefinitely, may be terminated by either party at any time, and, of course, is beneficial to the landlord. It's not wise to accept an oral agreement, which has no legal validity.

Before signing, ask your landlord for procedures for breaking a lease, should you decide to move. In general, you should give as much notice as possible, in writing, and expect to pay the entire remainder of the lease should a new tenant not be found.

Security deposits are used to cover damage to the apartment (deducted upon your departure). Thus, when you are returning the signed lease, make sure you have checked for any irregularities in the apartment, and specify them in writing—every crack in the walls or chip on an appliance—so that upon leaving you will not be charged for damage. No laws apply as to what constitutes a furnished apartment, so you should inquire about some of the items you require, such as a desk, a microwave, or a toaster. Ask the landlord for a detailed inventory of what is in the apartment and make sure it matches what is actually there.

## Short-term Rentals

If you cannot come to the city and spend time looking for an apartment before your actual move, consider either a short-term, furnished, fully equipped apartment or a residence hotel. Short-term, furnished apartments are less expensive than hotels, and with housing so tight, you might as well be comfortable during your search.

- **American Marketing Systems**, at 2800 Van Ness, is an agency that handles short-term (monthly) furnished and unfurnished apartments throughout the city (tels: 447-2000, 800/747-7784; fax: 440-1008; www.we-rent-sanfran.com).

- **Executive Suites**: (tel: 800/258-1973; fax 776-5155; www. rent.net/ads/executivesuites). Short-term furnished luxury studios, one- and two-bedroom apartments in San Francisco, the East Bay, and Sausalito.
- *Civic Center*—**Ashlee Suites**: 1029 Geary, at Van Ness (tel: 771-7396; fax: 771-7455). Studios to two-bedroom fully equipped apartments.
- *Downtown*—**The Steinhart**: 952 Sutter Street (tel: 928-3855). An older, restored, landmark building. Studios to two-bedroom furnished apartments, maid service.
- *Embarcadero*—**Golden Gateway Apartments**: 460 Davis Court, at Jackson (tel: 434-2000; fax: 989-5034). Stays of three months or more in an elegant complex. Health facilities and pool. Parking available.
- *Nob Hill*—**Nob Hill Place**: 1155 Jones Street, at Sacramento (tel: 928-2051). Quiet residence offers studios to two-bedroom apartments at prices fitting the area. Parking garages in the neighborhood.
- *Nob Hill*—**Pierre Suites/Nob Hill**: 835 Pine, near Powell (tels: 800/570-0252; 544-0252). Fine apartments of various sizes by week or month.
- *Nob Hill*—**Grosvenor Suites**: 899 Pine, at Mason (tel: 421-1899; fax: 982-1946). Studio to two-bedroom fully equipped suites, some with exquisite views of the city. Parking available.
- *Nob Hill*—**Nob Hill Chateau**: 795 Pine Street (tel: 986-5145; fax: 392-8161). Fully equipped studio and one-bedroom furnished apartments for rent by the week or month. Computer and fax lines, answering machines.
- *Wharf*—**Northpoint Executive Suites**: 2211 Stockton at Bay (tel: 989-6563). Fully furnished apartments of various sizes and amenities. Parking available. Swimming pool and health club.

Another option, although not particularly suitable for families, is the residential hotel, which offers one room and meals in a common dining room.

- *Downtown*—**Ansonia**: 711 Post Street (tel: 673-2670). Inexpensive hotel; breakfast and dinner served daily; no Sunday dinner.
- *Downtown*— **Cornell Hotel**: 715 Bush Street (tel: 421-3154; fax: 399-1442). Charming French-style hotel offering rooms and excellent meals, except Sunday.
- *Van Ness Corridor*—**The Kenmore**: 1570 Sutter Street, near Gough (tel: 776-5815; fax: 776-9659). Residence club in a quiet area, yet close to public transportation, supermarket, restaurants. Most meals included.

## Apartment Complexes

For permanent housing, some large apartment complexes handle their own rentals. These generally have a management office on the premises, which—at least theoretically—should make it efficient for repairs and service. In addition to considering these for long-term leases (if there are any available) you might also consider one of these complexes for the short term, so you can have some place to live and keep your furniture while looking for permanent housing. Some offer six-month leases or month-to-month contracts; in fact, six months is not unreasonable in thinking about finding satisfactory permanent housing.

- *Civic Center*—**Trinity Plaza**: 1169 Market Street, at 8th Street (tel: 861-3333). Studios and one-bedroom apartments, heated swimming pool. Moderate prices.
- *Embarcadero/Mission Street*—**Rincon Towers Apartments**: 88 Howard Street (tel: 777-4100). Two-tower set of apartments, from studios to two bedrooms. Short-term rentals available.
- *Embarcadero*—**Golden Gateway Center**: 460 Davis Court, at Jackson (tel: 434-2000; fax: 989-5034). Luxury apartments

and townhouses. Fitness center, tennis courts, swimming pool. Parking additional.

- *Embarcadero* — **Bayside Village**: The Embarcadero at Brannan (tel: 777-4850; fax: 777-2410). Studio to two-bedroom units, parking. Free shuttle bus to Financial District. Swimming pools, fitness center.
- *Lake Merced/San Francisco State* — **Parkmerced**: 3711 19th Avenue (tels: 888/218-0373; 587-6322). Moderately priced single-family townhouses and apartments in a large development near San Francisco State.
- *South of Market/Multimedia Gulch* — **City Lofts**: 175 Bluxome Street (tel: 495-8885). One- and two-bedroom live/work lofts, with a business center, a fitness room, and parking.
- *South of Market* — **St. Francis Place Apartments**: One St. Francis Place, 3rd Street at Folsom (tel: 888/704-8844; fax: 777-3972). Long- and short-term rentals of furnished one- and two-bedroom apartments.
- *Sunset* — **Sunset Towers**: 8 Locksley Avenue, at Kirkham (tel: 681-6800; fax: 681-1501). Near University of California Medical Center and Golden Gate Park. Studios to two-bedroom apartments. Parking, laundry, all conveniences.
- *Union Square* — **Trinity Towers**: 888 O'Farrell Street, near Polk (tel: 885-3333; fax: 885-3294). Loft apartments, townhouses, fitness center and swimming pool, underground parking, 24-hour doorman.
- *Van Ness* — **Fox Plaza**: 1390 Market Street (tel: 626-6900; fax: 863-3190; ARW Hospitality rental tel: 565-0625; fax: 554-0573). Rents and furnishes short-term and long-term apartments in this complex of studios to two bedroom apartments. Cats allowed, but no dogs.
- *Western Addition* — **Webster Tower and Terrace**: 1489 Webster Street, at Geary (tel: 931-6300). Modern studios, one- and two-bedroom apartments, and penthouses. Parking, rooftop terraces, shopping convenience.

- *Western Addition* — **The Fillmore Center**: 1475 Fillmore Street (tel: 921-1969; fax: 563-2019). Studios to three-bedroom apartments, penthouse, townhouse. Health club on premises. Shopping convenience.

# PURCHASING A HOME

Since most homes for sale are listed in the centralized database of the San Francisco Board of Realtors' Multiple Listing Service, real estate agents have access to the broadest range of available housing. Only about 10 percent of homes do not come to the open market; instead the owner of a top-end residence might ask a particular realtor to find a buyer privately. In San Francisco's tight market, where there are fewer homes for sale than buyers, this works well for realtors, but it also affects their commissions. Generally, realtors hope for a 6 percent commission (paid by the seller), but in a competitive market where homes turn over quickly, agents have become flexible and sometimes accept 5 percent.

The "fair market value" of a home is what a buyer will pay and a seller will accept. As mentioned, the lack of available properties and an influx of suddenly rich Internet entrepeneurs has created a "seller's market" in which buyers are very often forced to offer several hundred thousand dollars *over* the asking price to be the successful bidder, whether for a house or apartment. Generally, a home does sell at a price within the price range of similar homes on the market in its area, and your real estate agent should be able to give you an estimate of what each neighborhood's homes are going for.

Price ranges do fluctuate over time. When the stock market is rising (and the dot.coms are doing well), a seller may receive multiple offers, and when the stock market "corrects," these bidding wars may slow. Given this new type of buyer in the city, most attractive homes will receive multiple offers, so you will need to make a competitive bid immediately and be prepared to raise your offer quickly. In addition, because properties move so quickly,

79

you will need to have a mortgage up to a certain amount and the schedule of inspections and appraisals all pre-approved.

Work, if possible, with an agent with experience in the San Francisco market and with solid references; recommendations from friends and colleagues should help. Unfortunately, the best agents may be overbooked and may not have as much time as one who is fairly recent in the field. Nonetheless, in all cases be specific with your agent about your price limits and your needs; also indicate where you might be willing to compromise. Ask also about their relocation services. Below are three of the most well-respected throughout the city. All have several branches.

- **Tri-Coldwell Banker**: 1699 Van Ness (tel: 474-1750; fax: 771-1264; www. coldwellbanker.com)
- **McGuire**: 2001 Lombard (tel: 929-1500); 560 Davis (tel: 296-1000; www. mcguire.com)
- **Pacific Union:** 601 Van Ness (tel: 474-6600; www.pacunion. com)

Your agent should inform you of the weekend "open houses" in the neighborhoods you are considering. By looking at what is available in different areas and price ranges, you should quickly begin to understand values and how you may need to modify your own positions.

## Starting the Search

Most apartments for sale are condominiums in which each unit is privately owned along with a percentage of the common space. The few "community apartments" are what other cities call co-operative apartments, where residents share in the corporation that owns the building. These apartments are generally in buildings constructed in the 1920s, and as that was a time when real estate was inexpensive, these co-ops had large, open floor plans. Today, however, only a few of the biggest condominiums may have 2,500 square feet, and in general a new one-bedroom apartment averages

900 square feet and a two-bedroom about 1,200–1,300 square feet.

Small, stucco single-family bungalows line the streets in the western sections of the city, and large, well-designed homes are more frequent in the northern districts of Pacific Heights and the Marina, farther west at Seacliff, and in enclaves such as Cole Valley, Diamond Heights, and Sherwood Forest. All areas have low-rise apartment buildings, some have high-rise apartment complexes, and just about all have some semidetached row houses.

Victorian houses are San Francisco's pride. Although thousands disappeared in 1906, some 14,000 survived the fire and have been preserved, primarily throughout the Mission, Cow Hollow, Pacific Heights, and Alamo Square districts. Victorians may be garish or gracious, they may appear in a number of styles such as Queen Anne, Italianate, or Stick, they may be single-family homes or two-flats, or—as along Union Street—they may have been converted into stores and offices. No matter what their state, Victorians are always sought after and do not come cheap; a few still needing restoration are left, but for the most part they have already been refurbished and decorated in the glorious colors that have earned them the name of "San Francisco's painted ladies."

But Victorians, famous and expensive as they may be, are not all the city offers. If you are interested in historic houses, look also for the Brown Shingles popular in the 1890s, single-family homes built in reaction to the ornate Victorian. Made of natural materials, used simply and frankly, with cedar shingles and window trims of plain broad planks, they were still fairly Victorian in attitude. It wasn't until the early part of the next century that the one-story Craftsman Bungalow led the city away from its previous era. By the twenties, the compact California Bungalow, with its front porch and stucco walls, had become predominant in the then-developing western portions of the city. All these interesting styles still exist in the city and occasionally come up for sale.

Photo: San Francisco Convention & Visitors Bureau

*The right side of this Victorian was built in 1876 in the Italianate style, and the addition built in 1895, in the Queen Anne style.*

## Thinking About Price

First you should remember that San Francisco rates among the ten most expensive housing markets in the world and is the most expensive in the country. That said, you should next figure out which are the best resale locations in the city, such as in good school districts, in sunny areas, or in upcoming parts of the city, although these of course are the most expensive. Some districts — the Marina, Pacific Heights, Noe Valley, the Castro — are always in strong demand. Others are in upward transition, both in atmosphere and price — Hayes Valley, SOMA, Potrero Hill, Bernal Heights. Note that most neighborhoods have their own improvement associations, local residents who are vigilant about keeping the character of the area intact, which will, of course, maintain the value of real estate as well as that area's lifestyle. A general rule is "the better the view, the higher the price; the farther out into the fog, the lower the price."

Neighborhoods that are "coming up" are doing so quickly: a house that cost $180,000 in Bernal Heights just five years ago, for instance, may cost $350,000 today. The California Association of Realtors has said that "only 20 percent of households would be able to buy the city's median-priced home at $331,100." But "median" prices include the 10 percent that sell for above $1 million, as well as the 90 percent that may sell for $280,000, so affordable apartments and houses do exist. Yet the high end of the market is expanding and going higher: in 1998, some 11 homes in the city were sold for $5 million or more, and one outstanding two-bedroom 5,000 square foot apartment on Russian Hill sold for $15 million. Although these are exceptions, it is true that some 75 percent of the best properties receive multiple offers; in 1998–99, the winner bid at least 5–10 percent over the asking price.

If a job is bringing you to the area, inquire of the Human Resources department (during your compensation negotiation) as to whether the company offers housing incentives or a relocation package. Some do.

83

# STUDENT HOUSING

Fortunately, universities have housing offices to help find students appropriate housing; some have on-campus housing. For temporary and inexpensive accommodations, San Francisco has several youth hostels that offer basic domitory-style rooms for basic prices. Currently, the price per night runs to about $15, and there is a two-week maximum stay. If you are bringing valuables such as computers or printers, inquire as to their safekeeping; some have provision for safe storage, others do not. The two below are members of Hostelling International (www.hiayh.org), but there are others; see the Yellow Pages under Hostels. For the HI hostels, membership in Hostelling International is required: membership may be purchased on-site.

- **HI Fisherman's Wharf**: Fort Mason, Building 240 (tel: 771-7277; fax: 771-1468; www.norcalhostels.org). One hundred and fifty beds in an urban park on the Bay, formerly a military base. Credit cards accepted; reservations advisable. At the Marina and close to Fisherman's Wharf.
- **HI Union Square:** 312 Mason Street (tel: 788-5604; fax: 788-3023; www.norcalhostels.org). Two hundred and twenty beds in the heart of the downtown area; reservations required.

## Roommates

Sharing apartments is common, and roommate services offer referral services. In addition to the agencies below—most of which also handle regular rentals—look on bulletin boards at universities or at the Rainbow Grocery (see Chapter Thirteen).

- **Original San Francisco Roommate Referral Service**: 610-A Cole Street (tel: 558-9191; 800/446-2887; www.roommatelink.com)
- **Spring Street**: 3129 Fillmore Street (tel: 441-2309; www.springstreet.com)

- **Rent Tech**: 4054 18th Street, in the Castro (tel: 863-7368; fax: 552-8447; www.renttech.com); also at 1212A Union Street

## RETIREMENT LIVING

If you are planning to retire to San Francisco, as many people do, you might consider one of the attractive urban complexes that offer independent-living apartments plus assisted living and medical care programs. These complexes are convenient with respect to cultural events, the city's restaurants, and downtown shopping. Others dot the Bay Area, up into the Sonoma and Napa Valleys. *San Francisco* magazine frequently runs an advertising section on retirement living.

- **San Francisco Towers**: 1661 Pine Street (tel: 776-0500)
- **The Sequoias**: 1400 Geary Boulevard, near Gough (tel: 922-9700)
- **Coventry Park**: 1550 Sutter Street (tels: 921-1552, 800/722-1414)
- **The Carlisle**: 1450 Post Street (tel: 929-0200)

# Chapter Four

# LOGISTICS OF SETTLING IN

## GENERAL INFORMATION

For general information on living in San Francisco, dial **Local Source**, an automated 24-hour service that covers a variety of helpful subjects (tel: 808-5000; www.localsource.net/sanfrancisco). A listing of the four-digit subject codes can be found at the beginning of the Yellow Pages.

## ELECTRICITY HOOKUP

In most rental homes you will be expected to pay for your use of electricity and gas, but in some they are included in the rent. The electric utility industry in California has been deregulated, meaning that home owners may choose their own electricity provider. **PG&E (Pacific Gas and Electric)**, formerly the public monopoly in the state, continues to maintain the poles and lines for all electric service in California, and it is still the major provider of residential electricity and gas. PG&E's offices are open 8:30 am–5:30 pm weekdays (tel: 800/743-5000). New customers may be asked to pay a deposit, which will be applied (with interest accrued) to the monthly bill after one year if all bills have been paid on time.

For information on other registered electric service providers that meet the State's financial, technical and operational requirements, call **Electric Education Call Center** (tel: 800/789-0550). When considering a provider, consider the initiation and sign-up fees, length of contract, and how the electricity is generated.

Note that in the United States electricity is 110 volts, 60 hertz, and appliances brought from abroad that run on 220 volts will not run as they should. Fortunately, all housing comes with major appliances such as refrigerators and stoves, and sometimes with clothes washers and dryers. Otherwise, appliances in the United States are not particularly expensive, so it would be most efficient just to plan on purchasing what you need here. See Chapter Sixteen for appliance shops.

## TELEPHONE SERVICE

Local telephone service is provided by **Pacific Bell (Pac Bell)**. Long distance service may be handled by any one of a number of providers. Rates and services among carriers vary widely, so shop around; advertisements appear regularly in the media. Owing to inexpensive options and the advent of the Internet, rates are dropping rapidly. At this writing, plans costing 7¢ per minute nationwide at any time of day are being offered by **AT&T**, **MCI**, and others; some offer free or discounted service on low-use days. People who make international calls regularly should inquire about international telephone rates, which are also dropping quickly.

To connect your residential telephone, consult the White Pages, which details the rates, hookup and repair procedures, and all options such as call-waiting and voice mail; then call Pac

Bell (tel: 800/310-2355). Customer service responds in English, Cantonese and Mandarin, Spanish, Korean, Vietnamese, Filipino, and Japanese; see the telephone book under Pacific Bell for their specific telephone numbers.

### Telephone Books

Pac Bell delivers current telephone books when your new service is hooked up. New telephone books are issued annually in September. They are generally left in the lobby of apartment buildings or delivered to the door of private residences. Informational pages at the beginning of each book are multilingual, in English, Chinese, and Spanish.

The San Francisco **White Pages** are in one volume and include Brisbane, Colma, and Daly City; city, county and federal government listings are first, located by a blue edge to their pages. Business listings are edged in pink. The remainder, on plain paper, are residential listings. The **Yellow Pages**, also in one volume, are arranged alphabetically by category; a center insert also lists services with Internet addresses by category.

# TELEVISION AND RADIO RECEPTION

Basic television channels—the three national networks and some local stations—are free, but reception may not be good, depending on the area. Most people subscribe to cable television, which offers good reception on all channels and the option to subscribe at an extra charge to various movie channels. Call **AT&T Cable Services** (tel: 877/824-2288). The daily newspapers detail each evening's television programs, and the Sunday papers publish a weekly schedule.

With some 80 radio stations in the Bay Area, you can probably find just what you're looking for, in whatever language. FM reception may depend on what side of a hill you're living on, and you may need an outside antenna. AM reception is generally clear. The newspapers list the radio stations.

# ACCESSING THE INTERNET

All of the nationwide Internet providers have local access numbers in San Francisco and the Bay Area. If you have to find a new provider, you might ask your colleagues for their recommendations or take a look at the Internet magazines. If you need to check your e-mail before you are set up, try one of the Internet access points listed below, which should also have information about Internet providers. The **San Francisco Main Library** in the Civic Center provides Internet access, as do the Sony and Microsoft shops at **Metreon** in Yerba Buena, but they are usually crowded and suggest a time limit for access. **Kinko's** copy shops have Internet access and most are open 24 hours. Try also these cyber-cafes:

- **Club-I Internet Cafe**: 850 Folsom Street (tel: 777-2582)
- **Circadia Coffee House**: 2727 Mariposa Street (tel: 552-2649)

# MAIL DELIVERY

The Post Office delivers mail addressed to you at your new address without official notification, although you will have no doubt submitted a Change of Address card to your previous post office. There is one mail delivery per day, Sundays and holidays excepted. Until you have a permanent mailing address you may have mail sent to your name at General Delivery, San Francisco CA 94142. Pick it up at the Civic Center Station, 101 Hyde Street, at Golden Gate Avenue; hours Monday–Saturday, 10:00 am–2:00 pm. Bring identification.

Each postal "zip code" has a post office. All are open weekdays from 8:30/9:00 am to 5:00 pm; most, but not all, are open Saturdays for some portion of the day. For the post office nearest you and its hours of operation, see the informational section in the Yellow Pages; calling a central number also connects you to any post office (info tel: 800/275-8777).

# TRASH COLLECTION

Almost all new apartments and houses have in-sink garbage disposals to handle most food waste. For the rest, in large buildings, both trash collection and recycling of paper, glass, and metal are taken care of by the management. In small buildings, tenants themselves may have to place the blue recycling boxes by the curb on the days specified for that neighborhood. If you live in a house, you will have to arrange for garbage collection. Ask your neighbors or the previous owner of your home which scavenger company is used in your area. Bills are generally sent quarterly, and costs average about $12 per month.

# EARTHQUAKE INSURANCE

Homeowners may want to take out earthquake insurance, as part of the homeowners' insurance policy; inquire of your insurance agent. The **CEA**'s **(California Earthquake Authority)** "mini-policy" is available through many insurance agencies (CEA tel: 916/492-4300); other companies offer policies that are not part of the CEA system.

On a practical note, no matter where you are in the Bay Area, you should have a working flashlight in your home and perhaps some candles, a portable radio, a standard, non-electric telephone, and a few gallons of water—just in case. Always keep enough medication to tide you over and a small reserve of cash. Many stores in the Bay Area sell earthquake kits.

# OPENING A BANK ACCOUNT

Opening a bank account is easier than in some other countries. You will only need to provide a picture identification, an address, and enough money to make your initial deposit. When choosing a bank or a savings or loan association, make sure it is part of the federal insurance systems FDIC or FSLIC, to ensure that your funds will not be at risk. Consider a credit union, for they often offer good terms, both on accounts and fees, and on interest paid on time deposits and savings accounts.

Inquire as to all options open to you, especially their charges; with a sizeable deposit you may avoid the various user and monthly fees, and some offer no-fee checking. Ask if you may bank by Internet. Banks are affiliated with major networks such as CIRRUS or PLUS, which allows withdrawal of cash from automatic teller machines (ATMs); when choosing a bank, inquire whether it charges for using other banks' ATMs. Many shops and groceries accept bank cards, which, unlike charge cards, debit your account immediately.

You may be asked whether you wish to apply for a Visa/ Master Card. Inquire as to the rates of interest charged, for rates vary and low-interest cards are available. Note that it is illegal in California for merchants to use your credit card as identification; they may not write its number down on your check. Don't let this happen.

The two largest banks in California are Wells Fargo and Bank of America (BofA), and both have branches throughout the city. In any case, your bank should be convenient to your home or workplace. Banks are open weekdays only and are also closed on holidays.

# FINDING A LAUNDRY

You can find self-service laundromats in every neighborhood. Machines generally accept quarters only. Although many sell soap powders, it's better to bring your own; it's cheaper, and you can choose the kind you like. If you would like to be entertained while doing your laundry, try **Brain/Wash** at 1122 Folsom, between 7th and 8th Street (tel: 861-3663); wash your clothes, eat a meal and drink some wine, and listen to music or comedy.

Ask your neighbors for recommendations for dry cleaners, for there are many. Cleaning of standard items generally takes about three days, but most cleaners have "early bird specials:"

clothes that are brought in before a certain time (8:30 am or 9:00 am) may be picked up the same day after 5:00 pm; of course, many have home pickup and delivery. Hard-to-clean items take longer, as do items that require repair. **Meaders**, established in 1912, has four locations. Cleaners that advertise "hand finishing" or "French cleaning" do well with more delicate items; **Locust** at 3585 Sacramento Street (tel: 346-9271) and the nearby **Peninou French Laundry and Cleaners**, established in 1903, at 3707 Sacramento (tel: 751-9200) are two high quality cleaners. Cleaners do laundry as well as dry cleaning. See *Cleaners* in the Yellow Pages.

# GETTING YOUR HAIR CUT

Many of the city's hair salons are unisex. Prices vary widely, depending primarily on location. Salons near Union Square charge more than a local hairdresser in one of the outer districts. Tips are not included in the price, and every person — shampoo person, hair stylist, coat check — gets a tip based on level of service. A few chains — **Supercuts, The Beauty Store** — offer good prices and standard services. Of course the quality varies with the particular hairdresser at any salon, so you just have to experiment until you find someone you like. Salons may offer more services than you are used to: massage, music, art exhibits, etc; see also Chapter Fifteen under Spas for **Elizabeth Arden** and **77 Maiden Lane**, two elegant multi-service salons. Almost all shops are closed on Sunday and many on Monday. See *Beauty Salons* in the Yellow Pages.

- **Architects and Heroes**: 2239 Fillmore, near Sacramento (tel: 921-8383). Consistently voted one of the best hairdressers in the city. Open Sunday. Also at 580 Bush Street (tel: 391-8833).
- **Cowboys & Angels**: 207 Powell Street, Suite 400 (tel: 362-8516). Trendy, fun salon for young people who want to look wild and for corporate types who don't.
- **Mister Lee Beauty, Hair & Health Spa**: 834 Jones (tel: 474-

6002). Rated among the best in the city.

- **Snippity Crickets**: 3562 Sacramento (tel: 441-9363). Welcoming atmosphere for children's haircuts. Also in Berkeley. Open Sunday.
- **Vidal Sassoon**: 359 Sutter (tel: 397-5105). Popular salon, part of a nationwide chain.
- **Yosh for Hair**: 173 Maiden Lane (tel: 989-7704). Among the top hair styling salons in the city.

# READING A NEWSPAPER

As of this writing, San Francisco has two daily newspapers, the *San Francisco Chronicle* and the *San Francisco Examiner*. Both papers have recently been sold, however, and their future directions remain uncertain. Currently, on Sunday the two papers put out one combined issue. The *Oakland Tribune* and the *Berkeley Barb* serve the East Bay, as does the *Contra Costa Times*. In the South Bay, the *San Mateo County Times* and the *San Jose Mercury News* are the standards, and in the North Bay, the *Marin Independent*. All are available for subscription to be delivered to your door before dawn, as are such national newspapers as the *New York Times* and the *Wall Street Journal*.

Some of the most interesting and popular local newspapers, however, are free. *The Bay Guardian* is a liberal weekly that covers issues of interest throughout the Bay Area and reviews events and cultural activities. The *San Francisco Weekly* basically covers the same for the city. Both are issued on Wednesday and can be found in news boxes on street corners.

Most city districts have their own newspapers, with articles of local interest and ads for neighborhood services. *San Francisco Downtown*, for instance, covers the Financial, Retail and South or Market areas, *The Nob Hill Gazette* covers Nob Hill, and, obviously, *North Beach Now* covers North Beach, plus a section on South Beach. The *San Francisco Observer*, which serves "the heart of San Francisco," covers neighborhoods around the Haight, Hayes

Valley, Fillmore, and Duboce Triangle. Look for the tabloid for your community; many are delivered each month.

Various ethnic communities have their own newspapers. The *Tenderloin Times*, for example, is published in English, Chinese, Cambodian, and Vietnamese. Look for *Asian Week* at news boxes on city streets and in Japantown for *Nichi Bei Times*, a Japanese-English daily. The national *Sing Tao Daily* has an extensive section on California and is read by 100,000 Asians. *El Mensajero* is the bilingual weekly for the Latino Community, and *El Latino* is only in Spanish. *San Francisco Bay View* is a free weekly newspaper for the African-American community. There are others.

Leading the long list of gay publications are the bi-weekly *Bay Area Reporter* (Bar) and the *San Francisco Bay Times*. *Icon* is a lesbian newspaper, published monthly.

## Foreign Publications

European and Asian publications and some American hometown newspapers are found in a few shops around the city, and **Borders** on Union Square has a good selection. Chinatown's newsstands sell a good selection of Chinese papers, and you may find the free *Chinese TV Guide* tabloid in some restaurants and Chinese shops. **Kinokuniya Bookstore** in the Japan Center has an outstanding selection of Japanese publications. One news kiosk, on Sansome between Bush and Sutter, has a good selection of foreign and hometown newspapers, as do some newsstands such as **Eastern News**. See also Chapter Sixteen, under Foreign Bookstores.

- *Union Square* — **Harold's International News**: 524 Geary (tel: 441-2665)
- *North Beach* — **Cavalli Italian Bookstore**: 1441 Stockton (tel: 421-4219)
- *Chinatown Gate* — **Café de la Presse**: 352 Grant (tel: 398-2680)
- *Pacific Heights* — **Juicy News**: 2453 Fillmore Street (tel: 441-3051)

# FINDING YOUR SPIRITUAL HOME

Finding the right place of worship shouldn't be difficult. Generally the city's churches and synagogues are welcoming of anybody who wants to worship, whether affiliated with that religion or not. San Franciscans practice their religion in the way they do everything else—according to their own reasons and tastes—and it is said that only some 35 percent of the population is identified with a major religious denomination. Nonetheless there are multilingual options for daily or weekly worship for just about any faith. Most churches and synagogues sponsor educational and social programs for their congregants.

There are so many faiths—traditional denominations, evangelical, messianic, and those that worship in their own ways, such as the **Church of Saint John Coltrane,** an African Orthodox church that uses the music of the great jazz saxophonist in its liturgy—that they would be impossible to list here. And there are so many worship sites that they, too, would be impossible to mention. Instead, this small sampling should serve to show the diversity of opportunities in San Francisco. See the Yellow Pages under *Churches* or *Synagogues*. Some print their worship schedules.

- *Baptist*—**19th Avenue Baptist Church**: 1370 19th Avenue, at Irving (tel: 564-7721). The most active of the Baptist congregations. Services in English, Cantonese, Vietnamese and Arabic. Bible study in all languages.
- *Buddhist*—**Zen Center**: 300 Page Street (tel: 863-3136). Buddhist temple and information point for Buddhism in the Bay Area.
- *Catholic*—The major Catholic cathedral is **The Cathedral of St. Mary**, at 111 Gough Street, at Geary (tel: 567-2020). Masses in English and Spanish. For information on the Catholic community, schools, and churches, contact the Archdiocese office at 445 Church Street (tel: 565-3600).
- *Christian Science*—**First Church of Christ, Scientist**: 1700

Franklin Street (tel: 673-3544). Call for other places of worship and reading rooms.

- *Church of Christ* — **Civic Center Church of Christ**: 250 Van Ness Avenue, at Grove (tel: 861-5292). An international and multi-ethnic congregation of Caucasians, African Americans, and Asians.

- *Episcopal* — **Grace Cathedral**: 1051 Taylor Street, at California (info tel: 749-6310). This "modern Gothic" cathedral is the seat of the Episcopal Church in San Francisco, and hosts lectures, concerts, etc. Evening prayer, Evensong on Thursdays, carillon recitals and concerts, in addition to regular scheduled worship.

- *Islam* — For information on worship, call the **Islamic Center of San Francisco** (tel: 552-8831) or the **Islamic Bookstore and Islamic Society**: 20 Jones Street (tel: 863-8005).

- *Jewish* — **Congregation Emanu-El**: 2 Lake Street (tel: 751-2535). Reform temple. For information on any aspect of Judaism in San Francisco, call the **Jewish Community Information & Referral Service** at 121 Steuart Street (tel: 777-4545). Inquire about the annually issued *Resource*, an extensive guide to Jewish life in the Bay Area.

- *Methodist* — **Glide Memorial United Methodist Church**: 330 Ellis Street, at Taylor (tel: 771-6300). In the heart of the Tenderloin, Glide is the city's most celebrated religious gathering place. Sunday services are always crowded. This is the church most known in the city for social activism, feeding and providing job training for the poor and homeless.

- *Methodist* — **Park Presidio United Methodist Church**: 4301 Geary Boulevard (tel: 751-4438). Services in English, Chinese and Korean. Congregation involved in community projects.

- *Presbyterian* — **Noe Valley Ministry**: 1021 Sanchez, at 23rd Street (tel: 282-2317). The *de facto* community center for Noe Valley, this church is an interfaith gathering point, providing social events, meetings and concerts.

- *Quaker*—**Friends Quaker Meeting**: 65 9th Street (tel: 431-7440) Unprogrammed meeting. Socially active.
- *Unitarian*—**First Unitarian Universalist Church**: 1187 Franklin Street (tel: 776-4580). Congregation has worshiped here since 1888.

### Gay and Lesbian Worship

San Francisco's churches and synagogues are openly welcoming of gay and lesbians, singles or couples. Although active and integrated into the city's spiritual life, gays and lesbians are also forming supportive spiritual groups and worship sites of their own. Progressive in outlook, these communities are usually open to people of all sexual identities.

- *Catholic*—**Dignity San Francisco**: 1329 7th Avenue (tel: 681-2491)
- *Interfaith Christian*—**Metropolitan Community Church**: 150 Eureka at 18th St (tel: 863-4434)
- *Jewish*—**Congregation Sha'ar Zahav**: 290 Dolores Street (tel: 861-6932)

# REGISTERING TO VOTE

There are no time-linked residency requirements for voter registration; all citizens over the age of 18 with proof of a permanent address may vote. Call the **Department of Elections** at 633 Folsom Street, Room 109, for a registration form up to one month before an election (tel: 554-4375). Otherwise, before each election or primary there are usually people outside supermarkets registering voters.

# STORAGE LOCKERS

Last, if your new home is smaller than you had imagined and you need to store some belongings, consider a self-storage locker. Sizes range from those that would hold a few items to those in which you might store all your furniture while looking for housing. In these dry, well-maintained warehouses, there is 24-hour security; you retain the key to your own locker and have daily access. Sometimes there are waiting lists, but lockers do come available, and new warehouses are opening up. There are others outside the central districts, in the East Bay, and in Marin. See the Yellow Pages under *Storage — Self Service*.

- **Attic Self Storage**: 2440 16th Street (tel: 626-0800)
- **American Storage Unlimited**: 600 Amador Street (tel: 800/ 863-5820)
- **City Storage Loc-N-Stor**: 144 Townsend Street (tel: 495-2300); 500 Indiana Street (tel: 436-9900)
- **Crocker's Lockers**: 1400 Folsom Street (tel: 626-6665)

# Chapter Five

# FORMALITIES FOR FOREIGNERS

## IMMIGRATION

Perhaps the streets of the United States were not paved with gold as so many immigrants imagined when they came to these shores, but America has nonetheless been, since its earliest days, a land of opportunity. Whether people came to escape poverty or politics, America has always seemed to be—and often has been—the world's most beneficial haven. America has, in fact, gained its strength by being a "melting pot" of cultures, and it is immigration and assimilation that have created the world's most successful multi-ethnic nation. Immigration has waxed and waned over the centuries, owing to external factors such as wars or internal factors such as changes in societal attitudes. During the 1990s, the population of the United States grew by only 8 percent, but the percentage of foreign-born residents grew by some 30 percent. In 1996, some 900,000 immigrants came to the United States from 206 nations; Mexico and then the Philippines are the largest sending countries. One-third of all immigrants come to California, and about one-quarter of California residents are not native-born.

Although both the citizens and the government of the United States understand and believe that diversity enriches society, the country has always had mixed feelings about immigration: the subject of limiting immigration always comes up during economic downturns, for it is widely held that immigrants take jobs away from low-skilled American citizens.

The problem is compounded by the number of illegal immigrants who cross untended borders. For instance, since 1990, one million Mexicans have immigrated into the United States, some 80 percent of them illegally. Efforts to strengthen the borders have had some effect, but it is difficult to police the long border between the United States and Mexico. Thus, although some 170,000 illegal immigrants were deported in 1998, official efforts to limit immigration also tend to focus on legal immigration. A 1997 report to the United States Congress by the Commission on Immigration Reform recommended some immigration reform, but at this writing it is not yet clear which recommendations will be implemented.

Nonetheless, immigration laws are currently—and will no doubt remain—very complex, and it is important to consult the American Embassy in your country (or the consulate nearest you) long in advance of your desired emigration and to receive the most current information. Have ready as much documentation as possible concerning your personal history, health, qualifications, financial condition, and plans for your stay in the United States. You can receive detailed information on eligibility and requirements for immigrant visas on the Internet, from the websites of the State Department (www.state.gov; www.travel.state.gov) or the **Immigration and Naturalization Service (INS)**, an agency of the Department of Justice (www.ins.usdoj.gov). In the United States, you may also call the INS Forms Request Line (tel: 800/ 870-3676).

## Visas

All people entering the United States must have a valid passport, although in most cases Canadians may provide only legal proof of residency. Citizens of most western European countries, the United Kingdom, Argentina, Australia, New Zealand, Singapore, and Japan do not need visas for stays of under 90 days, but must complete the I-94 Nonimmigrant Visa Waiver upon arrival; almost everyone else must have a visa, obtained before departure from the American Embassy in your country or the nearest consulate; you will also need to complete the I-94 Form and keep it with you during your stay. Leave enough time to apply for and receive the visa; lines at visa offices can be long and employees harried. Depending on your country and situation, you can sometimes apply for the visa at your travel agent, while booking your flight.

Upon arrival at a port of entry, be prepared to wait in line at the immigration booth, to show your passport, visa, and return ticket (if appropriate), and to explain the reason for your visit. If you need help, immigration officers at the airport have information. In dire situations, you may wish to call your country's embassy in Washington, D.C. or its consulate in San Francisco (see below).

## Employment-based Visas

Do not expect to enter the United States and then to look for and find a permanent, legal job. There are, however, a variety of options for coming to the United States to work, depending on your skills, abilities, and experience in your field. It also often depends on how much an employer needs your unique services. The INS issues a booklet *Instructions for Completing Petition for a Nonimmigrant Worker, Form I-129*, which spells out in considerable detail all the categories of people eligible to work in the United States, the

101

circumstances of the employment, and how to apply. For immigrant worker visas, it is the would-be employer who makes the application for the I-140, which allows certain workers to apply for one of the E1-4 visas; these forms are not available outside the United States. Often, particular educational levels must have been reached, professional-certification requirements must have been met, or the applicant's experience so unique that the employer can show that no American citizens are qualified to fill the particular position. People with other specialty occupations such as licensed nurses are likely to receive permission to enter without much difficulty. Artists and entertainers must have demonstrated recognized achievements in their field, or national or international acclaim. The H1B visa is for high-tech workers; as of this writing, the annual allocation is 115,000 visas, and the cap is generally reached early in the fiscal year.

The publication mentioned above also spells out the requirements for those who may come to work permanently and those who may come to work temporarily. An example of a temporary position might be an internationally renowned professor who comes to a university to teach, or an acclaimed artist or entertainer who is coming to perform on tour. In California, applications may be had from the **Employment Development Office** in Sacramento (tel: 916/464-3400).

There are many categories for eligibility, including those for religious workers and those for entrepreneurs who are investing at least $1 million in an enterprise that creates a minimum of 10 new jobs in the United States. It is extremely helpful to check the State Department website.

Finally, do not expect to come and find illegal work, despite tales from your friends of how easy it is to find work in a restaurant or bar. Employers face stiff fines if caught employing non-documented foreigners, so this kind of job market is drying up.

## North American Free Treaty Agreement

To enter the United States under the North American Free Trade Agreement (NAFTA), Canadians and Mexicans should understand the conditions that apply to entry for business or work purposes. These are set forth in Justice Department Form M-316, *The North American Free Trade Agreement (NAFTA) between the United States, Canada and Mexico*, available at immigration offices, at United States consulates, and from Free Trade Specialists at most of the ports of entry between the United States and Canada/Mexico.

- *Canada* — **United States Embassy**: 100 Wellington Street, Ottawa, ON KIP 5T1 (tel: 613/238-4470)
- *Mexico* — **United States Embassy**: Paseo de la Reforma 305, Cuauhtémoc 06500, near the Monumento a la Independencia (tel: 01/5209-9100); consulates in Cuidad Juarez, Hermonsillo, Guadalajara

## Student Visas and Permits

Some 480,000 foreigners are studying in the United States, the majority in California. The highest percentage are Asians from Japan, China, and Korea. Universities welcome foreign students, providing their credentials meet the institutions' standards and all immigration criteria are met.

In most countries the **United States Information Agency (USIA/USIS)** maintains an Educational Advising Center. Centers can be found at U.S. embassies, Fulbright Commissions, non-profit organizations with overseas operations, and at local universities. These centers provide general information about the system of education and the admissions process in the United States, and they also offer individual advising (sometimes for a fee). Inquire of the American Embassy in your country. You can also get information from the State Department's website: click on "The Department," then on the region and country you are coming from; highlight the option "education" or "study."

103

To receive the visa that will allow you to enter the United States to study, you must already have been accepted at an accredited institution. Upon acceptance, you will receive from the Admissions Office the I-20 Certificate of Eligibility, which allows you to enter the school on a particular date. Take the I-20 to the American Embassy or your nearby consulate to apply for the appropriate visa: F1, J1, or M1. In addition to your passport and the I-20, you will need to show that your finances (or the finances of your sponsor) allow you to study without relying on income from working, although some work is permitted. Visas are generally valid during the duration of study. If you decide to postpone the entry date for any reason, you will have to start the process again and get a revised I-20 from the institution.

Although most universities have health clinics on their campuses, they all require foreign students to have health insurance, and most sell insurance plans that meet at least the minimum levels of the National Association for Foreign Student Affairs (NAFSA); if you have insurance, it must meet NAFSA's minimum criteria. Insurance requirements appear on the institution's application forms.

Part-time work on campus may exist at some universities, especially for graduate students who may be offered teaching/research assistantships. Although almost all foreign students must have taken the TOEFL test for admission to an American institution, the TSE (Test of Spoken English) may also be required for those interested in teaching assistantships. Spouses who enter the country with an F2 visa (dependent of an F-1 holder) may not work but may study full- or part-time as long as they are living with the holder of the F1.

For work and study programs, internships and seasonal work, contact the **Council on International Educational Exchange (CIEE)** or access their website for extensive information (www.ciee.org):

- *Australia*: University Center, Level 8, 210 Clarence Street (tel: 07/3849-8463; fax: 07/3849-8556)
- *France*: Centre Odéon Franco-Américain: 1, place de l'Odeon, Paris 75006 (tel: 01.44.41.74.74; fax: 01.43.26.97.45)
- *Japan*: Cosmos Aoyama Gallery Floor, 5-5367 Jingumae Shibuya-Ku (tel: 03/5467-5502; fax: 03/5467-7031)
- *United Kingdom:* 52 Poland Street, London W1V 4JQ (info tel: 171/478-2000; fax: 171/734-7322)
- *United States*: 205 East 42nd Street, New York, NY 10017 (tel: 212/822-2600; fax: 212/822-2699)

While in the United States, carry your student identification card with you. Also get the **International Student Identity Card (ISIC)**, an internationally recognized document which shows your student status and offers discounts on a variety of services and travel; you will need to bring proof of your registration as a student. Cards cost about $20, and travel agents often carry them, as does **Council Travel**, which is part of CIEE; for their offices worldwide, see their website above. In San Francisco offices are at 530 Bush Street (tel: 421-3473) and at 225 West Portal Avenue (tel: 566-6222). In Berkeley, Council Travel is at 2846 Channing Way (tel: 510/848-8604).

## Diversity Immigrant Program

The Diversity Immigrant Program is a lottery that offers 50,000 permanent residence visas each year. The program is divided into six regions: Asia; South America, Central America, and the Caribbean; Europe; Africa; Oceania; and North America (the Bahamas). No one country receives more than 3,500 diversity visas in any year. Applications for a visa date of two years in the future are generally due toward the end of October. Applications that arrive after the deadline are not considered. Check for current deadlines.

Certain countries within broad categories above are not entitled to apply, owing to the large number of applicants from those countries under other immigration programs. This includes Canada and Mexico, which have special programs under the North American Free Trade Agreement. At this writing, other countries excluded are China and Taiwan, Colombia, Dominican Republic, El Salvador, Haiti, India, Jamaica, Mexico, Philippines, Poland, South Korea, United Kingdom (except Northern Ireland), and Vietnam.

In general, an applicant must have been born in an eligible country and have either a high school education or its equivalent, or have two years of work experience in a job that requires at least two years of training to perform.

Inquire at the consulate nearest you for current information or search the INS website (www.ins.usdoj.gov). Basically, there are no entry forms: on a plain sheet of paper, type or print (in the English alphabet) your full name (surname first, and underlined), date and place of birth (and the same information for your dependents), plus your full mailing address. Attach with tape one recent photograph of 1.5 inches (37 mm). Sign the entry form; an original signature is required.

Put the entry form into a business-size envelope and as the return address put your full mailing address and place of birth. Mail it (regular mail only) to the address below. Note that the address for each of the six areas is the same, but that the zip code is different. If the application is sent to the wrong zip code, it will be disqualified. The address is: DV Program (add year of application, such as "DV01" for 2001) National Visa Center, Portsmouth NH USA. The zip code for each area of origin is:

- Asia: 00210
- South America, Central America, Caribbean: 00211
- Europe: 00212
- Africa: 00213
- Oceania: 00214
- North American: 00215

## Petition by a Relative

A U.S. citizen may petition to have a family member come to the United States. "Family members" include a spouse, parents, children, or siblings. First, the INS must approve an immigrant petition (INS Form I-130) filed by the relative in the United States. Upon approval, the State Department allocates an immigrant visa number to the overseas relative. With this, the overseas relative applies for the immigrant visa at the U.S. Consulate. This, unfortunately, is not a particularly efficient method of immigrating into this country, nor is it the most sure, for the number of immigrant visa numbers are limited and there is a preference system. First come spouses, parents and unmarried children under the age of 21; next come all the rest. Thus, even after the forms have been filled out, the $110 fee paid, and the appointment made for the interview, it may take many years for the application to take effect. Nonetheless, if you wish to follow this path to immigration, ask your relative in the United States to request the Department of Justice Form I-130, the *Petition for Alien Relative*. If you want to estimate the time it will take to receive the immigrant visa number, you can access the State Department's Visa Bulletin (http://travel.state.gov/visa_bulletin.html). Compare your number with the number the Department is then working on.

# CITIZENSHIP

After you have received your "green card" that allows you to stay and work in the United States, start thinking about citizenship. With certain exceptions, citizenship may be applied for after holding the "green card" for at least five years. Apply three months before the residency requirement is fulfilled.

An applicant for citizenship must be able to speak, read and write English (again, with certain exceptions, such as being over 55 years of age and having lived in the United States for 15 years), know the fundamentals of United States government and American history, and be of "good moral character."

## INS IN SAN FRANCISCO

The San Francisco District Office of the INS is at 444 Washington Street, near Sansome (tel: 705-4411). It is open from 6:45 am to 3:00 pm weekdays except Wednesday, when it closes at 2:45 pm. Waits can be extremely long. The office has forms and information; you may also order forms by telephone, if you know the number or name of the form you need (tel: 800/870-3676), or order them by fax: 844-5270, 855-9950).

If you need passport or immigration photographs or finger-print documentation, try the two shops below, across from the INS building. Both are open weekdays only.

- **Leetone Photo Center**: 615 Sansome Street (tel: 391-9890)
- **Corning Gold Photography**: 501 Washington Street (tel: 392-2223)

## FOREIGN CONSULATES

In the United States, embassies are in Washington, D.C., but countries with many residents or visitors in San Francisco maintain consulates here as well. Consulates are most helpful to their country's citizens during times of crisis: they replace lost passports and help in medical or legal emergencies by making referrals to appropriate doctors, dentists, or lawyers. They do not, however, help people get out of jail. Yet in all emergencies, they act as liaison between the family abroad and the person in the United States. It is a good idea to carry the telephone number of the consulate in your wallet; should trouble befall, it can be easily contacted.

For non-emergencies, embassies and consulates renew passports, record births, marriages and deaths, notarize documents, and provide advice on matters pertaining to citizenship in their country, such as filing taxes. Sometimes they offer information on local services, including lists of doctors and attorneys who speak your language, and translators.

Most consulates are open for consular affairs weekdays in the mornings only. Some have afternoon telephone hours. Find out when your consulate is open before going. On the national holidays of the United States and of your own country, the consulate will no doubt be closed. For a complete list, see the Yellow Pages under *Consulates & Other Foreign Government Representatives*.

- **Australia**: 1 Bush Street (tel: 362-6160)
- **Brazil**: 300 Montgomery Street (tel: 981-8170)
- **Britain:** 1 Sansome Street (tel: 981-3030)
- **Canada**: (visas and passports tel: 213/356-2700)
- **El Salvador**: 870 Market Street (tel: 781-7924)
- **France**: 540 Bush Street (tel: 397-4330)
- **Germany**: 1960 Jackson Street (tel: 775-1061)
- **Ireland**: 44 Montgomery Street (tel: 391-4214)
- **Israel**: 456 Montgomery Street (tel: 844-7500)
- **Italy**: 2590 Webster Street (tel: 931-4924)
- **Japan**: 50 Fremont Street, 23rd Floor (tel: 777-3533)
- **Malaysia**: 2 Embarcadero Center (tel: 421-6570)
- **Mexico**: 870 Market Street (tel: 392-5554)
- **New Zealand**: One Maritime Plaza (tel: 399-1255)
- **Philippines**: 447 Sutter Street (tel: 433-6666)
- **Russian Federation**: 2790 Green Street (tel: 202-9800)

# BRINGING

### ...Your Belongings

If your appropriate visa for residency is in order, there are no particular formalities for bringing your personal effects into the United States for your own use. If you have owned them for more than one year, there is no duty on import; antiques are also free of duty if they are more than 100 years old. It is, however, helpful to have an inventory and valuation of the belongings. For information, call the **United States Customs Service** (tel: 782-9210;

109

www.customs.ustreas.gov). Most international shippers are familiar with the paperwork and bureaucratic requirements for international shipment, and they are affiliated with moving companies in the United States.

## ...Your Appliances

As mentioned earlier, the United States uses 110-120 volt, 60 hertz electricity. Importing European appliances may be more trouble than it is worth, for appliances — large and small — are fairly inexpensive in America, and discount shops are found in every city. Most apartments and houses are equipped with stoves and refrigerators, and some with clothes washers and dryers.

## ...Your Car

All cars and vehicles coming into the country must conform with U.S. safety, bumper, and emission standards; the vehicle must have written certification that it meets emission requirements before it may be brought into the country. This may either be in the form of a statement from the Environmental Protection Agency (EPA), or a manufacturer's label in English that is affixed to the car. Unless the car was manufactured in the United States and exported, it is not likely that it will meet all standards. For information, write or telephone the EPA Programs and Compliance Division/Imports (6405-J), at 401 M. Street, S.W., Washington D.C. 20460 and ask for the *Automotive Imports Facts Manual* (tel: 202/564-9660; fax: 202/564-9596).

To bring a car into the country, you will need the shipper's original bill of lading, the bill of sale, foreign registration, and any other documents that cover the vehicle. The undercarriage of the car must be free of foreign soil, which can be accomplished by having the car steam-cleaned before shipment. Make sure you know in advance from your shipper the date the car will arrive, so that Customs can clear it. Imported cars (except some from Canada) should also have the International Registration Marker.

Except for the vehicles of returning U.S. government employees (including the military) and some citizens returning from employment abroad, foreign-made vehicles are generally dutiable at about 2.5 percent based on price paid. Contact the U.S. Customs Service at the Department of the Treasury, Washington D.C. 20229 (or any Customs office) for the brochure *Importing or Exporting a Car.*

## ...Your Pets

All dogs and cats being brought into the country must be examined at the port of entry before being allowed into the United States. (This also applies to pets that were taken out of the country and are being brought back in.) Dogs must be accompanied by a health certificate stating that they are free of diseases communicable to human beings. Both dogs and cats must be vaccinated against rabies at least 30 days before entry into the United States (except for animals under three months old). If the dog has been living in an area free of rabies, no rabies certificate is required; otherwise the dog should have a valid rabies vaccination certificate. For more details — and for details about other animals and birds — request the brochure *Pets, Wildlife: U.S. Customs* from The U.S. Customs Service, Department of the Treasury, Washington D.C. 20229 (or any Customs office).

## ...Your Money

There is no limit to the total amount of monetary instruments — cash, traveler's checks, negotiable securities — that may be brought into the United States, but if you bring in more than $10,000 (or if you receive that amount), you must file Form 4790 with the Customs Service.

## ...Your Medications

To bring medicines containing habit-forming drugs or narcotics (prescription-strength cough medicine, diuretics, heart drugs,

111

tranquilizers, etc) into the country, make sure all are properly identified and that you have a physician's prescription (or written statement that the medicine is used under a doctor's direction). Bring an amount that will tide you over until you can get a new prescription in the United States.

# CHAPTER SIX

# BRINGING THE CHILDREN

## GREAT FOR THE KIDS

San Francisco is a wonderful place to raise children. The area's moderate climate means that outdoor play is available just about any day of the year: parks and playgrounds dot the landscape, wide beaches offer endless play in the sand, and schools offer extensive extracurricular sports programs. The ethnic diversity of the city means that children will have a culturally stimulating environment in which to grow and learn. And the open friendliness of the city means a generally nurturing environment to those who avail themselves of opportunities presented. Well-behaved children are welcome in most restaurants, and even the most elegant restaurants have booster seats. Theaters, museums, private organizations,

113

*Children at play in a neighborhood park.*

the parks and other city agencies all have enriching programs for children. And the options for schooling, although seemingly complex and perhaps slightly discouraging at the outset, can offer a well-rounded education. Whatever you want for your child, you will no doubt find it in San Francisco.

## THINKING ABOUT SCHOOLS

First, think about schools. Choosing a school in San Francisco, whether elementary, middle, or high school, is not as simple as showing up on the first day of school in your neighborhood and expecting your child to receive a good education. In fact, it is wise to think about schooling well before you decide on the neighborhood where you might want to live, for the suburbs are an extremely attractive option in terms of schooling. With research and care, you should be able to find a good public school for your

114

child, or you may choose one of the excellent private schools, if tuition fees that may run as high as $15,000 per student are within your budget. If you can make a trip to San Francisco before your actual move, investigating schools should be among your priorities. Get advice from the Human Resources Department of your company, visit the San Francisco Unified School District headquarters, tour the schools you are considering, and talk to parents of children in those schools. Then, when you have found the right schools, follow carefully every procedure for application, for the most popular schools have the most applicants, and acceptance is not always assured.

There is no easy solution to schooling in the city of San Francisco. Public schools tend to be overcrowded and in the upper grades the large class size is not conducive to individual attention. Not all schools are equal in their facilities, programs, educational approach, or results, and budget cutbacks have forced major reductions in staff and in enrichment programs in areas such as art and music. Unfortunately, state and federal funding of schools is often inadequate; Gray Davis, the governor elected in 1998, has made raising the standard of education in California one of his highest priorities, but the enormous task will be difficult at best. Owing to the sheer number of children in public schools — some 5.6 million — California spends less per pupil than the national average and in 1997-98 ranked a low 46th in the country for *per capita* expenditures on education.

The above notwithstanding, the San Francisco school system educates the city's children. Public school students consistently rank above the national average in reading and math on the CTBS (Comprehensive Test of Basic Skills), a test that is given to every student to measure progress in those areas; another system-wide test, the Stanford 9 Test, compares ranks within the state and throughout the nation. But parents should remember that it also takes active parental participation to educate children in any city. Join parents' groups to understand the strengths and weaknesses

115

of your school. If arts or music programs in your child's school have been cut back, for example, make sure your child attends outside enrichment programs, either in structured public programs or through private lessons. Everything is available in San Francisco to supplement basic public school education; it just takes determination on the part of the parent to find it.

Other options exist. If you have several children to educate, you might want to consider a public elementary school and then perhaps a private high school. Legislation has recently lowered the number of students permitted in each public elementary school class, but public high school classes tend to be overcrowded, sometimes with upwards of 40 students in a class. Private high schools generally take a fair number of students from public schools, especially those who have tested well or who were in GATE programs (see below).

Private schools have distinct advantages. Although each has its own character, basically they all have smaller class size with a better teacher/student ratio, and they can give more individual attention to each child. Private schools (see below), of course, are expensive, but some do offer scholarships or other financial aid. And, although they are usually filled to capacity and the application process is stringent, there are many different types to choose from.

Try to start your research before arriving in San Francisco. Check the **San Francisco Unified School District (SFUSD)** website (www.sfusd.k12.ca.us). You might also contact **School Match, Public Priority System**, which has detailed statistics on public and private schools across the country (tel: 614/890-1573; www.schoolmatch.com). School Match can do a full search for the right school for your child. After you fill out a questionnaire detailing all your priorities, School Match will suggest schools in the area that match your preferences. The full search costs $97.50; individual reports and "snapshots" cost less.

## The Public Schools

In San Francisco, some 65,000 children attend the 77 public elementary schools (kindergarten through grade 5), 17 middle schools (grades 6–8), and 21 high schools (grades 9–12). Although a few schools offer grades K–8, most children attend a middle school. Not all schools are the same. Schools at all levels offer differing educational themes and teaching approaches; some offer academic programs while others stress technology, two are year-round, a few have language immersion programs (the language depending on the district), and some have better educational track records than others.

It is interesting to note that the highest percentage of the city's students are Chinese (27.4 percent), followed by Latino children (21.5 percent), and that Caucasians account for about 13 percent of the schooling population. Thus, no ethnic or cultural background dominates. Until 1999 the city officially maintained an ethnic and racial balance in the schools, but this was successfully challenged by the Chinese community on the grounds of discrimination. The SFUSD thus has been changing its procedures for application; it may no longer use ethnicity as a primary consideration in enrollment decisions, but may factor it in with location and economic need. One effect of the decision was the loss of almost $40 million in state funds for equalizing academic opportunities for African Americans and Latinos.

Every school offers a required core curriculum, and in addition to the themes mentioned above, some stress Bilingual Education, English-as-a-Second Language (ESL), Special Education, or the Gifted and Talented Education program (GATE); almost 15 percent of the city's students are enrolled in GATE programs. A wealth of information on public schools is available at SFUSD. SFUSD provides descriptions of each school's programs and their current "accountability report card." Much of this is also available on SFUSD's website, so if you have access to the Internet, you can obtain the information before you have to

117

Photo: Eleanor Burke

*The Marina Middle School.*

make your decisions. SFUSD, at 135 Van Ness Avenue (tel: 241-6000), also has information about the **OER (Open Enrollment Request)** application process (see below). In addition, information can be had from the **Parent Information Center** of the **Educational Placement Center**, within SFUSD (tel: 241-6085).

Every block and every street of the city is assigned to a public school "attendance zone." The sizes of these zones vary according to the number of school-age children living in them. The zones include all children, even those going to private schools. It would be ideal if popular schools were in each neighborhood and if each neighborhood had schools to accommodate all the area's kids, but this isn't the case. Thus, parents must apply for the public schools they believe would be best for their children. There is no guarantee, however, that they will be accepted. Yet, the application process is crucial to your child's education in this city.

A *regular* school is one in which children are assigned based on where they live. Most of the city's children go to schools in their attendance zone. Some of these schools can't accommodate all the children in their zone, so even if you are planning to send your child to the neighborhood school, you should apply for a place in that school during the OER process.

An *alternative* school may offer special curriculum programs or have higher standards for academic programs than a regular school. It may also have a higher degree of parent involvement. Sometimes students from particular zip codes which have had lower average performance results may be given higher priority for acceptance into an alternative school. Otherwise, acceptance is by lottery and based on the OER application.

Because they are so in demand, a few of the top high schools, the *application* schools, require a special application in addition to (or instead of) the OER. These include **Lowell**, **School of the Arts (SOTA)**, **Galileo**, and **Balboa**.

## For Non-native English Speakers

Several elementary schools within the school district (as well as preschools mentioned below) offer language immersion programs for children whose native language is other than English, and whose ability in English would not yet allow them to integrate fully into a regular English-language school. Languages include Japanese, Spanish, Chinese, and Korean. Inquire at SFUSD. In addition, **Newcomer High School** at 2340 Jackson Street offers a transitional program for newly arrived high school age students who lack adequate English language proficiency (tel: 241-6584). Students study at Newcomer High approximately one year before transferring to other high schools.

## Charter Schools

An increasingly recognized but somewhat controversial development is the use of public school funds to contract out the management of schools to private concerns. The almost 1500 "charter schools" nationwide have greater flexibility than municipality-run

119

schools in that they have autonomy in management of the schools, in hiring of teachers, and in the development of curricula and enrichment programs. Charter schools must, however, adhere to public school norms. In California, for example, they must keep track of the number of minutes of instruction for each age level, keep attendance records, and administer the annual achievement test. But standards are high: class size is usually reasonable and students receive more individual attention than in many public schools. Students often study longer hours each day and may have a somewhat longer term than a regular public school schedule. Included in the curriculum are enriched art, music and language programs which, unfortunately, have been reduced at the city's cash-strapped public schools. Teachers, who must hold teaching certificates, are also paid somewhat higher salaries. In San Francisco, the charter schools are the once-ailing Thomas Edison Elementary in Noe Valley, the Creative Arts Charter School, the Life Learning Academy, the downtown Leadership High, and Gateway High, for students with learning difficulties.

Charter schools are gaining popularity nationwide, and in 1999 President Clinton proposed spending $95 million in the following three years to bring the number of charter schools to 3,000. Yet the schools remain controversial: some educators believe that the schools are not accountable enough for their educational results across a broad spectrum of students. As in private schools, however, if the results are not forthcoming, parents will no longer support the schools. Ongoing parent involvement is fairly high, and standardized testing gives an indication of a child's progress. Nonetheless, allocating public funds to private concerns (rather than the community's voting for funds to improve the quality of municipality-run education) will remain controversial until the results are in. For information on charter schools, you can access the website of the **California Department of Education** (www.cde.ca.gov/charter).

120

## The OER

Selecting a child's school, of course, will be based on many factors other than just a school's location or reputation: the age, character, and language ability of the child should be considered, as well as the expected length of stay in San Francisco, whether permanent or temporary. The best way to determine which school is right for your child is to do your research: get the descriptions of schools and their "accountability report cards," visit schools if you can, and talk to parents of children in those schools. Then, begin the application process; the most popular schools have the highest number of applicants and the fewest openings.

The key to acceptance in the school you want for your child is the **OER (Open Enrollment Request)**. Each autumn the OER forms become available at schools or at SFUSD's Education Placement Center. The deadline for application is in January and it is strictly enforced; each year the date is slightly different, so make sure you are apprised of the date. Rank the schools you are applying for in order of preference. You are allowed to ask for four schools; one of them should be the regular school in your attendance zone if that is an option for you. SFUSD then compiles all the requests and matches them with the number of slots available in each school.

By March, the first round of acceptances are announced and the appeals process begins. In April, appeals are reviewed and the waiting lists are determined. In June, students who have not been placed are assigned to a school. Occasionally, vacancies occur at the last minute for students on waiting lists, but they should not be counted on, unless the school is in the "regular attendance district" of the child, meaning the neighborhood lived in.

## Public School Registration Requirements

A child must have turned five years old before December 2 to enter kindergarten during that year. Proof of birth date is required for entrance into a public school; this might be a birth certificate

121

or passport, for instance. As students must be legal residents of San Francisco, a proof of current address might include a recent utility bill in the name of the parent/guardian, a valid California driver's license, or a dated lease or property tax statement. Records from other schools attended should also be brought.

Kindergartners and first graders must have a complete physical examination before entering a public school. You will need to produce the child's immunization record. (Records from a foreign country must be reviewed by a local health facility.) DTP (Diphtheria, Tetanus, Pertussis), MMR (measles, mumps, rubella), Hib (Haemophilus influenza type B), and polio vaccination records will be reviewed. All children entering school are required to have a Tuberculin Skin Test, and if positive, will then need a chest x-ray. Immunization against Hepatitis B is required for incoming kindergartners.

### Preschools

Preschools are for children aged two to five. Preschooling has long been important in San Francisco, a city in which both parents are likely to work outside the home, and to which people migrate without having other family in the area to help take care of the kids. But preschool is important on other grounds: it is widely held that children who have been "socialized" by attending preschools perform better in their early school years than children who have not.

When investigating preschools, consider only those facilities that have been licensed by the State Department of Social Services. Licensing means that the facility has met the state's criteria concerning the physical plant (amount of fenced playground areas, number of toilets per child, safe food preparation area, etc) and that the staff has met stringent educational and experiential qualifications. But these are minimum criteria: when you visit a school, inquire about its staff-child ratio, its activities and play materials, its teaching approach (the ratio of teacher-provided structure to child-directed play), and its general philosophy for young children. Ask also about parent involvement and the process of feedback and evaluations concerning a child's progress.

Each school is different. No matter how positive a recommendation you receive from someone you know, you should visit the schools you are considering and determine for yourself whether the facility, the teaching methods, and overall environment are suitable for your child. First, you should decide which kind of preschool fits the personality of your child and your budget (and see if those have places available). There are independent, private preschools, those sponsored by religious agencies, and public preschools sponsored by the San Francisco Unified School District (SFUSD). See *Schools: Academic-Preschool & Kindergarten* in the Yellow Pages: in addition to alphabetical listings, many private preschools advertise their qualifications and special features on these pages.

The SFUSD's **Child Development Program** operates 43 Children's Centers that provide "supervision and instruction" for children from the age of two, provided they are toilet trained. Parents must be San Francisco residents. Eligibility is determined by income of families, and lowest income families are considered first; parents who can afford at least a portion of the tuition pay on a sliding scale. Some of the most popular centers have waiting lists. Call the Child Development Program for information (tel: 750-8500). Information can be had in English, Chinese, and Spanish.

You may be surprised by how costly the private preschools may be, despite some being incorporated as non-profit: fees may reach $500 per month, but some may offer financial aid, depending on need. *Cooperative* schools, in which the parents are expected to participate regularly, cost less, but you should be prepared to make a commitment to a particular time and activity at your child's school.

123

- *Independent* preschools are not affiliated with public or religious agencies. Many are neighborhood schools, serving the ethnic mix of that area. Some have bilingual programs, also depending on the neighborhood. There are dozens of these private, independent schools, so shop around. In addition to the Yellow Pages, if you are interested in a particular bilingual program, ask for information at the elementary school in the area you are considering, or of people who share your native language.

- *Agency-affiliated* preschools are sponsored by an organization such as the Jewish Community Center (JCC) or the Young Men's Christian Association (YMCA). Both have schools throughout the city. Each school sets its own approach; some have a religious component to the program, but others do not. *Religious* preschools are sponsored by a particular church or synagogue, not the agencies above. If you are interested in a religious component to your child's schooling, ask your church or synagogue for recommendations.

- *College and university* preschools are sponsored by the city's institutions of higher learning, servicing their faculty and students. Inquire of the university.

- *Montessori* schools are similar worldwide. They follow the teachings of Dr. Maria Montessori, who advocated stimulating, non-competitive activities in a structured atmosphere while providing creative freedom.

# PRIVATE SCHOOLS

Some 23,600 students attend the city's 36 private schools, and others commute to private schools in nearby towns. Private schools generally provide a high standard of education, small classes with a low student/teacher ratio, individual attention for children, and enriching extracurricular activities, all in a safe, nurturing, and stimulating environment. But this comes with a price tag. Tuition and other fees at private schools in the Bay Area are high, but they are generally in line with other private schools around the country. Some schools have financial aid programs and some offer reduced tuition if there are siblings in the school—it's worth checking them out. All in all, if you can afford it, you should at least check out private schooling during your investigation of schools. Some of the schools outside the city (especially in Marin) are extremely popular.

## Regulation/Accreditation

Private schools are not regulated by the California Department of Education, except that the physical plants of the schools themselves must meet the state's standards for any public business or building, relating to earthquake or fire. Thus, they may not conform directly to the same minimums for days or hours of school attendance, nor are their teachers asked by the state to meet particular experiential or educational requirements. This does not in any way mean that the schools do not meet—or even exceed— the minimum standards of the state. It only means they are not governed by state regulations. In general, parents send their children to private schools to exceed the minimum standards set by the state.

Elementary and high schools are generally *accredited* by one of a number of governing bodies, such as the Accrediting Commission for Schools or the Western Association of Secondary Schools. Religious schools may also (or instead) be accredited by their own religious accrediting body, such as the Western Catholic Education Association or the National Association of Episcopal Schools. Accreditation is a lengthy process during which the school must meet the requirements of the accrediting body, including standards for curriculum, teaching philosophy, etc.

## Types of Private Schools

There are several types of private schools and within them, their philosophies, goals, teaching approaches and curricula may differ widely. Some are traditional, others may be innovative in approach.

There are boys' schools and girls' schools, but most are co-educational. All should be able to provide detailed information during the application process. Some schools advertise their programs and philosophical approach in the Yellow Pages: see *Schools-Academic-Secondary & Elementary*. For a directory of California private schools ($17.50, plus tax and shipping), contact the California Department of Education: P.O. Box 271, Sacramento CA 95812 (tel: 800/995-4099). Unfortunately, the directory contains no evaluative statistics on the schools, but these can no doubt be had by writing to the schools directly. School Match, mentioned above, may have information as well. The schools themselves should be able to provide the parents of potential students with all the information necessary to make an informed decision.

*Non-profit* (or *independent*) schools are just that, and they are overseen by a Board of Trustees, often with parents on the Board or on committees that advise the Board. Many independent schools are eligible for outside funding and grants, and in order to receive them must meet the requirements of the funding agencies.

*Proprietary* schools may be a corporation or partnership, incorporated to make a profit, and although they are not necessarily governed by a board, they often have parents' committees that advise the administration, and being entirely dependent on tuition, are responsive to parents' concerns.

Most of the *parochial* (religious-based) schools in San Francisco are Catholic, although there are Jewish, Episcopal, and Baptist schools as well; inquire of your church or synagogue. Of the Catholic schools some are attached to parishes, some are independent and incorporated not-for-profit, and some—those affiliated with churches that were closed for budget-cutting—are now administered by the Archdiocese itself. Most have parent-teacher committees and some have advisory boards. For information, contact the **Archdiocese of San Francisco, Office of Catholic Schools**: 443 Church Street 94114 (tel: 565-3660).

The request must be in writing, and in addition to providing your name and address, you must indicate why you are requesting the information.

### The Admissions Process

Private schools are usually filled to capacity. Thus, any new slots are filled according to a priority system: first to be considered are children who have other siblings in the school, children who have attended that school's pre-school, or children of the school's alumni or teaching staff. Only after these children have been considered are outside applications taken.

In fact, the application/admission process is quite stringent and is lengthier and more detailed than application into a public school. The process starts earlier, and each school may have a slightly different schedule. Schools generally require an interview with both parents, and a "play" period with the child to evaluate readiness for the program. References from previous schools attended may be required. Most schools charge an application fee.

Have all your questions ready. Inquire about teaching philosophy, curriculum, amount of homework, ethnic diversity, after-school programs, expectations for parent participation, and information about all costs, not just tuition. For example, there are often extra costs for after-school "extended care," or for uniforms, if the school requires them.

## AFTER-SCHOOL PROGRAMS

As in any major city, children need to be supervised by an adult in their after-school hours, whether by a parent or in a structured program. Working parents should inquire about after-school "extended care" on the school premises, and whether there are places available and at what cost. The Child Development Program mentioned above offers after-school programs; call for information (in English, Chinese, or Spanish).

127

The **Recreation and Parks Department** sponsors a year-round after-school **Latchkey Program** for children 6–12 years of age. Programs are held in more than 30 of the Department's recreation centers around the city. During the school year, the hours are weekdays 2:00–6:00 pm, and during the summer 9:00 am–6:00 pm. These are structured programs: during the school year leisure and craft activities are encouraged (according to the specialty of the staff at a particular center), homework is supervised and a snack is provided. Summer programs feature arts and crafts, athletics, and field trips. These programs use a priority registration system, and there is a waiting list, especially for the most popular sites. Children in the Latchkey Program sign in upon arrival, sign out upon departure, and are expected to stay on site. Other "drop in" programs at Department centers are less structured and not as strictly monitored. Call for a brochure (tel: 337-4712).

Private schools also offer after-school programs for their students, invariably at extra cost. Each school's program is different, so if this is important to you, inquire during the application process.

# CHILD CARE

If you need child care, consider the non-profit **Marin Day Schools**, based at 100 Shoreline Highway, Mill Valley (tel: 331-7766; fax: 331-7066). It has 14 campuses around the Bay Area, including San Francisco, and has since 1981 provided child care and a developmental curriculum for children 6 weeks to 10 years old.

You might also contact the **Children's Counsel of San Francisco**, which has offices downtown, in the Mission, and at Bayview-Hunter's Point (downtown tel: 243-0700; www.childrenscouncil.org). Among its services, the Council provides workshops and counseling for parents needing child care, and referrals to licensed child-care providers in San Francisco; it does no screening of individual providers, so all interviews and reference gathering are up to the parent. Some subsidy funds are available for needy parents. **Wu Yee Children's Services** at 831 Broadway provides much the same services, with bilingual (Chinese) resources (tel: 391-4721).

Providers should be licensed by the Community Care Licensing Agency, and they are checked annually by the agency. Arrangements for child-care providers vary: some come to the parents' house and others take children into their own homes. Because some providers follow their own children's schedules, they maintain flexible hours, so inquire in advance about days when they might not be available and about vacations.

# EDUCATIONAL ENTERTAINMENT

Below is a small but representative sample of the range of opportunities for enriching entertainment in the area. Check occasionally with the San Francisco Visitors Center on Powell Street, for it has brochures on ongoing commercial activities and events that young children enjoy, including a list of city playgrounds. One commercial attraction is the **Basic Brown Bear Factory and Store** at 444 De Haro Street at Mariposa, a factory offering tours during which kids can see stuffed animals being made and stuff their own bears (tel: 626-0781); also at the Cannery (tel: 931-6670). For outdoor activities, make sure to bring a jacket for your child.

- **Rooftop at Yerba Buena Gardens**: A city block devoted to kids of all ages. Ice skating and bowling complex (tel: 777-3727), carousel, child-care center, and landscaped gardens. **Zeum** is an art and technology center for hands-on experience in exploring the high-tech and performing arts (tel: 777-2800).
- **Exploratorium**: 3601 Lyon Street, at the Palace of Fine Arts (tel: 561-0360). Hands-on science museum for kids of all ages (adults like it, too). Closed Monday.
- **Bay Area Discovery Museum**: 557 McReynolds Road, East Fort Baker, in Sausalito, just over the Golden Gate Bridge (tel: 487-4398). Hands-on multi-building museum for the entire family, focusing on natural sciences, art and multimedia. Hours change according to the season.

129

- **California Academy of Sciences** in Golden Gate Park (info tel: 750-7145). This complex includes an aquarium, planetarium, and natural history museum. Across the way is the **Japanese Tea Garden**, a pavilion with traditionally dressed waitresses serving tea. Also nearby is the 55 acre **Strybing Arboretum**, with its 7,000 plant and tree species, ponds, aquatic birds, etc.
- **M.H. De Young Memorial Museum**: Tea Garden Drive, Golden Gate Park (tel: 850-3658). Children's creative workshops, tours, and an "education room" with computer stations, reading areas, and art-appreciation activities.
- **Randall Museum**: 199 Museum Way, at Roosevelt (tel: 554-9600). Hands-on nature and history museum, with a petting zoo, woodworking shop, environmental learning garden. Summer classes. Closed Sunday and Monday.
- **Alcatraz Island**: Until 1963 a maximum security prison, now it is a tourist attraction, showing the daily lives of prisoners and guards. Check ferry schedules.
- **San Francisco Zoo**: Sloat Boulevard at 45th Avenue (tel: 753-7080). Extensive zoo with many attractions, including a children's zoo, a lion house, primate center, playground.
- **Underwater World**: Pier 39 (tel: 623-5300). Visitors progress on a moving walkway through this wraparound aquarium to see marine life of the Pacific Ocean.
- **San Francisco Maritime National Historical Park: Hyde Street Pier**: Foot of Hyde Street, near Fisherman's Wharf (tel: 556-3002). Explore 19th century sailing ships, a side-wheel ferry, schooners, and, incongruously, a World War II submarine. Operated by the National Park Service.

## RECREATION AND PARKS DEPARTMENT

Get to know the offerings of "Park and Rec," located in Golden Gate Park at McLaren Lodge, 501 Stanyan Street. Latchkey is only one of many programs for children; others include sports lessons, programs, and events. One of the most popular is the affordable **Camp Mather**, a rustic summer camp in the Stanislaus National Forest that allows families to spend a week together swimming and playing sports, participating in camp-like activities. Applications are taken in April and are selected by lottery; San Francisco residents are given priority.

# Chapter Seven

# OPTIONS FOR STUDY

## OPPORTUNITIES GALORE

The Bay Area has 35 degree-granting universities, colleges, and specialized technical schools, some the finest of their class in the country. Non-degree courses are also available in a surprising number of fields, traditional or New Age, and can further your life—or your lifestyle. Some representative samples of schools are listed below; their names should give an idea of what they are about, their websites should allow you access to their substantive information, and their addresses should allow you to contact them. The major universities are extremely competitive for admission. Even small technical schools require application in advance, and you may be asked to provide academic transcripts, references, proof of financial independence, and health insurance.

Foreigners wishing to study in the United States should follow the procedures detailed in Chapter Five. Be prepared to take the Test of English as a Foreign Language (TOEFL) as part of the application procedure. If you want to study in the United States, learn English first.

## ENGLISH LANGUAGE SCHOOLS

San Francisco is actually a multilingual city. Corporations that trade around the Pacific Rim are used to doing business in several Asian languages, staff in tourist shops can sell to just about any of their international clients, and the city-wide ethnic groceries and restaurants speak the languages of their clienteles. You'll hear more Chinese than English in Chinatown and along Clement, and more Spanish than English in the Mission — all with regional differences or dialects. But there are also communities of Russians and Koreans out along Geary, Vietnamese in the outer Tenderloin, and Japanese both around the Japan Center and in the Sunset. Pockets of other ethnic communities are multilingual as well.

Nonetheless, foreigners should make every effort to learn English as quickly as possible. If you do not speak English well, you will certainly be at a disadvantage with your competitors in business or your fellow students in school. Despite the plethora of multilingual publications, if you don't read English well you will not know as much as your neighbors as to what is happening in the city at any given time or even what opportunities are available. There are many registered English language schools in the Bay Area; choose one that suits your schedule and purse. For people who wish to apply for further study in the United States, the schools all offer TOEFL preparation. See also *Language Schools* in the Yellow Pages.

- **St. Giles Language Teaching Center**: One Hallidie Plaza (tel: 788-3552; fax: 788-1923; www.stgiles-usa.com). Morning or full-day programs, preparation for TOEFL and Cambridge exams, social occasions, and the I-20 for a student visa.

133

- **Brandon College**: 830 Market Street (tel: 391-5711; fax: 391-3918; www.brandoncollege.com). English as a Second Language, preparation for TOEFL and OTEIC, plus Business English. Housing assistance and social programs. I-20 for student visa.

## STATE-WIDE EDUCATION SYSTEMS

Four higher education systems are funded by the State of California. The most prestigious and stringent belong to the University of California system: in the Bay Area its major campus is in Berkeley, and its medical and other health-profession schools are in San Francisco, as is one of its law schools. Next come the enormous California State Universities, which in the Bay Area are San Francisco State, Sonoma State, San Jose State, and Cal State Hayward. Last come the city and community colleges: in San Francisco, San Francisco City College.

## UNIVERSITY OF CALIFORNIA

The University of California system offers some of the best education in the country, whether in its undergraduate colleges, graduate programs, or professional schools. The University of California, Berkeley, is one of the country's finest teaching and research universities, as is the Medical Center in San Francisco. Admissions are extremely competitive, and priority is given to California residents. Of some 30,000 applicants, only about 8,000 are accepted. No one ethnic or racial group constitutes a majority, which makes for an eclectic and diverse population.

- **University of California, Berkeley**: 110 Sproul Hall, Berkeley 94720 (tel: 510/642-6000; www.berkeley.edu)
- **UCSF Graduate Medical School:** 500 Parnassus (tel: 476-4044); also pharmacy (tel: 476-2372), nursing (tel: 476-1435), and dentistry (tel: 476-2737)
- **University of California Hastings College of the Law**: 200 McAllister Street (tel: 565-4600; www.uchastings.edu)

# CALIFORNIA STATE UNIVERSITY

The widespread California State University system is known for educating the bulk of California high school graduates. Although the number and type of high school courses required for admission are almost identical to that of the University of California system, the admissions process is less competitive. In San Francisco, **San Francisco State University** is at 1600 Holloway Avenue (tel: 338-1111; www.sfsu.edu). This 25,000 student "commuter" university offers undergraduate and graduate degrees, a law school, and several certificate and credential programs.

- **San Jose State**: One Washington Square, San Jose (408/924-1000)
- **Sonoma State**: 1801 East Cotati Avenue, Rohnert Park (tel: 707/664-2880)
- **California State University Hayward**: 25800 Carlos Bee Boulevard, Hayward (tel: 510/885-3000)

# CITY COLLEGE

**City College of San Francisco**, at 50 Phelan Avenue, is a community college that offers associate degrees and certificates, international trade programs, and a small-business institute (tel: 239-3000; www.hills.ccsf.cc.ca.us). It has ten campuses and more "instructional sites" in the city.

# PRIVATE UNIVERSITIES

In a class by itself among private universities, the beautiful campus of **Stanford** is nestled in the hills on the Peninsula, at Palo Alto. Its address is Stanford University, Stanford CA 94305 (tel: 723-2300; www.stanford.edu). Its undergraduate application process is extremely competitive: only around 13 percent of applicants are accepted; among those, 99 percent maintained a 3.0+ grade average in high school, and 86 percent were in the top 10 percent of their class. In the city are:

- **University of San Francisco**: Parker and Fulton Streets (tel: 422-6563; www.usfca.edu). Jesuit university founded 150 years ago. Undergraduate and graduate degrees in business, education, law, and many other fields.
- **Golden Gate University**: 536 Mission Street (tel: 442-7000; www.ggu.edu). Undergraduate and graduate degree programs at a university in the heart of downtown. Law school.
- **Academy of Art College**: 79 New Montgomery Street (tel: 274-2222; www.academyart.edu). A leading arts and design educator. Courses and degree programs in 10 visual arts majors, including film, computer art, video, graphic design, photography, advertising and industrial design. Bachelor of Fine Art and Master of Fine Art degrees.
- **New College of California**: 777 Valencia Street (tel: 888/437-3460; fax: 626-5171; www.newcollege.edu). Since 1971, this small college fosters "inquiry and critical thinking, and the integration of education with social action." Accredited by the Western Association of Schools and Colleges, NCOC offers BA degrees, weekend BA programs, a teacher credential program, a public interest law school, MFA and MA degrees.

## Specialized and Technical Schools

Specialized schools may offer full degrees or professional certificates and other credentials in particular fields. This representative sample should give you an idea of the range of education offered.

- **Heald Business Colleges**: 350 Mission Street (tel: 808-3000; www.heald.edu)
- **The San Francisco Law School**: 20 Haight Street (tel: 626-5550; www.sfls.edu). Long-established evening law school.
- **California College of Podiatric Medicine (Pacific Coast Hospital)**: 1200 Scott Street (tel: 563-8070; www.ccpm.edu)
- **American College of Traditional Chinese Medicine**: 455 Arkansas Street (tel: 282-7600; fax: 282-0856; www.actcm.org)

- **San Francisco Conservatory of Music**: 1201 Ortega Street (tel: 564-8086; www.sfcm.edu)
- **California Culinary Academy**: 625 Polk Street (tel: 800/229-2433, 771-3500; www.baychef.com)
- **University of the Pacific School of Dentistry**: 2155 Webster Street (tel: 929-6400; www.dental.uop.edu)
- **American Schools of Professional Psychology**: 999 Canal Boulevard, Point Richmond (tel: 510/215-0277; fax: 510/215-0299; www.aspp.edu). Graduate programs in clinical psychology.
- **San Francisco Art Institute, Extension Division**: 800 Chestnut Street (info tel: 771-7020; admissions tel: 749- 4554; www.sfai.edu). Ten-week classes in painting, photography, filmmaking, figure drawing.

# EXTENDED EDUCATION

Extended education courses and workshops may be short in duration but may offer certificates in some professional or technical fields. Others offer lifestyle courses such as "Wine Appreciation," or "Learning the Internet."

- **San Francisco State University, College of Extended Learning**: 425 Market Street (tel: 405-7700; www.cel.sfsu.edu). Continuing education opportunities, with classes held evenings and weekends.
- **University of California Berkeley Extension**: 55 Laguna Street (tel: 510/642-4111; www.berkeley.edu/unex). San Francisco campus for continuing education. A wide variety of courses and certificate programs, from "art to business and education to engineering." Call for catalogue.
- **The Learning Annex**: 291 Geary Street (info tel: 788-5500; www.learningannex.com). Non-credit courses on a variety of subjects, including computers and the Internet, health and healing, personal development, business and careers, and

finance and investing. Locations vary. Look for free catalogues in news boxes.

## COURSES FOR SENIORS

The universities and colleges all have programs that allow older adults to audit courses or, with some qualifications, to enroll as a student. The extension divisions welcome older students, and there are some opportunities specifically tailored toward seniors.

In Berkeley, look for **Alternative Lifelong Learning**, a member-run senior education program held at the North Berkeley Senior Center. Six-week courses, guest speakers, field trips. Note that as this is staffed entirely by volunteers, contact numbers may change (current tel: 510/530-3609).

- **Center for Learning in Retirement**: 55 Laguna Street (tel: 863-4518). UC's Extension Center offers workshops and study groups in a wealth of disciplines. Also offered are monthly walks and tours.
- **City College Older Adult Department**: 106 Bartlet Street (tel: 550-4415). Several campuses offer classes to people over 55. Call for a catalogue.
- **San Francisco State University, Urban Elders Program**: 22 Tapia Drive (tel: 338-2127). SFSU's "60 Plus" program offers either credit or audit classes. Call for a brochure.
- **Fromm Institute for Lifelong Learning (USF)**: 2130 Fulton Street (tel: 422-6805). "Retired" professors offer classes to people over fifty.

## LIBRARIES

To obtain a library card that allows book borrowing from any of the city's neighborhood public libraries, bring your driver's license or other picture identification, plus a document that shows your current address. There are libraries in many neighborhoods; some, in multilingual districts, offer books and periodicals in the languages primarily spoken in that area.

- **San Francisco Main Library**: 100 Larkin Street, in the Civic Center (tel: 557-4400). Extensive collections, a local history wing, work stations for connection to the Internet, and special-interest sections on history, gay and lesbian studies, art and music.
- **Mechanics' Institute Library and Chess Room**: 57 Post Street (tel: 421-1768). Long-established private reference and lending library. Periodicals, video and audio cassettes. Author readings and events. Chess Club is open to all members at any skill level. Classes and tournaments.

# Chapter Eight

# STAYING HEALTHY

## MEDICAL CARE IN SF

The quality of medical care in San Francisco is excellent. Practicing physicians who are also researchers at the area's major medical research centers and hospitals bring cutting-edge knowledge and techniques to their patients, assuring the best of care. There is no question of availability of excellent health care. There is a question, however, as to accessibility—how much access any individual has to the best care—and this concerns finances and health insurance.

## HEALTH INSURANCE

The United States has no national health insurance plan, but there are many options for obtaining insurance, provided you can pay for it. Workers may be covered through their employer's health plan, and some employers offer several to choose among. While discussing health benefits with your future employer, ask what the company's plan covers; many people don't know which health conditions or treatment procedures are covered until they are unexpectedly denied payment for some treatment. Not all companies offer health insurance to their employees; small businesses often do not, and employees thus must find coverage elsewhere, through their spouse or domestic partner, through associations or unions, or through an individual plan, which is more costly.

Even among individual plans there are several types. Some allow the holder to see any doctor at any time, others specify physicians belonging to their plans. Most usually have an initial amount that the patient must pay before the insurance begins to reimburse at the percentage allowed, and these "deductibles" vary. And not all insurance plans have the exact same coverage, not even within the same company. It's best to shop around, but not to take too long, for people without insurance are at great financial and health risk. See the Yellow Pages under *Health Plans*.

When choosing your physicians, inquire as to the insurance plans they accept. A few specialists—including some dentists—prefer not to allow insurance companies to dictate how they practice their profession and do not participate in insurance plans. Instead they require payment to be made at the time of treatment and, furnishing the appropriate diagnosis and treatment statements, ask patients to submit the insurance claims themselves. Invariably, the patient using non-participating doctors receives a lower percentage of reimbursement.

**Kaiser Permanente** is a major membership Health Maintenance Organization throughout the state of California and in other western states. With its own hospitals and physicians, its Personal Advantage membership offers comprehensive health care on all levels (tel: 800/464-4000). A Senior Advantage Program is also available for Medicare recipients and disabled persons (tel: 800/777-1238). Inquire about the Delta Care dental program.

141

Veterans of any branch of the United States military are entitled to use the services of the Veterans' Administration: contact the **San Francisco Veterans' Affairs Medical Center**, at 4150 Clement Street (tel: 221-4810).

## Emergency Services

In a dire emergency, dial **911** for police or ambulance response; for poison assistance also call the 24-hour poison control service: (tel: 800/876-4766). Response to a 911 health emergency call will be by a Fire Department ambulance. Paramedics will stabilize the patient, if necessary, and then transport to a hospital. In the case of accident or sudden trauma, the hospital will probably be San Francisco General, known for its trauma services, or for burns, St. Francis Memorial. In other cases, the ambulance will probably be directed to the nearest hospital, unless that hospital's Intensive Care Unit (ICU) has no beds available, and the ambulance is diverted to another emergency center.

All public hospitals have 24-hour emergency rooms, and many of them provide bilingual staff (Spanish, Russian, Chinese). All emergencies are treated, regardless of a person's ability to pay; once in stable condition, however, the patient may be transferred to a different facility. Each hospital has its own procedures for payment or insurance reimbursement. If you are covered by insurance in the United States, you should have no trouble sending the itemized bill to your carrier; most hospitals will do that for you. If you are covered in another country, you may be required to pay in advance and submit the itemized bill to your own carrier. The hospitals below with 24-hour emergency room telephone numbers are known for excellent care; those with specialties are also noted.

- *Castro/Hayes Valley* — **California Pacific Medical Center/ Davies Campus**: Castro and Duboce (emergency tel: 600-5555; tel: 600-6000)
- *Haight* — **St. Mary's Medical Center**: 450 Stanyan Street (emergency tel: 750-5700; tel: 668-1000)

142

- *Mission* — **San Francisco General Hospital**: 1001 Potrero Avenue (tel: 206-8000). The city's public hospital. Especially known for its trauma center.
- *Pacific Heights* — **California Pacific Medical Center/Pacific Campus**: 2333 Buchanan (emergency tel: 600-3333 tel: 600-6000)
- *Polk Gulch* — **St. Francis Memorial Hospital**: 900 Hyde Street (emergency tel: 353-6300; tel: 353-6000). Known for treatment of burns and spinal injuries.
- *Presidio Heights/Inner Richmond* — **California Pacific Medical Center/California Campus**: 3700 California Street (emergency room tel: 600-3333; tel: 600-6000)
- *Sunset* — **University of California, San Francisco**: 505 Parnassus Avenue (emergency tel: 353-1037; tel: 476-1000). Excellent hospital, attached to medical school.
- *Western Addition* — **Kaiser Permanente Medical Center/Geary Campus**: 2425 Geary Boulevard (tel: 202-2000). Care for members of Kaiser Permanente insurance plan.

## Pharmacies

When you first arrive in San Francisco, have with you enough medications to tide you over until you have found a doctor and pharmacy of your own. Foreigners should understand that many medications that are "over-the-counter" in other countries may require a doctor's prescription here. Ask your physician to write new prescriptions using both the trade and generic name of the medication. Bring a copy of your eyeglass prescription and an extra pair of glasses.

In addition to prescription medications, drug stores carry over-the-counter medications, vitamins, and a wide variety of familiar brands of health- and beauty-related items, plus foods, cold drinks, magazines and stationery, candies, and more. Cosmetic brands are generally well-known, and are less expensive than those found in the department stores. Neighborhood drug stores stay

143

open late, depending on the traffic in their area, sometimes until 8:00 pm or 10:00 pm. Most are open on Sunday.

If you have a health-related emergency and go to a hospital's emergency room, you will receive the appropriate prescription to treat your condition and enough medication to last until pharmacies open the next morning. The pharmacies below have 24-hour prescription departments. For over-the-counter remedies such as cough medicine or aspirin, you can also try 24-hour supermarkets.

- *Castro/Noe Valley* — **Walgreens**: 498 Castro Street (tel: 861-3136)
- *Outer Richmond* — **Walgreens**: 25 Point Lobos, at 42nd Avenue, near Geary (tel: 386-0736)
- *Pacific Heights/Marina* — **Walgreens**: 3201 Divisadero Street, near Lombard (tel: 931-6417)
- *Richmond* — **Rite Aid**: 5280 Geary Boulevard (tel: 668-2041)
- *Daly City* — **Walgreens**: 395 South Mayfair Avenue (tel: 650/756-4535)
- *South San Francisco* — **Walgreens**: 2238 Westborough Boulevard (tel: 650/873-0551)
- *South San Francisco* — **Walgreens**: 399 El Camino Real (tel: 583-8685)

## WOMEN'S HEALTH

The **University of California at San Francisco (UCSF)** has two centers in the Bay Area devoted to women's health care (at the Parnassus campus mentioned above and at UCSF Mount Zion on Divisadero Boulevard, at Post). Care includes cardiology and gynecology services, obstetrics, and breast cancer screening and treatment. The Great Expectations Women's Health Library and Resource Center offers resource materials and classes on women's health, including a Healthy Baby Program (tel: 476-6667).

The **Women's Program** of California Pacific Medical Center at 3698 California Street also consults on and treats all aspects of women's health (tel: 750-6500). Its comprehensive Planetree Library is at 2040 Webster Street (tel: 923-3681).

**Natural Resources**, at 1307 Castro, is a pregnancy, childbirth and parenting center, providing many excellent resources (tel: 550-2611). It offers classes and support groups during pregnancy and for new parents, has referrals listings for birth and child professionals, has a reference library, sells supplies and clothing at good prices, plus health-care products for mother and baby.

## ALTERNATIVE MEDICINE

San Francisco is one of the foremost cities in the United States for alternative medicine, including Eastern techniques and homeopathic healing. Traditional Western physicians in San Francisco are open-minded, probably to a greater degree than those in other American cities; for the most part they are willing to discuss non-traditional techniques and remedies with their patients, as well as to consider alternative options their patients present to them. Some of the hospitals also have Eastern-oriented medical clinics, and the major insurance companies now accept claims for acupuncture. Licensed acupuncturists work on their own or in conjunction with Western colleagues, and herbalists and homeopaths prescribe natural remedies. Therapeutic massage of varying internationally recognized techniques is available, as are classes for yoga and other relaxation methods. Massage is sometimes covered under health plans if prescribed by a physician or chiropractor.

Chiropractic, considered an alternative medicine in some countries, is considered mainstream in the United States, and chiropractic treatments for muscular and skeletal difficulties are generally covered by health insurance carriers, depending on the condition. There are many licensed Doctors of Chiropractic in the city; it's best to ask among your friends and colleagues for a recommendation.

For an excellent guide to services for natural living, look for the free semiannual publication *Bay Area Naturally* in natural food

145

shops and outlets. It includes descriptions and advertisements for holistic health professionals, "green" products and services, natural food restaurants, and natural food markets. *Common Ground*, another free tabloid, offers "resources for body, mind, and spirit." *Open Exchange*, which advertises courses and seminars in healthy living and healing, can be found in news boxes around the city.

- **American College of Traditional Chinese Medicine**: 450 Connecticut Street (tel: 282-9603). The clinic of this accredited school offers acupuncture and Chinese herb treatments for a variety of difficulties: upper-respiratory, gastrointestinal and cardiovascular problems, and more.

## Free Clinics

The **Community Health Network of San Francisco** provides low-cost health care to residents (tel: 206-4785). Funded by the city, clinics provide both primary and specialized care for people who have no health insurance and cannot afford access to traditional health care providers. In most, patients pay on a sliding scale geared to their ability to pay. Many of the clinics are staffed by professional volunteers—physicians, nurses, residents, interns —who donate their expertise to people who could not otherwise afford health care. Look in the City Government section of the White Pages under the *Health Department* and the subhead of *Health Centers*, and for emergency treatment, see above. The clinics listed below are well known:

- *Haight-Ashbury*—**Haight Ashbury Free Clinic**: 558 Clayton Street, at Haight (tel: 487-5632). Long-established clinic offering low-cost basic health services, HIV treatment, drug and alcohol detox, etc.
- *Hayes Valley*—**Lyon-Martin Women's Health Services**: 1748 Market Street, #201 (tel: 565-7667): Primary care clinic for women, providing treatment for acute and chronic conditions, physical examinations, gynecology, internal medicine, family

planning, and preventive health care. Special focus for lesbian and HIV-positive women. Sliding scale for fee payment.

- *Mission* — **Castro-Mission Health Center**: 3850 17th Street, at Noe (tel: 487-7500)

# DENTISTS

Although the quality of dental care in San Francisco is extremely high, finding the right dentist might take some time, depending on your needs and preferences. Thus, before moving, have any remaining dental work done, and bring with you current x-rays and copies of your dental records to give to your new dentist.

Your friends, neighbors, and colleagues may recommend dentists, but as with choosing any professional relationship, you will have to determine whether that person is right for you. This may depend not only on your physical needs, but whether you have dental insurance and whether the dentist you choose accepts it. For a recommendation, you might also call the **San Francisco Dental Society Referral Service** (tel: 421-1435). Be specific as to the type of dentist you are seeking, the type of work you need done, and any financial concerns.

Until you have found a dentist of your own, you might try the clinics of the dental schools in San Francisco. Both schools listed below offer inexpensive dental care by dental students under the supervision of faculty members who have first made the initial evaluation of condition and treatment. In addition to their regular clinics, both have weekday emergency services seeing patients on a first-come first-served basis, and after-hours emergency assistance. For 24-hour dental emergencies, you might also try San Francisco General Hospital, listed above.

- **University of California School of Dentistry**: 707 Parnassus Street (tel: 476-1891; after-hours emergency tel: 551-9036)
- **University of the Pacific School of Dentistry**: 2155 Webster Street (tel: 929-6400; info tel: 929-6501)

147

# HIV/AIDS

As San Francisco has been hit particularly hard by the HIV/AIDS epidemic, the city has extensive public resources for testing and care. Both San Francisco General and the Davies Campus of California Pacific Medical Center have well-known AIDS clinics (see addresses above). The **City Clinic** at 356 7th Street tests and treats sexually transmitted diseases at low cost or for free (tel: 487-5500); hours are Monday and Wednesday 8:00 am–4:00 pm, Tuesday 1:00–6:00 pm, and Thursday 1:00–4:00 pm. For an extensive list of helpful resources, see the Yellow Pages under *AIDS, HIV Education, Referral & Support Services*.

- The **Gay and Lesbian Medical Association** offers referrals to physicians and other medical services in the Bay Area, publishes helpful guides, and offers forums and seminars; it takes phone calls weekdays 9:30 am–5:30 pm (tel: 255-4547).
- **San Francisco Department of Public Health**: AIDS Health Project (tel: 502-8378). Free anonymous and confidential HIV testing.
- **California HIV/AIDS Hot-line**: (tel: 863-2437). Information on HIV/AIDS, safe sex, and a database of HIV-related services. In English, Spanish, Filipino.
- **A New Leaf**: 1853 Market (tel: 626-7000). Mental health and substance abuse programs for gays, lesbians, and bisexuals. Open weekdays, 9:00 am-5:00 pm.
- **AIDS/HIV Nightline**: Emotional support hot-line, open 5:00 pm–5:00 am every night (tel: 434-2437).
- **Stadtlanders Pharmacy**: 445 Castro Street, is the San Francisco branch of the nationwide pharmacy specializing in HIV/AIDS care (tel: 434-8600; www.stadtlander.com). Hours: 8:00 am–9:00 pm weekdays, 10:00 am–6:00 pm Saturday, noon–5:00 pm Sunday; 24-hour pharmacist available, and mail order is available on the Internet.

# CHAPTER NINE

# WORK AND BUSINESS ON THE PACIFIC RIM

From its earliest days, San Francisco has been a city of opportunities seen and grasped. Even today, whether you are coming to find a job or to start your own business, you will find that San Francisco opens its doors to those who are qualified—and who understand how the city works. Extensive informational resources are widely available and should be helpful for those who are determined to succeed.

If the Bay Area were an independent country, it would rank among the top 25 economies in the world. San Francisco plays a crucial part in the economy and trade of the vast Pacific Rim, and with some 30 of the world's largest banking institutions and offices here, it is sometimes called the "Wall Street of the West." Here are the headquarters for Bank of America and Wells Fargo, the Pacific Stock Exchange, and the Federal Reserve Bank of San Francisco. With the city's long-standing ties to Asia, finance and commerce along the Rim are increasingly becoming the most important part of the economy of the city and the region. Bay Area exports have grown more than 50 percent over just the last five years, while its overall economy grew by 9.2 percent.

You should think of the entire Bay Area as your resource, especially that geographically intangible — yet very real — concept called Silicon Valley, which stretches from San Francisco down to San Jose. Companies throughout the Bay Area are world leaders in high-tech innovation, manufacturing, and trade. This includes computers and software, telecommunications, semi-conductors, other electronics, and robotics. High-tech industries in the area attract almost 40 percent of the venture capital in the country, and knowledge-based industries account for just under 20 percent of the region's exports.

The largest corporations with headquarters in San Francisco are Bechtel and Levi Strauss, both American-owned. But foreign-owned companies also maintain a major presence in the area: Fireman's Fund Insurance, for example, with headquarters in San Francisco, is German-owned; Bank of the West is French-owned; and Shaklee is a Japanese company, to name just a few. It should be said, though, that as the Bay Area relies heavily on business with Asia and Latin America — two areas that were hit hard economically toward the end of the last decade — some major corporations regrouped for a time, bringing about job layoffs and a slowing of job growth.

Yet at the end of the last decade, San Francisco was ranked second only to Dallas as the most productive city in America. Its *per capita* average income of $35,000, however, was ranked as the highest. Part of this is owing to the professional caliber of workers and the fact that San Francisco is close to some of the most prestigious universities in the country — University of California and Stanford—which means that research plays a major role in the atmosphere of the entire region. In fact, more than half of those who work in the city have college or advanced degrees.

## THE JOB SEARCH

San Francisco has long been home to plentiful jobs in international trade and especially in tourism, where turnover is high. Recently, however, service-related businesses have been growing, while the economy of the region has been shifting to one based on knowledge. This means that people with all sorts of good computer skills —computer programming, telecommunications, data processing— and those who have education in the life sciences—biotechnology and scientific research—will be in increasing demand. The multimedia industry is one of the region's fastest growing, and both new jobs and new types of jobs are being created.

The above notwithstanding, unemployment in San Francisco hovers just under 3 percent. Thus, you should ensure that your résumé is attractively prepared and organized. If you have several distinct skills, for example, prepare different résumés with different emphases, depending on the job you are applying for. Be prepared also to network with any professional contact you may have and to make "cold calls" to the Human Resources departments of companies, rather than relying solely on your résumé and cover letter. Competition is fierce, and you must use every channel at your disposal. Think carefully about salary and your lifestyle, for the Bay Area has the highest cost of living in the state.

In order to apply for a job, you must prove that you are legally permitted to work in the United States; foreigners may be asked to take an English-language test. In addition, some companies will test you on the skills you claim to have and may ask for work samples and references.

If you are coming to the city without a job, start your search before arrival by looking at the website of the local newspapers to see what is available (e.g. www.sfgate.com). Once in the city, buy

151

the combined Sunday issue of the *San Francisco Examiner/San Francisco Chronicle* which has an extensive career section containing articles, advertisements for career development, and a major section of classified ads for job openings. Some free tabloid magazines can be found at news boxes on street corners.

- ***Open Exchange Magazine:*** a bimonthly publication sponsored by the Community Resource Institute, which develops learning technologies for personal growth and social change. Advertisements for seminars and courses, and by professionals offering help in a variety of fields from accounting and taxes to yoga and meditation.

- ***Jobs and Careers:*** lists hundreds of positions open (info tel: 800/49career; http://jobscareers.com)

- ***High Technology Careers***: a tabloid focusing on high-tech jobs (www.hightechcareers.com)

- ***Bay Area Business Woman***, a monthly newspaper with advertisements and articles of interest to professional women, plus a calendar of events (tel: 510/654-7557)

## Career Help

In addition to listing yourself with the employment agencies, try to take advantage of the organizations that help people to develop their capabilities, to present themselves well, and to understand the San Francisco job market: The **San Francisco Chamber of Commerce** (see below) sells an *Employment Guide*, listing agencies and services for job seekers.

- **Life Print** (formerly **Alumnae Resources**): 120 Montgomery Street, Suite 600 (tel: 274-4700; fax: 274-4744; www.ar.org ). Career development organization offering assistance to anyone beginning, advancing, or changing a career. Resource center, career advisor network, job listings, Internet access, seminars. Membership fee allows access to career counseling, workshops, career planning, and a quarterly newsletter, calendar, and access to their job list.

- **Experience Unlimited**: 3120 Mission Street (tel: 771-1776). Free service of the State Employment Development Department. Career Counseling, résumé assistance, etc.
- **Jewish Vocational Service and Career Counseling**: 77 Geary Street, Suite 401 (tel: 391-3600; www.jvs.org). Long established non-sectarian job counseling and employment agency. Workshops, networking, English instruction. Also at 4600 El Camino Real, Suite 207, Los Altos (tel: 650/941-7922).
- **Media Alliance**: 814 Mission Street, Suite 205 (tel: 546-6334; www.media-alliance.org). Non-profit association for communications and general media professionals. $45 fee plus $20 for access to job file.
- **San Francisco Chamber of Commerce**: 465 California Street (tel: 392-4520; www.sfchamber.com). Wednesday evening Job Forum, offered as a free community service. A rotating panel of experts from business, government and academia address a variety of job-finding problems. Not an employment agency, the Job Forum offers brainstorming and problem-solving to job seekers.

## Employment Agencies

The hundreds of employment agencies in the city offer temporary and permanent jobs. If you are willing to work outside San Francisco, inquire whether the agencies service the entire Bay Area. See Employment Agencies in the Yellow Pages, which has extensive advertisements, including agencies that specialize in fields such as the dental, insurance, or legal professions. The nationwide firm **Manpower** is in cities around the Bay Area (San Francisco tel: 781-7171; www.manpower.com).

- **Alpha Four**: 447 Battery Street, Suite 240 (tel: 995-9080; fax: 956-7161; www.alphafour.citysearch.com). Full-time and temporary placement for administrative, clerical, sales, finance, and graphic design positions.

- **ABAR Staffing Service**: 142 Sansome Street (tel: 773-2227; fax: 263-3690; www.abarstaffing.com). Full-time positions in finance, accounting, sales and marketing, management, and administration. Also in the East Bay.
- **Bach Personnel**: 2358 Market Street (tel: 626-4663; fax: 626-6159; www.bachpersonnel.com). "The Premier Gay/Lesbian Placement Agency," specializing in full-time, contract, and temporary positions.
- **Apple One**: 44 Montgomery Street (tels: 800/564-5644; 397-3201; www.appleone.com). Full-time positions around Bay Area. Also in Oakland (tel: 510/835-0217) and San Mateo (tel: 650/574-8252).

# STARTING A BUSINESS

Many people come to San Francisco hoping to open their own small retail business. In fact, despite the invasion of nationwide chain stores and franchises, locally owned businesses continue to characterize San Francisco, from tourist-oriented kiosks and locally owned upscale restaurants of all quality and prices to the most elegant fashion boutiques and furniture showrooms. Some businesses are successful, yet many fail, often owing to an incomplete understanding of how the city works. Much will depend on the amount of knowledge you have at the outset—including that all-important aspect of location—and how organized you are in your approach.

Businesses that depend on tourism are always a draw. Tourism is big business in San Francisco, its largest industry, sustaining more than 60,000 of the city's jobs. With 30,000 hotel rooms, hotel taxes alone account for $110 million that is added to the city's coffers. San Francisco International Airport filters 38 million passengers through its corridors every year.

Some 16 million visitors spend more than $5 billion in the city each year, a city that is often rated by travel magazines as the nation's most popular vacation spot. Other than vacationers, the

200 trade shows, conventions, and business meetings draw some 1.5 million. International visitors account for just under half of all hotel guests. Tourists and business visitors explore the city every day of the year, spending their money at tourist attractions, in the downtown and outer shopping districts, and especially at the city's restaurants.

## BUSINESS SETUP ADVICE

Before you do anything else, make sure you understand the legal and financial implications of opening a business and the risks involved. Start with the **U.S. Small Business Administration (SBA)**, at 455 Market Street, 6th floor, an agency of the federal government that helps people who want to open a small business (tel: 744-6820; www.sba.gov). Its Business Information Center offers informational workshops and seminars, counseling, computer access, and a resource library with information on business plans and starting a business (tels: 744-4244, 744-4242).

The SBA is also the largest source of long-term small business financing in the nation. Loans are made to qualified applicants by private lending institutions that participate in the SBA program, and a percentage of the loan (up to $750,000) is guaranteed by the SBA. Inquire of your banker or at the SBA for its booklet *Small Business Start-up Information*.

Women own some 27,000 businesses in San Francisco, and other minorities own some 15,000 businesses in the city. Women should inquire at the SBA about the Women's Pre-Qualification Loan Program, in which loan requests may be reviewed and approved by the SBA before application to the lending institution (SBA Women's info tel: 744-8491). The **Women's Initiative for Self Employment (WISE)**, a pilot program of the SBA, at 450 Mission Street, offers training in business assessment, marketing, finances and sales and counseling (tel: 247-9473). Fees are on a sliding scale.

155

Learn about the **Mission Economic Development Association (MEDA)** at 2601 Mission Street, 9th floor (tel: 282-3334; fax: 282-3320). This bilingual (Spanish and English) association in the heart of the Mission provides counseling, technical assistance, and loan packaging services (through the SBA and small lenders) to people wishing to set up a new business or improve an existing business.

The **Renaissance Entrepreneurship Center**, at 275 Fifth Street (tel: 541-8580; www.rencenter.org), is a non-profit entrepreneurial training organization supported by the San Francisco Community Development Fund and some private businesses. It offers classes in Introduction to Business, Business Planning, and Growing Your Business, plus courses in writing business plans and pricing products. Classes last 8 to 14 weeks.

The Business Reference Section of the San Francisco Main Library allows any card holder access to its services and database (tel: 557-4488). An excellent ongoing resource for current business information and annually issued business-related reports is the *San Francisco Business Times*, at 275 Battery Street, #940 (tel: 989-2522). Subscriptions are $70 per year.

For assistance with business plans and tax incentives, contact the **California Trade and Commerce Agency**, 801 K Street, Suite 1700, Sacramento 95814 (tel: 916/327-0079; www.commerce.ca.gov).

# NETWORKING

San Franciscans are friendly and open, both socially and professionally, so you should have little trouble meeting people and becoming an active member of the business community. Consider joining the groups below for business networking. If you are interested in volunteering at any of the dozens of worthwhile non-profit organizations in the city—another way to meet interesting people—contact the **San Francisco Volunteer Center**, at 425 Jackson Street, which coordinates volunteer opportunities in many community projects (tel: 982-8999; www.vcsf.org). Or contact the **Volunteer Centers of the Bay Area** (tel: 800/227-3123; www.volunteerbayarea.org).

The **San Francisco Chamber of Commerce**, at 465 California Street, is a non-profit membership association of almost 2,000 local businesses (tel: 392-4520). Working to attract businesses to the Bay Area, the Chamber sponsors luncheons, networking socials, and committee meetings, and organizes special events for members and non-members, plus the important Job Forum mentioned above. The Women in Business Roundtable is a bimonthly breakfast meeting with interesting speakers. Consider also some of the professional networking possibilities below.

- **Asian Business League of San Francisco**: 233 Sansome Street, Suite 575 (tel: 788-4664). Membership organization for Asians in business, providing seminars, workshops, networking events.
- **Bay Area Career Women**: 55 New Montgomery Street (tel: 495-5393; www.bacw.org). World's largest lesbian volunteer organization formed to eliminate discrimination. Business networking opportunities, social events, etc. Other chapters in the area.
- **City Club of San Francisco**: 155 Sansome Street, 10th Floor (tel: 362-2480). Multi-purpose professional and social club. Breakfast speakers, networking forums, special events.
- **Commonwealth Club of California**: 595 Market Street (tel: 597-6700). Prestigious public affairs group invites well-known and interesting people to speak at meal-centered meetings (breakfast, lunch, dinner, receptions). Special and social events geared to current issues; outings to cultural and sports events.
- **Golden Gate Business Association**: 2107 Van Ness Avenue (tel: 441-3651). Nation's oldest gay and lesbian business organization. Professionals, business owners, and artists belong to this group that offers networking events and a variety of business-related programs.

157

- **National Association of Women Business Owners — SF** (tel: 333-2130; www.nawbo-sf.org). Monthly dinner meetings, networking, business and social contacts.
- **Rotary Club of San Francisco** (tel: 923-0399). Call for meeting and luncheon sites.
- **World Affairs Council**: 312 Sutter Street, Suite 500 (tel: 982-2541). Programs on important foreign policy issues. Dinners with special, international guests, lectures from government officials, forums on current issues, special and social events.

# OFFICE SPACE

Office space in the city hovers at about a 6 percent vacancy rate. Corporate downsizing over the past few years and more stringent funding criteria have decreased the amount of new business construction in the city, which had once suffered from overbuilding and high vacancy rates. In addition, retention programs to keep business in San Francisco are fairly successful, and tenants are staying in their long-term office space. As less space is on the market, rents climb, and to compound the situation, commercial space is not rent-controlled. San Franciscans are concerned that steeply rising rents will be affordable only to national chains, and that small "mom-and-pop" businesses will be forced out. Some efforts by resident groups have been successful in keeping large chains out of their neighborhoods, but if prices continue to rise, they may not continue to be successful.

Thus, companies are beginning to colonize the heretofore industrial South of Market area, enlivened by the Moscone Convention Center, Yerba Buena Gardens (including Metreon), and the Museum of Modern Art. Multimedia companies have also established themselves in this area, which from South Park reaching out toward the Mission is now nicknamed "Multimedia Gulch." The new Pacific Bell baseball stadium is also increasing the attractiveness of the area for businesses of all sizes and levels.

Last, new development at Mission Bay is under way, and upon completion will bring more than a million square feet of university facilities, plus a varied residential and retail community.

## Temporary/Shared Office Space

Shared offices provide full services without a long-term financial commitment. You may rent a conference room for a meeting, or rent offices by the day, week, or month. See *Office and Desk Space Rental Service* in the Yellow Pages.

- **HQ Global Workplaces**: 44 Montgomery Street (tel: 781-5000); 2 Embarcadero Center (tel: 835-1300). Full conference, office, electronic, and secretarial services (www.hqnet.com). Other locations in Bay Area.
- **Office General Executive Business Centers**: 580 California Street (tels: 283-3200; 800/960-1818; www.officegeneral.com). Other locations in Bay Area.

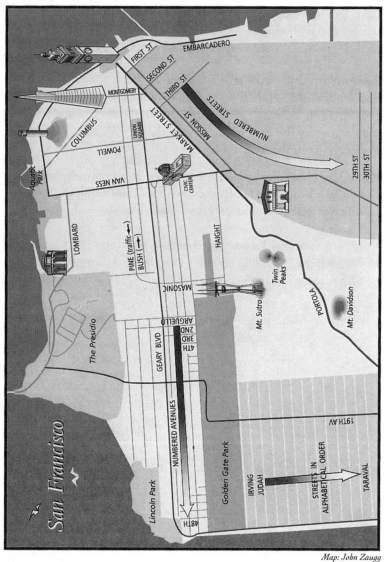

Map: John Zaugg

160

# Chapter Ten

# UP AND DOWN THE HILLS

## UNDERSTANDING THE CITY

The city plan of San Francisco should not be difficult to understand. Streets are laid out on more or less a grid, except where one of the city's 42 hills intrudes; on either side of a hill the name of a continuing street is most likely different. To understand the city, first take into consideration the role of the diagonal Market Street, which starts at the Bay and cuts southwest through much of the city. North of Market, the streets are named; south of Market, the streets are numbered. People often refer to these areas as "north of Market" or "south of Market."

North of Market, the street names have no particular order to them; you just have to learn them. South of Market, the north/

161

south streets are numbered, starting with First Street and continuing regularly to 30th Street, where Twin Peaks and then Mount Davidson loom above. At Twin Peaks, Market Street changes its name to Portola, and as it winds toward Ocean Avenue, the names and contours of streets follow no plan.

The numbered streets south of Market should not be confused with what everyone calls "the avenues." These begin at Arguello, which runs from the Golden Gate Park panhandle to the Presidio. These straight streets run north/south from Second Avenue (there is no First Avenue) to Forty-Eighth Avenue, at the edge of the sea. Making orientation even easier in this area, south of Geary Boulevard begin the alphabetically consecutive streets (running east/west), starting with Anza and Balboa, and—after jumping Golden Gate Park—continuing to Wawona, just north of Sloat.

If none of this makes sense at first, take heart: most intersections throughout the city have large green signs above them, indicating the cross street, which is helpful when driving, for street signs may occasionally be missing or hidden by foliage.

Small city maps, found at bookshops, can be carried in a briefcase or purse, but there are no pocket-sized street atlases for San Francisco. Some maps—mostly of the downtown and tourist areas—may be had at the San Francisco Visitors Center. More detailed, indexed maps can be purchased at some gasoline stations, and members of the **California State Automobile Association (AAA or "Triple A")** may obtain free maps at 150 Van Ness Avenue (tel: 565-2012). A detailed street atlas to keep in your car may be bought at bookstores. The Yellow Pages have a few helpful maps of neighborhoods, downtown streets, public transportation routes, and city zip codes.

# THINKING ABOUT TRANSPORT

Transportation is an important issue in San Francisco. The population of this small city almost doubles each workday, when more than 200,000 commuters file into the city—in vehicles, on ferries, on trains. Rush hours may be among the busiest in the country, as vehicle access into the city is limited to two bridges and two major highways coming up from the Peninsula. Traffic problems are compounded by the millions of tourists who come to the Bay Area every year, many of whom either drive their own cars or rent one to go out into the countryside. Traffic is also a problem on weekends, as residents themselves head to the country and suburbanites come into the city. Thus, if you decide to live in a suburb and work in the city, you will have to think carefully about commuting strategies. In the city itself, driving and parking in the city center can often be difficult, depending on time of day and the number of delivery trucks double parked.

Compounding the problem, the city's municipal transit system has been beset by problems. Mayoral candidates promise during campaigns to fix them, then once elected state that problems are being addressed. Nonetheless, San Franciscans consistently rate public transit—along with unaffordable housing—as the city's worst problems; people who use the system, however, do manage to get to work on time, and the system is more or less reliable. Many people walk to work, some use bicycles, and several banks of parking meters downtown are designated for motorcycles.

## Walking

San Francisco, despite its hills, is a walking city, and people walk whenever and wherever they can. According to California law, all vehicles must stop for a pedestrian in a crosswalk (except at extremely busy intersections). Surprisingly, for the most part, they actually do. Occasionally an impatient driver will pretend not to see the person crossing, or a tourist in a rented car might not know the law, so it is still important to pay attention to traffic and cross when safe. Obey the traffic signals and the "Walk" or "Don't Walk" signs. And note that jaywalkers who cross outside the designated crosswalks do not have the right of way.

When crossing the street, watch for cars that are turning right on a red light. Also, watch out for cars that dash through the intersection *after* the light has turned red. This is a major problem in San Francisco, one the police has yet to solve. Do not assume that the instant the light has turned green in your direction, it is safe to cross.

## Bicycling

San Francisco rates among the top ten urban centers in the country for bicycling. The city encourages bicycling for daily transportation, and commuting by bicycle is popular. There are a few bicycle lanes on city streets, including a major lane in both directions on Valencia Street. Color-coded signs on bike routes indicate the direction (primary crosstown routes in full color or neighborhood routes in green and white), and odd numbers indicate north-south routes while even numbers are for east-west routes. The routes try to avoid the hills. To aid commuters, bicycle lockers have been installed at several public garages, and some Muni routes are experimenting with bike racks. Always lock your bike to an anchored, solid object with a U-lock. For information on the Bicycle Program, call the Commuter Hotline (tel: 585-2453). Bicyclists are expected to obey all the laws pertaining to motorists, not that many do. For bicycling as a sport, see Chapter Fifteen.

## MUNI

The **Muni (Municipal Railway)**, San Francisco's public transportation system, accommodates more than a half million passenger rides each day (info tel: 673-6864; recorded timetables: 923-6336). Muni's 81 routes are covered by diesel and electric buses, cable cars, and the city's light rail streetcars known as Muni Metro. Of the 81 lines, 16 are express buses, making limited stops along their routes. All types begin operation at about 5:00 am and run until about 1:00 am; in the early morning the city is serviced by nine Owl lines.

The front of each vehicle displays the route number/letter and name, destination, and type of service: black/white lettering indicates local buses with many stops, green/white lettering indicates limited stops, and red/white lettering means express service. Buses are numbered (e.g. 38-Geary), and streetcars are lettered (e.g. J-Church). The bus stops themselves indicate which buses/streetcars stop there and their schedule. Buses stop only at designated bus stops, and not even in the pouring rain is the driver likely to open the door for you one inch away from the bus stop.

For a single trip, exact fare is required: adults currently pay $1; children over 4, seniors over 65, and students and disabled people with a discount card pay 35 cents. If you plan another trip within a few hours, ask for a "transfer" while paying your fare. Transfers, which are free, allow two additional trips within the time limit displayed on them, usually about $1\frac{1}{2}$–2 hours, although some drivers are more liberal in where they mark the expiration.

For regular use of Muni, it's best to buy a **Fast Pass**, the weekly or monthly pass that allows unlimited access to any Muni vehicle, including cable cars (and to BART and Caltrain within San Francisco). There's no need for transfers, no need to search for dollar bills or change. Fast Passes are widely available, and prices vary according to category: see the Muni Timetables booklet that is sometimes in a rack at the front of the bus. Disabled persons should get the Regional Transit Connection Discount Card (tel: 923-6070). All streetcar stations are wheelchair accessible; call for further information (tel: 923-6142).

## Cable Cars

Cable cars—since 1873 the city's most famous form of transportation—are certainly the most thrilling way to see San Francisco, as they clang charmingly up and down the hills on their underground cables at just under 10 miles per hour. But for occasional use they are expensive: currently they cost $2 per ride, unless you have a Fast Pass. And during the height of the tourist season it's

165

hard to find a seat inside. Generally it's the tourists who like to sit on the outside in the fog and the wind, while the locals head into the inside seats.

The cable cars run on three lines—the Powell/Mason and Powell/Hyde lines, which begin at Powell and Market and head toward Fisherman's Wharf, and the California Street line, which begins at Market and California and terminates at Van Ness. Stops are every few blocks and are either marked with a maroon and white sign on the curb, or by a yellow line between the rails. Wait on the sidewalk, signal the gripman to stop, and board only when the car is fully stopped. Theoretically, automobiles are supposed to stop to allow people to cross to the cable car, but they don't always, so watch carefully when stepping off the sidewalk when the cable car is approaching.

## BART

**BART (Bay Area Rapid Transit)** is a 5-line, 72-mile commuter railway that stops at some 39 stations on its route between the East Bay and Colma/Daly City (info tel: 650/992-2278; www.bart. org); it is wheelchair accessible. Efficiently run, BART accommodates more than 250,000 passenger rides each day. Bus lines are set up throughout the Bay Area to take people directly to BART. The service starts around 4:00 am (later on weekends) and shuts down around midnight. Trains run approximately every fifteen minutes, more often during rush hours. Check the schedules, for on weekends the trains run every 20 minutes and on Sundays the service is further reduced. Several informational brochures are available at BART stations.

To determine the fare to your destination, check the information charts which are displayed in each station. For regular commuting, buy a multi-trip ticket, which saves time and money The magnetic ticket is read by the computerized turnstiles at the entrances and exits. If you buy a one-trip ticket, save it in order to exit the station at your destination.

*One of San Francisco's beloved cable cars.*

*Taking BART makes commuting into the city easy.*

167

## Commuter Transit

Regularly scheduled buses and ferries bring commuters into the Financial District each day from around the Bay Area. Most ferries have differing weekday and weekend schedules, and some also have service to tourist attractions or to sports events. For recorded information on public transport and driving in the Bay Area, call **TravInfo** (tel: 817-1717).

- *East Bay* — **AC Transit** (Alameda-Contra Costa Transit) offers bus service to San Francisco and connects to BART stations in the East Bay (call TravInfo).
- *Marin/Sonoma* — **Golden Gate Transit** (GGT) offers fixed-route bus service from Marin to downtown San Francisco, and ferry service to the Ferry Building from Larkspur and Sausalito (tel: 923-2000; Marin tel: 455-2000); modified service on weekends. Bus service to and from Marin county locations, or leave your car at the "Park & Ride" parking lots. Call for the *Bus & Ferry System Map*, which details all the services and locations. All ferries are wheelchair accessible, and **Whistlestop Wheels** is GGT's intercounty paratransit service for disabled passengers who are enrolled (tel: 454-0964).
- *Marin* — **Blue & Gold Fleet**: Commuter ferries from Tiburon to Ferry Building, all-day ferry between Pier 41, Sausalito, and Tiburon (tel: 773-1188), and service to Alcatraz and Angel Island.
- *East Bay* — **Harbor Bay Maritime Ferry** (tel: 510/769-5500). Weekday commuter ferry between Harbor Bay Isle and the San Francisco Ferry Building.
- *East Bay* — **Alameda Oakland Ferry** (tel: 510/522-3300). Commuter service between Alameda, Oakland, and San Francisco.
- *Peninsula* — **Caltrain**: Daily train service between San Francisco and San Jose, stopping at stations in the South Bay and Peninsula (tel: 800/660-4287). The terminus is San Francisco's

Fourth Street Station, at Fourth and Townsend. The new extension of Muni has made access to the Financial District easier, but to Market Street it's only about a 10-minute walk. Fares are based on distance; buy tickets at the Caltrain stations.

- *Richmond* — **Red & White Fleet**: Weekday rush hour commuter service, with two trips in each direction on weekdays between the Ferry Terminal and Harbour Way (tel: 673-2900).

- *San Mateo* — **SamTrans** (San Mateo County Transit District): Bus service within San Mateo County and commuter service to San Francisco Financial District. Also services San Francisco International Airport and the Colma BART station (tel: 800/660-4287).

## Taxis

Taxis in San Francisco do not cruise the streets regularly as they do in many other major cities. There are taxi stands at the major hotels downtown, but at rush hours, on rainy days, or when there is a major convention in town, there may be no taxis to be had, even at the stands. Trying to call one on the telephone can be frustrating at any hour, but if you're out of the direct city center, it's still best to call a cab well in advance of the time you'll need it, and then confirm just before its expected arrival that it is, indeed, on the way. Some hospitals, hotels, and apartment complexes have direct lines to the taxi companies, and any restaurant will call a taxi for you when you are ready to leave.

Taxis may be yellow, blue, or red and green, but all have the name of the cab company and the number of the cab in prominent letters on the sides. The top light of the taxi is illuminated when it is vacant. If an empty cab passes you by even though you are flagging it down, it has probably been called on the radio to go to a particular address. In San Francisco, the meter does not start running until you have entered the cab. Tip about 20 percent.

You can either give the taxi driver the exact street address where you're going, or you can indicate the two cross streets, such as "the corner of Washington and Battery." If you think you know the best route to get there, tell the driver on which streets you want to go. Generally, however, the driver is aware of the traffic conditions at that time and will take you the shortest and quickest way possible.

- Citywide Cab (tel: 920-0700)
- DeSoto Cab (tel: 970-1300)
- Luxor Cab (tel: 282-4141)
- Veteran's Cab (tel: 552-1300)
- Yellow Cab (tel: 626-2345)

# DRIVING IN THE CITY

The most important thing about driving in San Francisco is to drive defensively. The congested downtown streets, the few major arteries, and the hills and the sun in drivers' eyes all contribute to the highest rate of traffic accidents in the state (although not involving pedestrians). Do not let the hills intimidate you. People drive up and down the hills every day, and some major routes go over the steepest of hills. When stopping at a traffic light while driving up a hill, leave at least ten feet between you and the car ahead, in case that car rolls back a little when starting up again. On some steep hills, you may have to downshift to maintain the car's power level, and some streets are marked with the percentage of grade and warnings to trucks not to attempt them. Make sure you have a pair of sunglasses in your car when you drive. If you drive toward the East in the morning or toward the West in the afternoons—especially when maneuvering the hills—the sun can be blinding.

When parking on a hill, "curb your wheels." This means if your car is heading down a hill, turn the front wheels toward the curb, to keep it from rolling. If your car is heading up a hill, turn the back part of the front wheels toward the curb to keep it from rolling back down. If you do not, your car will be ticketed.

Streets are narrowest in the downtown area, and it is on these streets, of course, that delivery trucks routinely double park, forcing cars to merge and causing traffic jams. Try to glance two to three blocks ahead while you are driving, to determine whether your lane is clear. Drivers in San Francisco are not particularly generous in allowing cars to cut into their lanes, so it's best to leave yourself as much time as possible to change lanes.

Many of the streets east of Van Ness are one-way; past Arguello, however, most streets — except for a few major arteries — are two-way. Two important one-way streets are Bush, which heads east ("Bush to the Bay"), and Pine, which heads west ("Pine to the Pacific"), for their lights are "timed," meaning that if you maintain a certain speed (and if there are no obstacles), you should not meet any red lights once you are in the traffic flow.

Some downtown streets have "diamond lanes," reserved for buses and for cars turning right at the next corner. Cars may turn right on a red light, after having come to a complete stop and allowed all pedestrians in the crosswalk to cross; some busy intersections, however, have signs saying "No turn on red." Left turn on red from a one-way street and into another is permitted under the same conditions.

Rush hours are generally 7:00–9:30 am and 4:00–7:00 pm. Streets leading to the bridges or freeways begin to be crowded by 3:30 in the afternoon, and traffic is slow until early evening. Local radio and television stations report traffic conditions every few minutes during rush hours and regularly throughout the day. You can also call TravInfo.

Do not be shocked at the price of gasoline; Northern California motorists pay the highest prices in the country. Some San Franciscans rely on public transportation, but despite the various expenses a car entails, most people find one necessary.

Last, all car passengers must wear seat belts, and occasionally a ticket will be given for failure to do so. Children under four years of age and under 40 pounds must wear a child restraint.

The California State Automobile Association is the best source of information for cars, driving, routes and maps, licenses, and insurance and permits. It also provides its members with excellent emergency road services. Offices are open 8:30 am–5:00 pm weekdays.

## THE PARKING PROBLEM

About 800,000 cars circulate each day in this city of only 750,000 people. There are not enough parking spaces, so parking is a major complaint among residents. The closer to the bay, the harder it is to find a parking space. Downtown, parking meter spaces are generally reserved until 6:00 pm for commercially licensed vehicles to load and unload merchandise. Other meters may run on a half-hour basis. People who do find a parking space tend to stay there and return periodically to "feed" the meter, which is supposedly illegal; sometimes "meter maids" (parking police) mark the tires of cars with chalk to indicate the time they passed by; if the car is still there the next time the meter maid passes, it will be ticketed.

Parking garages and outdoor lots help with the problem, but they are crowded and prices vary: it depends on their location, whether they are city-owned or private, whether you are a short- or long-term parker and what time of day you park; early morning entry may allow a flat day rate, and evening parking also may incur a flat fee, paid in advance. In the popular areas around North Beach, Chinatown and Fisherman's Wharf, a $2.00 charge for 20 minutes is common, pretty expensive if you're planning a leisurely evening out. But if you're staying only 20 minutes, it might be worth it. The garages mentioned here are reasonable in price; there are others around the city, and fortunately supermarkets and most shopping centers have their own free parking lots.

- *Union Square*: Sutter/Stockton Garage
- *Union Square*: Under Union Square, enter on Geary
- *Yerba Buena*: Fifth and Mission Garage

- *Japantown*: Entrances on Post and Geary, off Webster
- *Chinatown*: Portsmouth Square Garage, enter on Kearny, just past Clay
- *Financial District:* St Mary's Square Garage, enter from Kearny, north of Pine
- *North Beach*: Vallejo/Stockton Garage, enter from Vallejo
- *Richmond*: Geary and 16th Avenue, on second floor, above shops.

When you make a reservation at a restaurant, ask about parking; valet parking is often available, but can be expensive, for the price displayed does not include the expected tip to the parker. Some restaurants and cinemas offer validated parking in nearby parking garages; your parking ticket stamped by the restaurant or theater entitles you to a discount on the charge.

In high-traffic districts, residents may park indefinitely on non-metered streets with a permit issued by the **Department of Parking**, at 370 Grove Street (info tel: 554-5000); you must have proof that the car is registered in California and that you live where you say you do. Street signs indicate the permit needed for that area, and they also specify how long non-permit cars may park during certain hours. Signs also indicate which day of the week and time the street is to be cleaned; if your car is parked there during those hours, permit or not, it will be ticketed and towed. Unfortunately, street cleaning days decrease even further the number of available parking spaces. (If you see a street on which no one is parked, don't thank your lucky stars that you found a parking space: look to see if this is street cleaning day.)

None of this makes it easier to find a space on Chestnut Street if you want to go to a film on a Saturday afternoon or to Ninth Avenue for dinner. Nonetheless, avoid parking illegally, for anything other than an overtime meter incurs a high fine. Look on the parking meter itself to determine its hours and days of operation; don't assume that parking is free on holidays, especially in tourist areas. Fines are extremely steep for parking where the curb is painted red (prohibited) or blue (handicapped parking), in a crosswalk, or where the curb has been cut out for wheelchair access. And do not even think about parking in a bus zone. A white curb is for passenger pickup and drop-off, and a green curb is for 10 minute parking. Yellow is for commercial vehicles, and the hours and days of parking limitations should be painted on the curb. A green, yellow and black zone is for taxi cabs. As mentioned above, some downtown streets prohibit parking during morning or evening rush hours; for infractions, your car will most likely be towed. These streets are usually marked "tow-away zone."

## Driver's Licenses

All applicants for a California driver's license must submit proof of legal presence in the United States. (This might include — among other documents — a birth certificate, U.S. passport, Certificate of Naturalization, Canadian Passport, or Mexican Border Crossing Card with a valid I-94.)

Residents of San Francisco — defined as people who are making their home here or who have taken a job here — must apply for a California driver's license within 10 days to the **DMV (California Department of Motor Vehicles)**, at 1377 Fell Street (tel: 557-1179; www.dmv.ca.gov). If you have a valid license from another state, you may not be required to take the driving test; all applicants, however, must take the written "rules of the road" test and a vision test. All applicants must give a thumbprint and have a picture taken. DMV offices are located in towns throughout the Bay Area. A driver's license is generally valid for four or five years, and expires on your birthday of that year.

If you are here only on a temporary basis, however, you may drive for one year with a valid license from your home state. This applies also to citizens of Western nations; others must possess a current International Driving License. If you do not drive but would like an official identification card, bring identification, Social Security number, and proof of address to the DMV.

## DUI

Do not drink alcohol and drive. It is dangerous, and the police crack down on drivers who have been drinking (even if the driver doesn't appear to be "drunk"). If you intend to drink, designate a non-drinking driver for that evening. Fines for DUI ("driving under the influence") are steep, and if there is a serious accident, may even involve a term in prison. The DWI ("driving while intoxicated") is not generally used in California, for prosecutors do not need to prove that a driver is intoxicated to take the driver to court. In California it is illegal to drive with a blood alcohol level of 0.08 or more; the fact that a driver doesn't know the blood alcohol level is not an excuse under the law.

### Registering Your Car

Within 20 days of establishing residency in California, you must register your out-of-state car. (Residency means paying resident-based tuition at a school, having a job, filing for home owner's tax exemptions, obtaining any kind of lease or contract, or any other benefit that non-residents do not obtain.) In order to register the vehicle with the DMV, you will need to fill out the application, pay the current fee, and produce the title to the car and a "smog certificate" (available at many full-service gasoline stations). The car must be inspected by the DMV.

If you are coming to California for only a few months, you need not register your car, and may drive with your own state's license plates. This may pose a problem if you rent an apartment in a neighborhood which requires parking permits to park on the street; you can't get a permit for a car not registered in California. In this case, it's best to rent a space in a garage nearby, or make sure in advance that your apartment has a garage space.

### Automobile Insurance

California state law requires that all drivers be financially responsible for their actions while driving and for the vehicles they own;

if you have an accident not covered by your insurance, your driver's license will be suspended. In fact, car dealers do not permit you to take possession of a new car without proof of insurance; make sure to arrange for it in advance. The minimum amount your insurance must cover per accident is $15,000 for a single death or injury, $30,000 for death or injury to more than one person, and $5,000 for property damage; given the litigious nature of American society, however, these minimums may not protect you well enough, depending on your financial circumstances. If you are bringing a car with you, you may be able to transfer your insurance if the company does business in California; check in advance with your carrier. Otherwise, some major insurance companies that service California are **Allstate**, California State Automobile Association (AAA), **Farmers**, **Mercury**, **State Farm**, and **20th Century**. Rates vary considerably. Many companies have discounted rates for drivers with proven safety records, some give discounts for cars with alarm systems, some have discounts for professionals, and some offer towing services.

## PURCHASING A CAR

Advertising supplements for new cars appear in each Friday's daily newspapers. Used cars are advertised in the classified ad sections, especially on Sundays. When purchasing a car, it is best to determine the dealer's factory invoice price on the car (not the "sticker price" which is affixed to the window). Several services help buyers get the best deal possible.

Members of the Cal State Auto may use its Vehicle Pricing Service to receive suggested retail prices on new and used vehicles, and to buy a new car at a fair price, without haggling (vehicle pricing tel: 800/272-2877; vehicle purchasing service tel: 800/477-1222; www.csaa.com/carbuying). When you indicate the make, model and options of the car you want, "Triple A" will tell you which dealers in the area have agreed to sell at the pre-arranged price.

176

# HANDICAPPED ACCESS

San Francisco is wheelchair friendly. Buses have operator-assisted ramps for wheelchairs, all BART stations are wheelchair accessible, and curbs throughout the city are cut to a slope for easy access to sidewalks and crosswalks. Hotels and restaurants are wheelchair accessible, and most public rest rooms have wide stalls that will accommodate wheelchairs.

Drivers with handicaps may apply to the DMV for a permit to park in any of the blue-marked parking spaces reserved for handicapped drivers. Your doctor should have a form that entitles you to such application. As mentioned above, people with physical disabilities are entitled to a public transportation discount card.

The Department of Tourism issues *California Travel Planning Guide*, which is available at the Visitor Center in Halliday Plaza. If you have a problem, contact the 24-hour Crisis Line for the handicapped (tel: 800/426-4263).

The **San Francisco Paratransit Broker** arranges reasonably priced taxi transportation for people with physical disabilities who are enrolled in their program (tel: 543-9650).

# THE CALL OF NATURE

It shouldn't be hard to find a clean public bathroom in San Francisco. Downtown, in addition to rest rooms in the large hotels and department stores, there are a few French-style coin-operated *sanisettes*, standing lavatories with toilet and sink; when you are finished, open the door to exit, and as it closes behind you, the toilet flushes and the entire facility is sterilized. Supermarkets generally have rest rooms for customer use, as do shopping centers. Fast-food restaurants, bars, and coffee shops may expect you to purchase at least a cup of coffee to use their rest room, and some small restaurants on the tourist path have clear signs indicating that rest rooms are for customers only. Rest rooms at service stations may require that you ask the attendant for a key. In most places, if you ask to use a rest room, you will not be refused.

177

# CHAPTER ELEVEN

# GASTRONOMIC DELIGHTS

A LITTLE BIT RUSTY AT THE START OF THE CRAB SEASON?

## SAN FRANCISCO—THE BEST?

San Franciscans believe their city to be the gastronomic capital of America. Residents of a few other American cities may dispute this claim, but the seemingly endless numbers of tourists who patiently await their tables at the city's crowded restaurants tend to confirm that San Francisco's offerings rise to the top. But how has this come to pass? The answer is itself a stew, combining the city's particular geography, climate, history—and attitude.

Begin with the ingredients: the area's moderate climate and the city's proximity to rich, fertile, agricultural lands, to the Pacific Ocean, and to the country's top wine-producing region. See the fishing boats coming in early each morning to the piers off

Jefferson Street, and you will never doubt that the fish is fresh, year-round. Drive south or east, passing the rich vegetable fields and flourishing orchards that supply the city's restaurants directly, and you can tell what is in season and what will be on the menu at that time. Or pass the miles of grape-laden vines as you head up to warm, sunny Napa or Sonoma—just an hour north of the city— and then don't be surprised to find outstanding wines made at those vineyards in restaurants all over town.

Now stir in a bit of history. The city's unusual approach to food combinations has grown from its own cultural diversity. From its earliest days, San Francisco was a town where people ate out. It started with the Gold Rush, when thousands of miners with money—or gold nuggets—in their pockets, came down from the hills for a taste of "civilization." Restaurants of all types flourished. Even at that time, the cooks were immigrants—Italians, Hungarians, French, and Chinese—melding their own cooking traditions with the ingredients on hand. After the flurry of the Gold Rush and the Silver Rush died down, eating establishments remained.

Since then, each wave of immigrants has taken and given to the tastes and aromas of the city: Italian food with Oriental overtones, Vietnamese food presented in the style of the French, and pan-Asian or pan-Latin cuisines. Although you might hear such appellations as *eclectic* or *international,* the more common culinary term for this bringing together of traditions and tastes is *fusion,* describing an approach in which each flavor contributes to the overall dish but is identifiable in itself. But fusion is not new in San Francisco, and in fact, fusion of cultures, cuisines, and traditions—with each contributing but still identifiable in itself—is what has always defined the city itself.

## Attitude of San Franciscans

Adding spice to the answer of why San Francisco's restaurants are so exceptional, is that San Franciscans demand they be so. San Franciscans also love to eat out—at restaurants of all levels—

179

and with a mean household income of about $60,000, residents spend about $2,500 per household per year eating out. Thus, no one needs to settle for just a "good dinner." Although it is not true that San Francisco has more restaurants than people, with some 3,500 eating and drinking establishments, it may well have more restaurants *per capita* than other cities. Thus, diners get a wide choice, and they set the tone. In fact, the city works on the premise that the entire experience of eating should be fun. San Franciscans consider eating out to be one of their major cultural—albeit playful—experiences, and they demand, and get, the best.

"The best" does not necessarily mean the most expensive restaurant or those that are lavishly reviewed. An innovative Thai restaurant might be the best in its class, and an otherwise undistinguished Italian restaurant might well have the best calamari—to some diners' tastes. Other restaurants may tickle diners' fancy with their decor, and some now are offering entertainment—foreign movies or live music—along with the dining experience.

Also, particularity rules. Gone are the days when Italian food meant spaghetti with tomato sauce; now San Franciscans may select among their favorite Ligurian- or Roman-style restaurants, even choosing a place for one particular dish. (This holds true for fish restaurants as well, where people may throng to a particular restaurant for its way of cooking one type of fish.) And gone also are the days when Chinese food meant Chicken Fried Rice; now San Franciscans pick carefully among Hunan, Chiu Chow, or Cantonese cuisines, and they know which restaurants serve the best *dim sum*. The best San Franciscan restaurants demonstrate a strong sense of place.

But even the cuisines do not tell the entire story. San Franciscans also demand that restaurants, no matter the style of cuisine, mirror their lifestyles. The restaurants themselves should be attractive. The food they eat should be healthy and look good, whether it is a luxurious dinner in an elegant restaurant or a hearty meal in a neighborhood pub. Food in San Francisco can also be high art. What is known as California Cuisine — which originated at Berkeley's **Chez Panisse** and which has now been adopted around the globe — epitomizes this trend. Emphasizing regional, in-season ingredients, California Cuisine presents a beautiful yet simple-seeming and healthy effect (sometimes with a touch of humor) although the exotic combinations of ingredients and presentation may not be simple at all.

Yet even with California Cuisine, distinctions blur. Some restaurants known for California Cuisine also use Asian flavors and presentations, others might borrow from the Italian, some might just call themselves Modern American, or even that generic term of *fusion*. What San Franciscans want, in short, is everything all at once: excellent and healthful food imaginatively prepared, a great view, an attractive space, and friendly service. Some of the city's most inventive chefs — at luxury restaurants such as **Aqua, Fleur de Lys, La Folie, Campton Place** and **Jardeniere** — offer a "tasting menu" that allows diners to sample several of the evening's dishes, including starters, entrees, and desserts. If San Franciscans, as some people claim, "want eveything now," at least in terms of dining out, they seem to be able to get it.

### Resources
It is a passion of San Franciscans to seek the best restaurant for every meal. Weekends find people out early eating hearty breakfasts or, later, a delicately prepared brunch. Weekday lunchtime sees crowds in most of the downtown business-style restaurants, people looking not just to eat but for a culinary experience. (It is wise to reserve for lunch, just as much as for dinner.) And dinner is a constant process of happy exploration in any neighborhood, sometimes the more offbeat, the better. Currently, expanding out of the tried and true districts, San Franciscans are seeking out the restaurants and bars in what is sometimes called Baja Mission (on the edge of Potrero Hill), the Inner Sunset nexus around 9th Avenue, and the new offerings near the baseball park.

It would be impossible to describe all the city's excellent restaurants here. There are so many international cuisines and traditions that these chapters can give only representative samples of the diverse culinary experiences the city offers. To aid in your pleasant search, buy one of the guides dedicated entirely to eating out in the Bay Area. The best, which covers both restaurants and food markets, is *A Food Lover's Guide to San Francisco*, by Patricia Unterman, a local food writer who knows San Francisco's restaurants better than anyone else. Loosely arranged by district and within district by category, her book makes it easy to find anything you want to know about food in the area. *Access San Francisco: Restaurants* presents a comprehensive selection, also arranged by neighborhood. The famous *Zagat's* rates restaurants according to diners' choices; in recent years, **Boulevard** has been rated the city's most popular restaurant, with Aqua the runner-up.

Although this book emphasizes establishments patronized by locals, do not overlook those in the tourist guides, for the elegant places that the hordes of tourists are clamoring to try — **Fifth Floor**, Fleur de Lys, **Farallon**, Jardiniere, **Stars** — are truly exceptional. In addition, these guides — such as the always-interesting *Time Out San Francisco* — usually describe some out-of-the-way places of all cuisines and price ranges that they believe capture the spirit of San Francisco.

Look also at the daily newspapers and weekly tabloids, which review and rate restaurants and often conduct readers' polls, which accounts for the myriad restaurants that boast that their specialty (sushi, hamburger, pizza, barbeque, salsa, etc) has been judged the best in the city. They probably all have, by one judge or another. *The Bay Guardian* and *San Francisco Chronicle* also regularly publish surveys of the "best" in dozens of categories, always interesting, always with a surprise. Beauty of the establishment is often rated, and some — such as Farallon and Jardiniere — are imaginative in their decor. If noise bothers you, pay attention to the decibel ratings in restaurant reviews, as the current trend for a lively atmosphere has resulted in large open spaces with high ceilings, which greatly increases the noise.

## Reserving a Table

Most but not all restaurants take reservations. The currently fashionable restaurants require reservations to be made one month in advance, and if you do not call exactly when specified, you might not get a table; sometimes, however, tables are available at off-hours, such as 5:45 pm or 10:00 pm. As a general rule, the better the restaurant, the longer in advance you should book. This also holds true for the restaurants that play live music, or those with a view—**The Waterfront** and **Greens** at water level, or the **Carnelian Room** soaring 52 floors above. To find out about table availability and making a reservation on the Internet, you might try **Open Table** (www.OpenTable.com).

On the other hand, there's no harm in calling to see whether there has been a cancellation. Ask whether the restaurant serves dinner at the bar to walk-in customers, for bar food is of the same quality as in the rest of the restaurant. (Some restaurants have open kitchens, and sitting at the counter/bar allows you to watch the chefs perform their magic.) Sitting at the bar is an attractive option for solo diners, although San Franciscan restaurants are welcoming to people dining alone.

Most restaurants can accommodate you if you make a reservation the day before or even on the morning of the day you intend to dine, and in some, if you don't reserve in advance, you can wait for a table to be vacated. Restaurants generally figure 90 minutes for a couple to remain at a table and two hours for a party of four. The maître d'hôtel will be as honest as possible—given the unpredictable time a party may linger—in assessing the waiting time, or indeed, if there is a chance to get a table. If you have to wait, the maître d' will almost always offer a seat at the bar.

Not all restaurants take reservations. Some of the fish restaurants do not, or will take reservations only for parties of more than six people; this also holds true for the Asian establishments and many small, neighborhood restaurants. In popular places where there is a line, there will usually be a waiting list; seating is first come first served, according to the tables available and the number of people in the party.

Do not forget that tourists love San Francisco restaurants. When a large convention is in town, it can be impossible to get a table at a restaurant that might have been reviewed in a guidebook or that was recommended by the convention planners. Make your reservation as far in advance as you can and call if you must cancel; don't just not show up. No one minds if you cancel; they're glad you have called. Some restaurants require confirmation of the reservation the day before, and a few ask for your credit card number, explaining that you will be charged a fee if you do not show up.

Despite the foggy, cool evenings, San Franciscans love to eat outside; some restaurants have patios sheltered from the wind by glass screens with gas heaters under an overhanging roof. These popular establishments are likely to be crowded on warm spring or autumn nights (and always for brunch on weekends), so make sure you reserve in advance, and mention that you'd like a table on the patio or one with a view. The reservations taker usually says, "we'll see what we can do," meaning that you will probably get a table you want, given the traffic flow at the time.

Dress is generally casual, and it is rare to find a man wearing a suit, except for holidays or special occasions. In the most fashionable restaurants, a man might wear a sports jacket, without a tie, and women slacks, sweaters, and a blazer. However, it's always good to dress appropriately to the establishment and the occasion. In most neighborhood restaurants and smaller cafes, casual dress is the rule; even blue jeans and sneakers are acceptable. One casual Berkeley establishment humorously advertises "food so good, you might want to wear your nice jeans."

## Opening Times

San Francisco is an "early town." Because the Pacific Time Zone is three hours behind New York's financial markets, financial workers start working before dawn and eat lunch and dinner early. Because they most often eat before performances, not after, do not expect to get into popular restaurants around Union Square or at the Civic Center in the early evening (or on days when there are matinees) unless you reserve well in advance. On the other hand, you can generally get a table if you are willing to eat a little later, after a performance has started.

Restaurants start to serve breakfast around 6:30 am, begin lunch at 11:30 am, and those that don't stay open all day may start dinner service at 5:30 pm, taking their last orders around 10:00 pm. Some restaurants in the Financial District close by 9:00 pm, and a few are open weekdays only.

A few restaurants—**Black Cat**, **The Globe**, **Chow**, **Brazenhead**, and **Absinthe**—fill the void in late-night dining, while **Lisa's on Folsom**, and **Yuet Lee** and a few others in Chinatown satisfy the need for a late-night Chinese food fix. **Sparky's**, **The Grubstake**, and **Mel's** offer burgers into the wee hours. The hours of neighborhood restaurants generally reflect the habits of the locals. Asian restaurants usually serve all day, as do the coffeehouses. Fashionable restaurants may take their last orders around 10:30, but neighborhood eateries are generally closed by then.

Most of the large restaurants serve dinner every day, but serve lunch only on weekdays. Most of the Asian restaurants are open daily as well, although any small family-run establishment may close one day a week. Days of closure vary, but generally it is either Sunday or Monday.

## The Menu

The menu depends on the season. Some restaurants print their menus daily, and in others servers recite the list of that day's special dishes. These invariably reflect the fishermen's catch and the

185

produce that is then most plentiful in the markets. Pay attention to the specials, for they generally offer the best value for the money. Do not hesitate to ask how a dish is prepared, and in the case of an oral recitation of the specials, to ask the price, if the server omits it.

If you have dietary restrictions, specify your needs to the server in advance, so that you can be assured of ordering a meal that you can eat. The server will ask the chef what is in the dish you are considering, and then you can decide. In general, you send back a meal only if it isn't cooked properly or if it is different from what is described on the menu.

Order only as much as you want. Restaurants are used to people ordering two appetizers, to splitting appetizers and main courses between two diners, or serving just an appetizer and a dessert. And every establishment, from the grungiest dive to the most fashionable temple of gastronomy, will cheerfully wrap your unfinished meal to take home.

Coffee may be served at any time during the meal and generally with the dessert, not after; all restaurants offer decaffeinated coffee and many offer espresso and cappuccino. Tea drinking is becoming trendy, and most restaurants now offer a selection of teas, including decaffeinated versions and herbal infusions.

## What Will It Cost?

An excellent dinner in a neighborhood Asian or Latino restauraunt may cost as little as $10, including a beer or soda, and an excellent meal in one of the city's top restaurants may cost as much as $100 per person, with several glasses of wine. The average per-person dinner tab is currently $35, on a par with New York. Yet what matters to San Francisco diners is value for the money, and in general, eating out in San Francisco is an affordable pastime.

Chinese and other Asian restaurants may offer a lunchtime special of soup, a hearty main course with plenty of rice, plus tea for about $5.00. Dinner specials may be slightly, but not much, higher in price. In fact, because the best restaurants are crowded year-round, and the inexpensive restaurants are affordable at any time, few have "early bird specials," for people arriving (and leaving) before normal dining hours. Occasionally restaurants offer specials with a coupon from the newspapers.

### Paying the Bill

All the major restaurants accept credit cards. In the United States the tip (gratuity) is generally not included in the bill, although some restaurants will add 15 percent for a party of at least six people. The standard tip is 15–20 percent, depending on level of service; 20 percent is becoming more common for good service. In San Francisco, the sales tax is 8.5 percent, and when figuring the tip, many people just double the tax that appears on the bill. This assumes the service was good; if not, point it out to the manager or tip accordingly.

It is best not to assume that the small Asian eateries accept credit cards, although many do. Even some of the popular neighborhood restaurants don't, so if this is of concern, call ahead or carry enough cash. A few will accept a local check, so long as you provide a picture identification. In some Asian establishments you may not understand the bill because it is written in Chinese on a small piece of paper only somewhat resembling a bill. On the other hand, the amount may be so cheap—under $20 for two people—that a rarely made mistake of a few cents doesn't matter much.

# SMOKING

Smoking is not allowed in any public place in San Francisco, not in any public building, restaurant, theater, sports arena, nor on public transportation. A recent law passed to prohibit smoking in bars raised a loud protest, but even before the law was enacted, San Franciscans were capable of shooting dirty looks and saying something pointed to anyone they thought was smoking too close to their "smoke-free zone."

187

# SAN FRANCISCO'S OWN

It is true that San Francisco's cuisine blends international flavors, but the city boasts its own local favorites, worth seeking out. The season (November–May) for the sweet, meaty **Dungeness crab** is eagerly awaited, and people keep track of the weather, for stormy weather makes for a bad catch. Cracked crab, served cold with a cocktail or butter sauce, or Crab Louie, a crab salad with a Thousand Island type dressing, are served in most fish restaurants during crab season. Outside crab season, the crab is likely to have been frozen or imported. Asian restaurants serve well-sauced crab dishes, and many people think the upscale Vietnamese restaurant **Thanh Long** at 4101 Judah Street in the Outer Richmond serves the best in the city; dinners only, closed Monday (tel: 665-1146).

Filet of sole is on the menu worldwide, but the local varieties—**petrale**, **rex**, or the delicate **sand dabs**—are particular to this area. Two of the oldest fish houses in the city are known for their excellent preparations:

- **Sam's Grill**: 374 Bush Street, near Kearny (tel: 421-0594). For almost 150 years, Sam's has served excellent fish. Try the sand dabs and rex sole. Closed weekends.
- **Tadich**: 240 California Street (tel: 391-1849). Perennially popular, Tadich's has been serving seafood in San Francisco since 1849, making it the oldest in the city.

If every fishing port has its favorite seafood dishes, San Francisco's is **cioppino**, a fish stew based loosely on the Ligurian *ciuppin*. It also resembles the French *bouillabaisse* and the Spanish *zarzuela*. Basically, cioppino features locally caught crab in season, other fresh shellfish and fish (especially the local rockfish, like cod), all stewed in a spicy tomato broth. Note that squid, a favorite seafood in San Francisco, is called by its Italian name *calamari*, even in some Asian restaurants. Eat the stew with San Francisco's **sourdough bread** (see Bakeries, in Chapter Thirteen).

*Eating lunch by a fountain in the sun.*

- **Alioto's**: 8 Fisherman's Wharf, at Taylor (tel: 673-0183). Despite the tourist atmosphere, this is one of the best cioppinos in the city.
- **Rose Pistola**: 532 Columbus Avenue (tel: 399-0499). Excellent cioppino and other Ligurian dishes. Live jazz.

## CALIFORNIA CUISINE

As mentioned above, California Cuisine is a modern American style of cooking that emphasizes fresh, regional ingredients in creative combinations and presentations. **Chez Panisse** at 1517 Shattuck Avenue, Berkeley, is still the high temple of California Cuisine (tel: 510/548-5525; cafe tel: 510/548-5049). Delicious and beautiful ingredients in magically pure combinations look deceptively simple on the plate yet are addictive to the palate. Make reservations for the restaurant (downstairs) at least a month in advance and expect an outstanding culinary experience during an expensive price-fixed meal, with one entree selection per evening. In the cafe (upstairs) reserve the same day and expect a delicious, imaginative selection at more moderate prices.

189

- *Downtown* — **Postrio**: 545 Post Street (tel: 776-7825). A temple to California Cuisine. Outstanding dishes, creatively prepared.
- *Mission/Potrero* — **Gordon's House of Fine Eats**: 500 Florida Street (tel: 861-8900). Billing itself as "modern American," Asian overtones can be found amid the blend of American traditions.
- *Mission* — **Luna Park**: 694 Valencia, at 18th Street (tel: 553-8584). Chic yet funky atmosphere, good California cuisine, and a bar that serves up great margaritas and other trendy drinks.
- *North Beach* — **Moose's**: 1652 Stockton Street (tel: 989-7800). Eclectic menu, great bar, famous for the Mooseburger.
- *South Waterfront* — **Delancey Street Restaurant**: Embarcadero at Brannan (tel: 512-5179). Upscale "ethnic American bistro" staffed by people who have "hit bottom" and are now being rehabilitated. Closed Monday.
- *Sunset/NorthBeach* — **The House**: 1269 9th Ave (tel: 682-3898); 1230 Grant Ave (tel: 986-8612). Asian/Mediterranean/California Cuisine in a spare setting.

## The Old ...

As mentioned, San Francisco became an eating-out town during the Gold Rush, when miners came down from the hills for a good time. Tadich's (see above) is the oldest restaurant in the city, and others, some dating from the 1860s, also pride themselves on maintaining traditions of "old San Francisco."

- **Fior d'Italia**: 601 Union Street, at Stockton (tel: 986-1886). Claiming to be the oldest Italian restaurant in the country, this standard, fairly expensive Italian restaurant has been in this location since 1886.
- **Fly Trap**: 606 Folsom (tel: 243-0580). Only a few streets away from its 1898 location, this rather hidden restaurant still serves grilled food in an old-time setting. Closed Sunday.
- **Jack's**: 615 Sacramento Street (tel: 421-7355). In the same

location for more than 135 years, Jack's has recently been restored, with period furnishings. Fresh and hearty food, traditional favorites, plus "California" dishes.

- **John's Grill**: 63 Ellis Street, at Powell (tel: 986-0069). Since 1908, John's has served hearty food. Live jazz.
- **Maye's Oyster House**: 1233 Polk, between Bush and Sutter (tel: 474-7674). Serving Italian food and seafood since 1867, Maye's has an old-time feel, despite its modern piano bar.
- **Schroeder's**: 240 Front Street, near Sacramento (tel: 421-4778). Solid German food such as sauerbraten and sausages, served here for more than one hundred years. Open weekdays.
- **The Old Clam House**: 299 Bayshore Boulevard (tel: 826-4880). Since 1861, this fish house has been offering fresh seafood in an old-time setting. Open daily.

## ... The New

Although many restaurants borrow liberally from world regions, San Franciscan restaurants excel in presenting a meld of flavors and traditions that reflect the city's own cultural diversity. Fusion cuisine may blend several culinary traditions, at least one of them Asian, and often the exotic result seems more than the combination of the parts.

- *Cole Valley* — **EOS**: 901 Cole Street (tel: 566-3063). Popular for East/West cuisine, and its excellent wine list and wine bar. Less noisy upstairs. Dinner daily.
- *Downtown* — **Oritalia**: 586 Bush Street (tel: 782-8122). Mediterranean and Eastern blends, such as a Chinese cioppino. Dinner only.
- *Marina* — **The Blue Monkey**: 2414 Lombard Street, at Scott (tel: 776-8298). Excellent Thai fusion cuisine.
- *Mission* — **The Rooster**: 1101 Valencia, at 22nd Street (tel: 824-1222). Country cooking with European, Asian, and Latin flavors, in a rustic setting.

- *Noe Valley*—**Firefly**: 4288 24th Street (tel: 821-7652). Popular neighborhood eatery preparing "American food with no ethnic boundaries." Wonderful desserts. Dinner only.
- *Polk/California*—**Crustacean**: 1475 Polk Street (tel: 776-2722). Like its sister restaurant Thanh Long: Euro/Asian menu featuring Dungeness crab, garlic noodles, and other interesting dishes.
- *Polk/Broadway*—**Yabbies Coastal Kitchen**: 2237 Polk Street (tel: 474-4088). Excellent establishment specializing in fish dishes with Asian-Mediterranean overtones.
- *SOMA*—**XYZ**: 181 3rd Street at Howard (tel: 817-7836). Popular restaurant next to W Hotel, serving seafood with Japanese overtones, and other fusion-style dishes.

## ... and the Basic

To the rest of the world American food means steaks, roast beef, barbeque, fried chicken, burgers and fries, and San Francisco does not disappoint. But here—although you can find **McDonalds** and other international burger chains—even the purveyors of down-home ribs and burgers do so with their own San Francisco twist:

- **Max's Diner**: 311 3rd Street (tel: 546-6297). Huge sandwiches, burgers, and desserts, plus a sports bar.
- **Big Nate's Barbecue**: 1665 Folsom, near 12th Street (tel: 861-4242). Ribs, chicken and sausage links in this takeout storefront owned by Nate Thurmond, the famous basketball player. A few tables for eat-in.
- **Bill's Place**: 2315 Clement Street (tel: 221-5262). For more than 25 years, consistently rated among the best for burgers and crispy fries.
- **Brother-in-law's Barbeque #2**: 705 Divisadero Street (tel: 931-7427). Delicious brisket and "short-end ribs," plus greens, beans, spaghetti, and corn bread. Take out, for there are only two small tables in front for eating-in.

- **Cliff's Bar-B-Q & Seafood**: 2177 Bayshore Boulevard (tel: 330-0736). Ribs of all sorts, spicy or not, excellent brisket, fish and turkey burgers. A few tables.
- **Hamburger Mary's**: 1582 Folsom at 12th Street (tel: 626-5767). A city tradition, advertising "Great food, Fun Bar, Crazy Staff." Excellent meals served to a rather interesting clientele.
- **Memphis Minnie's Bar-B-Que Joint**: 576 Haight Street (tel: 864-8461). Great smokehouse ribs, brisket, Andouille sausage, and a good selection of sides. Closed Monday.
- **Mo's Place**: 1322 Grant Avenue (tel: 788-3779). Among the best burgers in town. Also at Yerba Buena Gardens on the second level of the bowling alley-ice skating rink.
- **Powell's Place**: 511 Hayes Street (tel: 863-1404). Delicious fried chicken, yams, and greens. Pork chops, beans and rice, and other soul food. Daily specials.
- **Harris' Restaurant**: 2100 Van Ness Avenue (tel: 673-1888). Excellent steaks, good decor, from a famous California cattle rancher.
- **House of Prime Rib**: 1906 Van Ness Avenue (tel: 885-4605). Succulent prime rib, carved at your table.

# FISH

Expect all restaurants to serve fish, and for it to be fresh. As the menu depends on the day's catch, the entire city pays close attention to the weather and fishing conditions. It is a disappointment when the Dungeness crab catch is low, or when storms prevent the taking of sand dabs and rex sole. Restaurants that don't print their menus every day generally announce fish dishes as specials of the day. Often they will give the origin of the fish. If they don't, you can ask where the fish was caught.

In a restaurant, a serving of fish is generally about $5^{1}/_{2}$ or 6 ounces. Don't neglect the fish dishes in Asian restaurants: although the portion of fish may be smaller, the flavors meld together with the vegetables and sauces of each region's culinary traditions.

The elegant, trendy Aqua and Farallon specialize in fish, and **Scott's** in the Embarcadero Center is always reliable. Sam's and Tadich's (see above) remain favorites, and if their ambience is staid, the quality of the food is not. There will no doubt be a good fish restaurant in your own neighborhood. Try also these below, and see the following chapter for Asian restaurants.

- *Castro* — **Anchor Oyster Bar**: 579 Castro Street (tel: 431-3990). Small restaurant serving delicious pastas, seafood, and clam chowder, with a delightful aroma of garlic throughout.
- *Civic Center* — **Hayes Street Grill**: 320 Hayes Street (tel: 863-5545). Great fish on a menu that changes daily. Tell the staff if you have a performance to make in the Civic Center, and service will be speedy.
- *Inner Sunset* — **PJ's Oyster Bed**: 737 Irving Street (tel: 556-7775). Long before 9th Avenue became chic, PJ's was serving fresh oysters, chowder, and other excellent Southern dishes to neighborhood locals, and it still does.
- *Polk Corridor* — **Swan's Oyster Depot**: 1517 Polk Street (tel: 673-1101). Lunch only at the counter of this excellent almost century-old fish market. Outstanding chowder, oysters, seafood salads.
- *Western Addition* — **Alamo Square, a Seafood Grill**: 803 Fillmore Street, at Fulton (tel: 440-2828). Fish any way you like it. Dinners daily; Sunday brunch.

# VEGETARIAN AND KOSHER

Catering to a healthy, fitness-oriented crowd, even the best "carnivore" restaurants offer well-presented vegetarian selections. Italian restaurants offer meatless pasta dishes and the ubiquitous Asian restaurants have vegetarian dishes. The city's totally vegetarian restaurants offer the same high-quality food as the others.

You will not find many kosher restaurants under rabbinic supervision in San Francisco. The preponderance of vegetarian restaurants, however, should allow people who keep kosher to enjoy the cuisines of San Francisco with few problems.

- *Chinatown* — **Lotus Garden**: 532 Grant Avenue, in Chinatown (tel: 397-0707). Chinese vegetarian restaurant. Closed Monday.

- *Chinatown* — **Lucky Creation**: 854 Washington Street, near Stockton (tel: 989-0818). Very popular local vegetarian eatery in the heart of Chinatown. Try the tofu roll with mushrooms. Closed Wednesday.

- *Civic Center* — **Ananda Fuara**: 1298 Market, at 9th Street (tel: 621-1994). Hearty breakfasts, curries, pizza, salads, and sandwiches, vegetarian and vegan. Open until 8:00 pm Mon–Sat; closed 3:00 pm Wed.

- *Civic Center* — **Millennium**: 246 McAllister, near Hyde (tel: 487-9800). This "optimal health cuisine restaurant" serves elegant and imaginative combinations of vegan, organic, low-fat foods … and luscious desserts.

- *Downtown* — **Sabra Grill**: 419 Grant Avenue (tel: 982-3656). Glatt kosher Middle Eastern restaurant.

- *Haight* — **Ganges Vegetarian Restaurant**: 775 Frederick Street (tel: 661-7290). Curries and regional Indian dishes in a pleasant setting across from Kezar Stadium.

- *Marina* — **Greens**: Building A, Fort Mason, next to the Marina Green (tel: 771-6222). Always crowded, this upscale restaurant with its big windows sits almost in the bay. The delicate vegetarian creations all have a "Zen" flavor. Closed Monday, open Sunday for brunch. Reservations a must.

- *Outer Sunset* — **Shangri-La Vegetarian Restaurant**: 2026 Irving Street (tel: 731-2548). Good neighborhood restaurant, with an extensive menu and low prices. Vegetarian but not vegan.

- *Outer Sunset* — **Joubert's Restaurant**: 4115 Judah, at 46th Avenue (tel: 753-5448). Vegetarian and vegan cuisine from South Africa. Dinners Wed–Sun.

- *Union Square* — **This is It Grill**: 430 Geary Street (tel: 749-0201). Glatt kosher Middle Eastern restaurant.

# FOREIGN CUISINES

Because Asian restaurants are found on just about every commercial street, the next chapter is devoted solely to "Eating Out in Asia." Yet so many other foreign cuisines are represented in the city that it would be difficult to mention only a few of the French, German, Spanish, or Moroccan. Quite naturally, given the history of the city, other prominent cuisines are the Latin American and Italian, and those described below are merely a few suggestions of the diversity San Francisco offers.

## Latin American

As with most ethnic cuisines, Latin American cooking in San Francisco is not just "Mexican food." It is true that *taquerias* abound, but in San Francisco the ingredients are regionally based, using good-quality meats and fish, relying on fresh vegetables and fruit, and with rice and beans as tasty side dishes. Some places advertise, for the healthy set, that they use no lard. Spicy *salsas* are often competitively rated, and some restaurants will boast that they were judged to have the "best salsa in S.F." by some panel at some time. What this means is that the tomato salsa is made with fresh ingredients, but the degree of chunkiness and fire varies from place to place. The Mission, as one would expect, is home to the most authentic Mexican establishments, plus Peruvian, Salvadoran and Nicaraguan restaurants, which have slightly different flavors and traditions. Combinations of cuisines are coming to be known as *nuevo latino*. Note that the **Taqueria Can-Cun**, often rated as the best Mexican restaurant in the city, has several locations in the Mission.

- *Cuban/Puerto Rican* — **El Nuevo Frutilandia**: 3077 24th Street (tel: 648-2958). Only 10 tables in this eatery that serves authentic Caribbean cuisine: Cuban pork sandwiches, plantains, and delicious fresh-fruit smoothies. Closed Monday.
- *Mexican* — **Los Jarritos**: 901 South Van Ness Avenue (tel: 648-

8383). Small family restaurant offering excellent Mexican dishes at low prices. Wonderful menudo.

- *Mexican* — **Mom Is Cooking**: 1166 Geneva Avenue (tel: 586-7000). Excellent, inexpensive outpost in the Excelsior District.
- *Mexican* — **Cafe Marimba**: 2317 Chestnut Street, at Scott (tel: 776-1506). Upscale, interesting combinations, good margaritas, in a lively Marina atmosphere. Closed Monday.
- *Mexican* — **Maya**: 303 2nd Street (tel: 543-6709). Elegant Mexican seafood dishes, beautifully prepared.
- *Nicaraguan* — **Nicaragua Restaurant**: 3015 Mission Street, near Cezar Chavez (tel: 826-3672). Locals have been coming here for more than 20 years for the delicious Central American regional dishes.
- *Peruvian* — **Fina Estampa**: 2374 Mission, near 20th Street (tel: 824-4437). Peruvian specialties such as fish soups, ceviche, marinated beef dishes. Spanish-style *tapas*. Closed Monday.
- *Salvadoran* — **El Zócalo**: 3230 Mission, near 29th Street (tel: 282-2572). *Pupusas* (like a filled tortilla). Fish soup and other excellent fish and shrimp dishes, fried plantains, etc.
- *Salvadoran* — **De Rosario**: 1796 San Jose Avenue (tel: 334-1863). Comfortable Mission restaurant serving pupusas, *platanos*, and other Salvadoran basics.

## Italian

Although traditional southern Italian cuisine — pasta, tomato sauce, and garlic — can still be found in just about any Italian restaurant, even this basic combination is becoming increasingly refined and imaginative. Some restaurants now feature the buttery, rich cuisine from the north, fish dishes from the coasts, the simple yet flavorful dishes of Rome, or even the specialized hearty cuisine of a small area past Trieste that is now part of Yugoslavia. And, of course, each restaurant features its region's wines. (For pizza, see below.)

In the old days, Italian workers coming back to North Beach could eat a full meal for fifty cents. Wine — especially during

Prohibition — was made in the basement and served in coffee cups. Now, this area is still the focus for Italian restaurants — although prices are slightly higher. Yet there are dozens of interesting Italian restaurants in all corners of the city; here are just a few favorites.

- *Embarcadero* — **Il Fornaio**: 1265 Battery Street, at Levi's Plaza (tel: 986-0100). Monthly specials feature the differing regions of Italy; the standard menu always authentic. Outdoor dining.
- *Fillmore* — **Laghi**: 2101 Sutter (tel: 931-3774). Excellent pastas, main courses, breads, and an interesting wine list from the Emilia-Romagna region.
- *Hunter's Point* — **Dago Mary's**: East on Evans, off 3rd Street, just past the entry gate at the Hunter's Point Shipyard (tel: 822-2633). Since 1931, this old-world, basic Italian and fish restaurant has thrived in an unlikely location. Weekday lunch only, 11:00 am–3:00 pm.
- *Mission* — **Delfina**: 3621 18th Street (tel: 442-4055). Small, reasonably priced, and friendly restaurant serving simple yet elegant and imaginative combinations.
- *North Beach* — **Albona**: 545 Francisco Street, in North Beach (tel: 441-1040). Unusual spices from the Istrian region on the Adriatic make the Yugoslavian/Italian combinations interesting. Closed Sunday and Monday.
- *North Beach* — **Ideale**: 1315 Grant Avenue, in North Beach (tel: 391-4129). Roman specialties, lightly sauced fresh pasta dishes and roast meats.
- *Polk/Van Ness* — **Acquerello**: 1722 Sacramento Street, off Polk (tel: 567-5432). Luxurious restaurant, with north Italian specialties, homemade pastas, wonderful antipasti.

### Pizza

Although a few restaurants serve the individual Italian-style, thin-crust pizza cooked in a wood-fired oven (**Il Fornaio** and **Pazzia** come to mind), most pizzas are American, in that they come in a number of sizes suitable for sharing, and the toppings are more dense. Most of these noted neighborhood favorites also serve pasta and other Italian dishes. Most chains offer home delivery.

- *Broadway*—**Tommaso's**: 1042 Kearny Street (tel: 398-9696). The city's oldest pizzeria, and some say still the best. Dinner only; closed Monday. Parking is difficult.
- *Downtown*—**Blondie's Pizza**, at 63 Powell, at Market (tel: 982-6168). Dead center in the tourist area, this is nonetheless a popular pizzeria for locals who are downtown.
- *Fillmore/Cow Hollow*—**Extreme Pizza**: 1730 Fillmore Street (tel: 929-9900) and 1980 Union Street (tel: 929- 8234). Some of the city's best pizza. Create pizza the way you want, and take it home to bake.
- *Mission*—**Pauline's**: 260 Valencia St, near 14th (tel: 552-2050). Try the pesto pizza. Dinner only; closed Monday.
- *North Beach, etc.*—**North Beach Pizza**: 1499 Grant Avenue at Union (433-2444). Popular pizzeria, serving a wide variety of pizza toppings, plus Italian entrees. Several other locations.
- *Potrero Hill*—**Goat Hill Pizza**: 300 Connecticut, at 18th Street (tel: 641-1440). Sourdough crust, excellent pizzas, live music on weekends. Monday night, all you can eat.
- *Union Street*—**Amici's East Coast Pizzeria**: 2033 Union Street (tel: 885-4500). Also in North and South Bay.

# GRABBING A BITE

Eating fast in San Francisco does not necessarily mean "fast food." Storefront sandwich shops and cafes provide sandwiches, salads, and hot dishes with an international flavor for eating in or taking out. San Franciscans love to eat lunch out of doors. Eating *al fresco* is not always easy, for the wind is often fierce, and frankly, the air can be cold. This does not deter San Franciscans, who pour out of offices, off construction jobs, or out of delivery trucks, to eat outside under any feeble ray of sun.

199

Chinese restaurants generally serve their eat-in clientele quickly, and these eateries are jammed at lunchtime; almost all have takeout menus. Some office, shopping, and entertainment complexes (**Rincon Annex**, **Metreon**, and **Crocker Galleria**, for example), have food courts, with stalls lining a central set of tables for fast eating, and the four-building **Embarcadero Center** abounds with quick-eating solutions. Small chains such as **Briazz** sell sandwiches to go, and even their ready-made items cater to the tastes of San Franciscans, with many vegetarian and low-fat offerings. The latest trend is the wrap—interesting combinations of foods wrapped in a tortilla—and **World Wrapps** and others offer inexpensive, interesting lunches. But hearty lunches such as burritos or chili can be had to take out from small storefronts around the city, or slices of pizza at any of the dozens of pizza storefronts. Juice bars such as **Jamba Juice** offer smoothies and protein drinks for those who really have no time.

- **Peasant Pies**: Two locations (Noe Valley and Sunset districts). Individual filled savory and sweet pies to take out. Some stuffed with seafood or poultry, others vegan; the dessert pies are all vegan. Addresses: 4108 24th Street, at Castro (tel: 642-1316); 1039 Irving, at 11th Street (731-1978). Pies also available at some supermarkets.
- **Pasta Pomodoro**: Nine restaurants offering inexpensive Italian food to eat in or take out.
- **Fuzio Universal Pasta**: Chain of inexpensive pasta restaurants with dishes to eat in or take out.
- **Noah's Bagels**: City-wide chain. Bagel sandwiches featuring smoked salmon and cheese spreads make for an inexpensive and hearty lunch. Hot bagels to take out.
- *Civic Center*—**Saigon Sandwiches**: 560 Larkin Street, at Eddy (tel: 474-5698). Vietnamese sandwiches of meatballs, roast chicken, or pork, plus vegetables, spices, and a delicious sauce.
- *Embarcadero*—**Yank Sing**: 427 Battery Street (tel: 781-1111).

*San Franciscans dining al fresco.*

Takeout department adjacent to the ever-crowded *dim sum* house. Also at 49 Stevenson Street (tel: 541-4949) and (weekdays only) Rincon Center (tel: 957-9300).

- *Haight*—**Two Jack's Seafood**: 401 Haight Street (tel: 431-6290). Excellent takeout fried fish dinners, in a funky Haight atmosphere.
- *Tenderloin*—**Ba Le**: 511 Jones, near Geary (tel: 474-7270). Vietnamese grocery with prepared food ready to take home. Spring rolls, sausages, rice noodles, meat on skewers, and everything for a delicious Vietnamese meal. Table service.

## WEEKEND BREAKFAST

Sunday brunch can be found on the menu of numerous restaurants and hotels, but eating a hearty Sunday breakfast—pancakes, red flannel hash, French toast and omelettes—is also a distinct social occasion, at places like **Mel's Diner** or **Max's Diner**, or at a number of rather sparsely decorated neighborhood cafes. These are wildly popular, so be prepared to add your name to the list and to wait.

Some of the cafes open only for breakfast and lunch, and many are closed Monday, after the Sunday crush. A few take cash only.

- *Cow Hollow*—**Doidge's**: 2217 Union, near Fillmore (tel: 921-2149)
- *Downtown*—**Dottie's True Blue Cafe**: 522 Jones Street (tel: 885-2767). Closed Tuesday.
- *Glen Park*—**Tyger's Coffee Shop**: 2798 Diamond (tel: 239-4060)
- *Haight*—**Pork Store Cafe**: 1451 Haight Street, near Ashbury (tel: 864-6981)
- *Hayes Valley/Castro*—**It's Tops**: 1801 Market Street (tel: 431-6395)
- *Lower Haight*—**Kate's Kitchen**: 471 Haight Street, near Fillmore (tel: 626-3984)
- *Mission*—**Boogaloos**: 3296 22nd Street, at Valencia (tel: 824-3211)
- *Pacific Heights*—**Ella's**: 500 Presidio (tel: 441-5669)
- *Potrero Hill*—**Just For You Cafe**: 1453 18th Street (tel: 647-3033)

## COFFEEHOUSES

Cafes in each neighborhood reflect the character of their clientele, but North Beach seems driven by the mystique of coffee. Once, North Beach's coffeehouses welcomed Italian workers coming back from the docks, and now they comfort anyone who wants to sit for a while and relax. Many of the most famous of the North Beach coffeehouses—**Caffè Puccini**, **Steps of Rome**, **Caffè Greco**, **Caffè Roma**—line a few short blocks of Columbus, between Broadway and Union. Others, such as **Caffè Malvina** and the famous **Cafe Trieste**, are nearby.

Of the 100 coffeehouses in the city, most offer some kind of pastry selection to go with the coffees, teas, or Italian sodas, and some also serve light meals and salads. What is important is that in any coffeehouse, you may order something refreshing and then sit for as long as you like. Even in the most undistinguished-looking establishment, the quality of the coffee (and selection of aromatic teas) may be very good. As with everything else, San Franciscans are espresso snobs, knowing just which cafe serves the type of coffee they like (often it's **Illy**). Some people rail at the ubiquitous **Starbucks** intruding into neighborhood businesses; others like the chain's coffee and reliable atmosphere. For Irish coffee, try the ever-popular **Buena Vista Cafe**, at 2765 Hyde, near Ghirardelli Square (tel: 474-5044). (See Chapter Thirteen for coffee roasters.)

- *Financial District* — **Torrefazione Italia**: 295 California (tel: 274-1634). Deep leather couches and a friendly atmosphere in which to enjoy the good Italian coffees.
- *Lower Haight* — **Bean There**: 201 Steiner (tel: 255-8855). Modern, airy coffeehouse, with pleasant decor and welcoming ambience.
- *Noe Valley* — **Lovejoy's**: 1351 Church Street (tel: 648-5895). Probably the most charming tea room in the city, with antiques and a cosy English atmosphere.
- *North Beach/Chinatown* — **Imperial Tea Court**: 1411 Powell Street, at Broadway (tel: 788-6080). Unusual Chinese teas to purchase in bulk or to enjoy on the premises, each one brewed to bring out its unique flavor.
- *Outer Sunset* — **Java Beach Cafe**: 1396 La Playa Boulevard, at Judah (tel: 665-5282). A beach atmosphere, good coffee, and a relaxed atmosphere.
- *Pacific Heights* — **Tea & Company, World Tea House**: 2207 Fillmore Street, at Sacramento (tel: 929-8327). Nice place to relax with a cup of tea or coffee and a fresh pastry.
- *Potrero Hill* — **Farley's**: 1315 18th Street (tel: 648-1545). Funky and popular neighborhood coffeehouse.
- *Richmond* — **Caffe Dante**: 3101 Geary (tel: 386-2057). Friendly Italian coffeehouse with excellent coffee, pastries, and sandwiches.

# ICE CREAM

All national brands of ice cream, frozen yogurt, and sherbet are available in supermarkets, and **Ben & Jerry's**, **Häagen-Dazs**, and **Baskin-Robbins** have outlets in the city. Better, however, are the neighborhood ice cream parlors, some of which are listed below, and most of which create their own offbeat, exotic flavor combinations. **Double Rainbow**, **Ghirardelli Chocolate Shop and Soda Fountain**, and **Swensen's** are famous San Francisco institutions, and the **Gelato Classico** shops offer Italian-style preparations.

- *Castro/Pacific Heights* — **Rory's Twisted Scoop**: 1300 Castro Street (tel: 648-2837); 2015 Fillmore Street (tel: 346-3692). Homemade ice cream. Tables outside at Fillmore Street.
- *Inner Richmond* — **Toy Boat Dessert Cafe**: Clement at 5th Avenue (tel: 751-7505). Welcoming, traditional ice-cream parlor on inner Clement.
- *Mission* — **Mitchell's Ice Cream**: 688 San Jose, near 29th Street and Guerrero (tel: 648-2300). Extremely rich (16 percent butterfat) concoctions, often rated the best in the city.
- *Mission* — **Bombay Ice Creamery**: 552 Valencia Street (tel: 431-1103). Flavored with Indian herbs and spices. Closed Monday.
- *Outer Sunset* — **Marco Polo Italian Ice Cream**: 1447 Taraval Street (tel: 731-2833). Exotic Asian flavors, plus delicious traditional combinations.
- *Potrero Hill* — **Daily Scoop**: 1401 18th Street (tel: 824-3975). Friendly, neighborhood ice cream parlor.
- *Richmond* — **Joe's Ice Cream**: 5351 Geary, near 18th Avenue (tel: 751-1950). Great flavors since 1959, always popular.
- *Sunset* — **Polly Ann Ice Cream**: 3142 Noriega, near 38th Avenue (tel: 664-2472). More than 400 tasty and exotic flavors in a tiny, cheerful shop.

# CHAPTER TWELVE

# EATING OUT IN ASIA

## AN ASIAN TOWN

If it's all just Chinese food to you, it won't be after you've lived in San Francisco a while. Differing aromas from the hundreds of Chinese, Vietnamese, Thai, Korean, and Japanese restaurants permeate the city, enticing an Asian population that numbers upwards of 175,000 and the rest of the city as well. Each neighborhood has its Asian restaurants, and some areas cater to particular nationalities: Japantown and Chinatown of course, but also Larkin Street for Vietnamese restaurants and provisions, Clement Street for a lively mix of Asian establishments, and Irving Street in the Outer Sunset for its own eclectic mix from the Far East.

Fortunately for San Francisco's discerning diners, there are simply too many Asian restaurants to describe here, so just a few representative samples are given, along with a description of their culinary approach. Become a true San Franciscan and make your own list of favorites.

# FIRST, THE CHINESE

Chinese restaurants are in the majority in San Francisco. Both complex and subtle, Chinese food is almost always economical: a hearty lunch in a neighborhood Chinese restaurant may cost under $5.00, and a dinner not much more. In a society not rich enough to offer a slab of meat or a quarter-chicken to each person, Chinese cooks learned to base their dishes on the inexpensive rice or noodles, topped with the region's vegetables and a flavored sauce. To this might be added a few ounces of meat or poultry, or along the coast, fish. For thousands of years this method of cooking has provided a nutritious diet of carbohydrates, vegetables, and an adequate amount of protein.

Despite some similarity in philosophy, the cuisines of China differ widely, owing to differences in regional ingredients, soil and climatic conditions, and of course, ancient traditions. Here, although the ingredients come from this one fertile area, many Asian restaurants focus on one region's cuisine, and often this can be identified by their names, such as **The Hunan**, the **House of Nan King**, **Parc Hong Kong**, or **The Taiwan**. Even these, however, may include in their repertoire special dishes from other regions—Cantonese dishes in a Hakka restaurant, or Shanghai dishes in one that says it is Cantonese.

The restaurants differ in style, quality, popularity, and price, as do all others. In Chinatown especially, you cannot judge the quality of the food by how the place looks. Some unpretentious, basic-looking dives serve the best food in their class (although you might hesitate to take an out-of-town colleague there) and some of the most reputable-looking places may not be as good.

With Chinese food, price does not determine quality.

Chinese chefs, like others in the city, cater to Western tastes by cooking with low or no oil and some, such as **Brandy Ho**, **Sage,** and **The Hunan**, proudly advertise that they use no monosodium glutamate (MSG). Hearty, healthy, Chinese breakfasts are also gaining in popularity, especially the thick rice porridge known as *congee* (or *juk/jook*) from the south of China; it can come with meatballs, fish—even jellyfish. Or from northern China, try the dough dishes such as "Chinese donuts" and warm bowls of soybean milk, either salty or sweet.

## Differing Cuisines
It was **Cantonese** immigrants who originally brought their cuisine to these shores during the mid-19th century. Canton specializes in a delicate cuisine, lightly flavored and sauced, thus preserving the character of the ingredients, especially the mild fish and chicken pieces that are added to the fresh vegetables. This also holds true of the cuisine from **Hong Kong**.

Slightly more piquant, with highly flavored, sometimes sweetened sauces are the seafood dishes from the city of **Chiu Chow**, which sits just at the northern edge of Canton. Even farther north, on the Pacific coast by the mouth of the Yangtze River, **Shanghai** developed a heavy and hearty cuisine, with strongly flavored dishes braised in dark soy sauces.

- **Fountain Court**: 354 Clement, at 5th Avenue (tel: 668-1100). Interesting Shanghai cuisine in a neighborhood eatery. Crowded on weekends for *dim sum*.
- **Harbor Village**: 4 Embarcadero Center (tel: 781-8833). Excellent *dim sum* at lunch and delicate seafood dishes. Overflows with families on weekends, but the food is worth the wait.
- **Oriental Pearl**: 760 Clay Street, near Kearny (tel: 433-1817). Cantonese and Chiu Chow seafood cuisine. *Dim sum* at lunch.

207

*Photo: Eleanor Burke*

*Daily menu outside a Chinese restaurant.*

More expensive (and better appointed) than the majority of Chinese restaurants in the area, the menu is also more imaginative.

In the north, where rice does not grow plentifully, dough dishes provide the major starch. Noodles served with a variety of sauces and toppings, dough-wrapped dumplings, and dishes made with pancakes are standard. Because Peking (now Beijing) was the capital of the empire, some particularly delicate dishes were created for the Mandarins who ruled. **Peking/Mandarin** cuisine also offers some of China's more imaginative dishes.

- **San Tung**: 2240 Irving Street (tel: 661-4233); also at 1031 Irving (tel: 242-0828). Neighborhood restaurants in the Sunset, featuring excellent dumplings and noodles.
- **Firecracker**: 1007 Valencia Street (tel: 642-3470). Popular and noisy spot for imaginative Beijing cuisine, offering low oil and lots of garlic. Closed Monday.
- **Mandarin:** Ghirardelli Square (tel: 673-8812). Upscale Northern Chinese restaurant with beautiful views.

In the hot southern portion of China, **Hunan** and **Szechuan** have always been poor districts. Their cuisines were developed to keep people cool and to preserve perishable meats. Hot and spicy food, the Chinese believe, keeps people cool internally, so Hunan food especially is very salty and extremely spicy. Chilies and salt also encourage people to eat more rice and drink more tea, so that they eat only a little meat. Smoking preserves meats, and smoked hams and ducks and heavy, spicy sauces characterize this cuisine, which is very popular in San Francisco. Szechuan food does not approach the fire of the Hunan, although it too is quite spicy.

- **Hunan Restaurant**: 924 Sansome Street, off Broadway (tel: 956-7727). Small chain of excellent restaurants, often rated the best Hunan food outside of China. Extremely spicy dishes (that can be modified to your taste) and smoked meat dishes.

*Photo: San Francisco Convention & Visitors Bureau*

*The Mandarin Restaurant in Ghirardelli Square.*

**Hakka** means "guest." The Hakka were wanderers, nomads who adapted their own cuisine to the regions where they stopped, incorporating those regions' cuisines into their own. Try the creative dumplings, the hearty clay pot dishes, and the salt-baked chicken, all traditional Hakka favorites.

- **Ton Kiang**: 5821 Geary Boulevard, near 22nd Avenue (tel: 386-8530). Salt-cooked chicken, clay pot dishes, fermented, wine-flavored dishes, seafood, and some of the city's best *dim sum*, any time of day.
- **Dragon River**: 5045 Geary, at 14th Avenue (tel: 387-8512). Flavorful Hakka and Cantonese dishes in a neighborhood restaurant in the Richmond.

With some dishes emanating from the north of China and others from the island itself, **Taiwanese** cuisine tends to blend several Chinese cuisines and features dough-based staples such as dumplings and pancake dishes. Some also favor the "hot pot" **Mongolian** cuisine in which a pot of boiling broth is brought to the table along with raw vegetables and meats/fish, to be prepared by the patron.

- **Taiwan Restaurant**: 289 Columbus Avenue, at Broadway (tel: 989-6789); 445 Clement (tel: 387-1789). Noodle dishes and seafood.
- **Coriya**: 852 Clement, at 10th Avenue (tel: 387-7888). Hot pot and Taiwanese cuisine.
- **Happy Valley Chinese Seafood**: 1255 Battery Street, in Levi Plaza (tel: 399-9393). Mongolian hot pot and seafood dishes.

### Dim Sum

*Dim ʃum* ("small bites") is popular for lunch and brunch. In *ðim ʃum* restaurants, carts with stacks of little bamboo baskets containing steamed or fried dumplings (filled with seafood, chicken, pork, vegetables — or tasty combinations thereof) are wheeled by the tables for the diners to choose among. *Bow* (large steamed rolls with barbequed pork), *ʃiu mai* (pork dumplings), *ha gow* (steamed shrimp dumplings), egg rolls, and pot stickers (fried dumplings) are standards. On the table are small carafes of soy sauce, vinegar, and hot sauce, to mix and use as you choose.

*Dim ʃum* is usually served at midday, although to cater to Western tastes, *ðim ʃum* houses in San Francisco may offer it in the evening as well. A traditional *ðim ʃum* house will usually open at about 10:00 am and close mid-afternoon. In San Francisco, however, these restaurants may also serve a regular menu at midday and stay open with their regular menu in the evenings. In some restaurants the little dishes and baskets left on the customers' tables are counted in order to determine the bill; in others, the waiter marks on the bill how many items have been chosen.

211

In the smaller eateries in Chinatown, the waiters may not speak English, so just point to dishes that look appealing. *Dim sum* is not expensive; if you don't like what you've chosen, you're not risking much. Of course, if you see chicken feet, you'll know right away what they are.

- *Financial District* — **Yank Sing**: 427 Battery Street (tel: 781-1111); 49 Stevenson Street (tel: 541-4949). The Rincon Center branch is open weekdays only (tel: 957-9300).
- *Chinatown* — **Gold Mountain**: 644 Broadway (tel: 296-7733)

## JAPANESE CUISINE

Japanese food emphasizes harmony, and dishes are arranged to be as pleasing to the eye as to the palate. Japanese cuisine is delicate, featuring low-fat fish, gently sauced dishes, braised meats, tofu, fresh vegetables, several types of flavorful noodles, and, of course, the increasingly sought-after *sushi*. The lightly battered and fried *tempura* fish and vegetables are popular, as is *sukiyaki*, the meat and vegetable casserole cooked at the table. The many varieties of *sake* — a clear rice wine — may be consumed hot or cold; experiment with different sakes at some of the new sake bars that are opening up in conjunction with regular wine bars, in Japanese restaurants, or on their own.

Authentic and varied Japanese restaurants are clustered in and around the Japan Center but most neighborhoods have their own favorites, both for cooked dishes and for sushi, which is one of San Franciscans' favorite foods. Because sushi is so much in demand, it is fortunate that residents of different neighborhoods think the sushi bar in their own district is the best. This means delicious sushi is available throughout the city any day of the year.

If you are a beginner at sushi, consider **Isobune** at 1737 Post Street in the Japan Center (tel: 563-1030). Little boats carrying freshly made sushi dishes sail along an oval canal, displaying the preparations as they move along. Choose those that look appealing.

Prices are reasonable, so as with *dim sum*, if you select a dish you don't care for, you haven't risked very much. Isobune is a friendly place: sushi lovers sitting next to you will be happy to advise you on selections if you're not sure.

- *Cow Hollow* — **Ace Wasabi's Rock 'n' Roll Sushi**: 3339 Steiner Street, at Chestnut (tel: 567-4903). Great sushi in a loud, trendy, typical San Francisco atmosphere. Open only for dinner, and always crowded.
- *Inner Sunset* — **Ebisu**: 1283 9th Avenue (tel: 566-1770). Small, popular eatery with good sushi and other dishes.
- *Inner Sunset* — **Hotei**: 1290 9th Avenue (tel: 753-6045). Japanese noodle cuisine in a charming setting.
- *Japan Center* — **Mifune**: 1737 Post Street (tel: 922-0337). Soba and udon noodles with a variety of add-ins, to make a delicious, inexpensive meal.
- *Mission* — **Blowfish Sushi to Die For**: 2170 Bryant Street (tel: 285-3848). Some of the city's best sushi, plus an imaginative and well-created menu.
- *Mission* — **Tokyo Go Go**: 3174 16th Street, near Valencia (tel: 864-2288). Eclectic and trendy, serving interesting, fun sushi combinations at moderate prices. Closed Monday.
- *Richmond* — **Kabuto**: 5116 Geary Boulevard (tel: 752-5652). Full Japanese menu, excellent sushi, friendly service. Dinner only. Closed Sunday and Monday.

# SOUTHEAST ASIAN CUISINES

Of course, in San Francisco there is always more to try, and dozens of Southeast Asian restaurants show off their differing cultural and historical traditions. Many use rice or noodles as a base, and most specialize in seafood dishes. Because the climate of these countries is generally hot, the food can be quite spicy; you can order "medium spicy" or "not spicy" if you think the fiery peppers will not suit your palate.

213

- *Thai*—**Thep Phenom**: 400 Waller Street (tel: 431-2526). Spicy seafood dishes, curries with coconut, duck curry, squid salad, catfish with lemongrass; dinner only. **Modern Thai**: 1247 Polk Street, near Bush (tel: 922-8424). Upscale Thai cuisine in a pleasant setting; closed Tuesday. Many other Thai restaurants in the city.

- *Vietnamese*—**Slanted Door**: 584 Valencia Street (tel: 861-8032). Trendy but authentic, serving five-spice roast chicken, clay pot dishes, papaya salad. **Pacific Restaurant-Thai-Binh-Duong #2**: 337 Jones Street, in the Tenderloin (tel: 928-4022). Excellent spring rolls and *pho*, the Vietnamese soup of noodles, meats, vegetables, and bean sprouts. Lunch only. **La Vie**: 5830 Geary (tel: 668-8080). Popular Richmond restaurant blends the Chinese influence from the north and the French from the south. Dishes are interesting and flavorful.

- *Korean*—**Seoul Garden**: 1702 Post Street, in Japantown (tel: 346-3486). Marinated fish, pork, or chicken *shabu shabu* (that you barbeque at your own table on charcoal braziers). Dishes accompanied by rice, pickles, and salads. *Kim chee*, a fiery hot cabbage accompaniment is not for the faint of heart. Others include **Heavenly Hot Restaurant**: 4627 Geary (tel: 750-1818); **Korea House**: 1620 Post Street (tel: 563-1388); **Brother's Restaurant**: 4128 Geary (tel: 387-7991).

- *Singaporean*—**Straits Cafe**: 3300 Geary Boulevard (tel: 668-1783). A melange of Pacific seafood cuisines, Indian curries, and other exotic aromas, with attractive dishes set out on banana leaves.

- *Cambodian*—**Angkor Wat**: 4217 Geary Boulevard (tel: 221-7887). A delicious mingling of Asian tropical flavors, of coconut milk and lemongrass, yet with overtones of France.

- *Burmese*—**Nirvana**: 544 Castro Street (tel: 861-2226). Melange of Indian, Chinese and other Southeast Asian aromas. Excellent noodle dishes, five-spice roast chicken, and fish. Substantial use of garlic and relishes.

## Pan-Asian

As is to be expected in a city where differing cultures meet head on, the trend now is for Asian restaurants to meld their own differing cuisines to create a *Pan-Asian* flavor, a slightly more restrictive yet imaginative approach to *fusion cuisine*. Some offer full menus, others are mainly noodle houses.

- *Castro* — **Tin Pan**: 2251 Market Street (tel: 565-0733). Excellent and popular Asian bistro serving noodle dishes and other flavorful dishes in a friendly atmosphere.

- *Cow Hollow* — **Betelnut**: 2030 Union Street (tel: 929-8855). Crowded and fun, serving Pan-Asian cuisine with flavors of China, Indonesia, and Vietnam. Expensive. Walk-in traffic eats at the bar.

- *Embarcadero* — **Longlife Noodle Company & Jook Joint**: 139 Steuart Street (tel: 281-3818). Lively Pan-Asian establishment serving innovative noodle dishes and *jook*. Inexpensive. Also at Metreon, in Yerba Buena.

- *Haight* — **Citrus Club**: 1790 Haight Street, at Shrader (tel: 387-6366). Popular, inexpensive noodle house that avoids heavy oils, using citrus flavors instead. Closed Monday.

- *Marina* — **Zao Noodle Bar**: 2301 Chestnut Street (tel: 928-3088). Flavors from Southeast Asia: "health and wisdom in a bowl." Also at 2406 California Street (tel: 345-8088) and in Palo Alto.

- *SOMA* — **AsiaSF**: 201 9th Street, at Howard (tel: 255-2742). Crowded, noisy, and good-natured, this restaurant/cabaret catering to both straights and gays offers good food and a "gender illusion" show on the catwalk. Closed Monday and Tuesday. Nightclub downstairs on weekends.

# Chapter Thirteen

# EXPLORING THE MARKETS

LEFT TWO PACES
RIGHT TEN PACES
AND WE'LL BE
HOME MA

## OUTDOOR MARKETS

Outdoor markets, often called "farmers' markets," sell the region's freshest seasonal produce, usually of better quality and often at lower cost than that of supermarkets. In addition to these year-round markets in the city, there are farmers' markets in most of the towns of the Bay Area, including one that is exceptionally varied at the Marin Civic Center in San Rafael on Thursday and Sunday.

Look for produce that is certified "organic," meaning that it was not treated with chemical pesticides or fertilizers and that the soil is rotated according to healthful standards. Organic meats come from animals raised without growth hormones or antibiotics,

216

and without pesticide-treated feed. Organic groceries tend to cost slightly more.

- *Wednesday and Sunday*: Market Street at United Nations Plaza. Large inexpensive market, with many stalls for Asian produce. Flowers, fish, herbs, etc.
- *Saturday:* Green Street at the Embarcadero. Upscale market, with the highest quality of produce, fresh breads, pastas, fish, meats, and several stalls that sell freshly cooked foods to eat at tables nearby.
- *Saturday*: Alemany Boulevard at Crescent, near Highway 280. Enormous international farmers' market. Go early before the crowds arrive. Or go late when some produce is reduced in price.
- *Tuesday*: Justin Hermann Plaza, at Market and Steuart Streets, during the clement months.

*Market day in downtown San Francisco.*

217

# SUPERMARKETS

The **Safeway**, **Bell's**, **Albertson's**, and **Cala Foods** chains have stores throughout the city. All are open daily at least until 9:00 pm and are often open for some portion of the day on holidays; the Cala on Geary and the Marina Safeway are open 24 hours daily. In addition to their freshly cut meats, fish, produce, and staple goods, supermarkets carry alcoholic beverages, magazines, and over-the-counter medications. Some have prescription-filling pharmacies, either within or next door. All the large supermarkets accept major credit cards and bank debit cards. Many also have ATM machines on the premises if you need cash.

The merchandise at San Francisco supermarkets is usually guaranteed, so if there is something wrong with a product you have bought, most will take back the item provided you have a receipt. On perishable items, look on the package to make sure that the expiration date has not passed; if it has, supermarkets will generally exchange the item. (Foreigners should note that in the United States, dates are written with the month, day, and year, in that order.) Several supermarkets stand out for their particularly fine selections; prices match the quality.

- *Pacific Heights* — **Mollie Stone's**: 2435 California Street, near Fillmore (tel: 567-4902). Elegant market with excellent fresh and smoked fish counters, well-cut meats, beautifully prepared meals to take out, cheeses, organic produce. A small cafe. Parking lot.
- *Portola* — **Pommon's Tower Market**: 635 Portola Drive (tel: 664-1600). Well-stocked independent market, with an excellent meat and fish department, plus an interesting deli counter.
- *Presidio Heights* — **Cal-Mart**: 3585 California Street, in Laurel Village (tel: 751-3516). Extremely upscale and well-maintained supermarket. Interesting deli section and independently run meat department. Fresh breads, excellent produce.
- *Sunset* — **Andronico's**: 1200 Irving Street, at Funston (tel: 661-

218

3220). Upscale supermarket with a superior takeout department (hot and cold), a salad bar, and seating nearby. Excellent
butcher and fish department, a table just for different olives, a
wealth of cheeses and fresh breads, interesting produce. Other
locations.

## Health Food Supermarkets

In addition to their preservative- and chemical-free fresh and
packaged food products, the shops below also carry vitamins,
natural cosmetics, and brochures and books on natural living in
the Bay Area. **Real Foods** is a chain that has locations throughout
the Bay Area. All are open on Sunday.

- *Polk/Van Ness* — **Whole Foods Market**: 1765 California Street
  (tel: 674-0500). Large, well-stocked health food supermarket,
  with an extensive takeout section of prepared foods, artistically
  prepared meats to take home and cook, excellent fresh fish,
  bakery. Generally expensive, but extremely high quality.
  Parking available, but lot is crowded at peak shopping hours.
  Also in Mill Valley and Berkeley.
- *SOMA* — **Rainbow Grocery**: 1745 Folsom Street (tel: 863-
  0621). Cooperative, worker-owned health food market, with
  an excellent selection at good prices. Some parking available.

## Discount Supermarkets

Discount supermarkets may not carry all the particular brands
you like, but those that do are generally of good quality, and the
price is right. Occasionally you have to buy in bulk, by the case.

- **Smart & Final**: Three locations. Packaged foods, cleaning
  items, janitorial supplies. Extra savings with Smart Advantage
  card. Ample parking. Others throughout the Bay Area.
- **Trader Joe's**: Two locations. Extensive selection of packaged
  and frozen goods, dairy products, snack foods, bakery items,
  and spirits. Other locations throughout Bay Area.

219

- **Foods Co**: Two locations. Warehouse supermarket with a well-rounded selection at good prices. Ample parking.
- *South of Market*—**Grocery Outlet**: 1717 Harrison Street (tel: 552-9680). Also known as "Canned Foods Warehouse." Excellent prices but inventory changes, so stock up on items you like. Ample parking.
- *South of Market*—**Costco**: 450 10th Street (tel: 626-4288). Warehouse selling all sorts of items, mostly in bulk. Packaged and fresh foods, frozen items, alcoholic beverages, and much more. Small membership fee.

## SHOPPING FROM HOME

Inquire whether your supermarket has home delivery, for not all do. Some, such as Whole Foods Door to Door, offer telephone/fax/e-mail ordering (tel: 800/529-5761; fax: 972/774-0865; e-mail: iscom@aol.com). You can also order grocerices online (www.peapod.com; www.webvan.com). Www.planet-organics.com offers local organic produce grocery items.

## SHOPPING IN ASIA

Shopping in Chinatown can be an other-world experience, especially on Saturday and Sunday. Crowds of people carrying overflowing bags push and shove as they walk down Stockton, Powell, or the side streets. They, however, will no doubt have found excellent prices and high quality fish and poultry, and produce of all sorts. Both produce and packaged goods are displayed outside the shops in boxes or on shelves, and this contributes to the traffic jam. Because signs are in Chinese and not all personnel speak English, sometimes shopping is a challenge. Nonetheless, Chinatown is a great place to shop if you're not faint of heart. Parking is impossible, and parking lots on the periphery can cost up to $2.00 for 20 minutes. Either hoof it or take public transportation. No matter how you get there, don't miss Chinatown on market days, quintessentially San Franciscan.

*Fresh fish at a Chinese market.*

Asian markets, however, are visible throughout the city, both in supermarkets and small shops. The specialty markets—fish markets and butchers—are listed within their categories; see below.

- *Chinatown*—**Happy Supermarket**: 1230 Stockton Street (tel: 677-9950). Large bustling supermarket. Live fish in tanks, meats, produce.
- *Japantown*—**Super Koyama**: 1790 Sutter Street, at Buchanan (tel: 921-6529). Modern Japanese grocery. Fresh ingredients for sushi, sukiyaki, soups, and most Japanese meals. Fish and meat freshly cut. Good produce.
- *Japantown*—**Uoki Market**: 1656 Post Street, between Buchanan and Laguna (tel: 921-0515). Busy Japanese grocery, with fish freshly prepared, produce, canned goods.
- *Mission*—**New Bombay Bazaar**: 548 Valencia, near 16th Street (tel: 621-1717). Large store for Indian packaged goods, spices, herbs. Audio-Video selections. Small eat-in/takeout place next door. Closed Monday.

221

*Photo: Eleanor Burke*

*A Chinese market.*

- *Outer Sunset* — **Twenty-Second and Irving Market**: 2101 Irving Street (tel: 681-5212). A multicultural market with a little of everything from everywhere, and Asians, Russians, and Arabs come to find it here. Excellent produce.
- *Richmond* — **Richmond New May Wah Supermarket**: 547 Clement Street (tel: 668-2583). Two entrances to this large supermarket, one for fresh fish and meats, the other for produce and packaged goods.
- *Tenderloin* — **New Chiu Fong**: 724 Ellis Street, near Polk (tel: 776-7151). Vietnamese supermarket with an extensive selection: fresh meats and poultry, produce, herbs, packaged goods.

# SMALL ETHNIC GROCERIES

In addition to the ubiquitous Asian shops, don't miss the small ethnic delicatessens with their international selections. Most have packaged goods as well as deli counters for fresh-made specialties. Of course the Mission will have more Latin American shops, Chinatown and Japantown their own shops, Outer Geary the Russian stores, and North Beach the Italian. Here are just a few.

- *Italian* — **Lucca Ravioli Company**: 1100 Valencia Street at 22nd Street (tel: 647-5581). Old-time deli offering ready-to-cook pasta dishes, homemade pizza, sausages, sauces, wines, cheeses, etc. Closed Sunday.
- *Italian* — **Molinari**: 373 Columbus Avenue, at Vallejo (tel: 421-2337). Freshly cut sandwiches, smoked meats, buffalo milk mozzarella and other cheeses, sausages; a selection of everything Italian. Closed Sunday.
- *Jewish* — **Moishe's Pippic**: 425-A Hayes Street, at Gough (tel: 431-2440). Chicago-style Jewish deli, open at breakfast and lunch. Good corned beef, Chicago hot dogs, etc.
- *Latin American* — **Casa Lucas**: 2934 24th Street (tel: 826-4334). Open-front store selling fresh produce, herbs, Mexican sausages and cheeses. Everything for Latin American cooking.

- *Mexican* — **La Palma Mexicatessen**: 2884 24th Street (tel: 647-1500). Excellent tortillas, fixings for burritos and tacos, freshly made chips. Ingredients for Mexican cooking.
- *Middle Eastern* — **Haig's**: 642 Clement, near 8th Avenue (tel: 752-6283). Haig's famous hummus and baba ganoush can now be found in some supermarkets, which is fortunate, for parking near Clement Street can be difficult. Packaged goods, tables to eat in. Closed Sunday.
- *Russian* — **Gastronom Deli & Bakery**: 5801 Geary Boulevard (tel: 387-4211). Excellent smoked meats and fish, Russian salads, and packaged goods. Also at 2801 Judah Street (tel: 664-1835).

# BAKERIES

San Francisco is proud of its sourdough bread, crusty and flavorful, with a vaguely sour and slightly chewy interior. It originated here during the Gold Rush, when French baker Isadore Boudin melded sourdough yeast into a French baguette. Today, many restaurants bring sourdough loaves or rolls to the table, and supermarkets sell it sliced in loaves, as classic baguettes, and even as sourdough English muffins. **Boudin**, with outlets around the city, still sells sourdough breads and rolls, baguettes, other breads, sandwiches, etc, and has just celebrated its 150th anniversary.

Bakeries serve their neighborhood's ethnic populations: North Beach is known for its Italian pastry shops, the Mission along 24th Street for excellent Mexican baked goods. Supermarkets now stock locally baked breads, bagels, and pastries; look for fresh breads baked by **Acme**, **Metropolis**, **Parisian**, **Semifreddi**, and the **Noe Valley Bakery**. **Eppler's** is a full-line bakery that is popular and **Just Desserts** is renowned for its delicious cakes. Below are a few of the city's fine bakeries — ones you might miss if you don't know that neighborhood.

- *Bayview* — **Wendy's Cheesecake Bakery**: 4942 3rd Street (tel:

822-4959). Cheesecake, sweet potato pie, pecan pies, etc. Barbeques. Closed Sunday.

- *Chinatown*—**Eastern Bakery**: 720 Grant Avenue (tel: 392-4497). One of Chinatown's more extensive bakeries, offering prepared pork buns and pot stickers, other baked goods, plus mooncakes—pastry with a variety of sweet fillings.

- *Cow Hollow/Marina*—**Bepples Pies**: 1934 Union Street, at Laguna (tel: 931-6225) and 2142 Chestnut Street, at Steiner (tel: 931-6226). Delicious fruit pies, and meat and vegetable pies. Eat in or take out.

- *Hayes Valley*—**Citizens Cake**: 399 Grove Street at Gough (tel: 861-2228). Breads, pies, sticky buns, and wood-oven pizzas. Opens at 7:00 am weekdays, 9:00 am weekends.

- *Mission*—**Golden Crust Pies & Baker's Delight**: 3233 24th Street (tel: 824-7117). Delicious home-baked pies and breads in an unassuming shop. Don't miss it!

- *North Beach*—**Liguria**: 1700 Stockton Street (tel: 421-3786). Just Italian *focaccia* bread: plain, tomato, onion, raisin. Sometimes there's discounted *focaccia* in the freezer. Go early, for when they sell out, the shop closes.

- *North Beach*—**Italian French Baking Company**: 1501 Grant Avenue (tel: 421-3796). Excellent homemade breads, rolls and pastries.

- *North Beach*—**Victoria Pastry Co**: 1362 Stockton (tel: 781-2015). For more than 80 years, the ever-popular Victoria has been selling Italian pastries, cakes, pies, etc.

- *Pacific Heights*—**Bay Bread**: 2325 Pine Street (tel: 440-0356). Excellent hearth-baked artisan breads, made with organic flour, from the retail store of this restaurant supplier. Olive bread, herbed *fougasse, brioche*, and others. Closed Monday.

- *Pacific Heights*—**Pâtisserie Delanghe**: 1890 Fillmore Street, at Bush (tel: 923-0711). Homemade French pastries such as sweet rolls filled with fresh fruit and custard, eclairs, cream puffs. Closed Monday.

- *Richmond* — **Moscow and Tblisi Bakery**: 5540 Geary Boulevard (tel: 668-6959). Wonderful, always crowded, bakery selling excellent rye breads, filled *piroshkis*, and Russian pastries.

# CHEESE

Cheese in the United States tends to be pasteurized, so there may be fewer of the delicate flavors and varieties found in other countries. Supermarkets generally have cut cheeses, and some of the better stores mentioned above (Andronico's, Whole Foods, etc) have superior selections. A few dedicated cheese shops carry an extensive stock, and most also carry interesting gourmet items and some wines.

- *Cole Valley* — **Say Cheese**: 856 Cole Street (tel: 665-5020)
- *Polk/Broadway* — **Leonard's 2001**: 2001 Polk Street (tel: 921-2001)
- *Twin Peaks* — **Creighton's Cheese and Fine Foods**: 673 Portola (tel: 753-0750)
- *Glen Park* — **Cheese Boutique**: 666 Chenery (tel: 333-3390)
- *Mission* — **24th Street Cheese Company**: 3893 24th Street, at Sanchez (tel: 821-6658)
- *Western Addition* — **Country Cheese**: 415 Divisadero Street (tel: 621-8130). Closed Sunday.
- *Pacific Heights* — **Artisan Cheese**: 2413 California Street (tel: 929-8610)

# FISH

Living so close to the sea, there's no reason for you to settle for less than the freshest of seafood. All varieties of domestic fish are available according to the season, and with refrigeration standards so high, fish from other regions is also good. But local waters offer some fish you might not have heard of; once you've tasted local sand dabs, petrale, and rex sole, you'll be hooked. During Dungeness crab season, supermarkets sell crab already cooked and cleaned; fish markets may sell them whole, or cooked and cleaned.

Supermarkets carry many varieties of seafood already cut and packaged, and not relying on local weather conditions, may stock Atlantic salmon or other non-local fish. Whole Foods, Andronico's and other superior supermarkets, however, tend to use local suppliers; a few have sushi chefs cutting fresh sushi. Dedicated fish markets throughout the city are also excellent.

Although many of the old fishing piers have been taken over by tourist attractions, the fishing fleet still docks at "Fish Alley," on the Jefferson Street promenade, between Taylor and Jones. If you don't mind cleaning your own fish, try buying whole fish direct from the fishermen on Saturday morning; go early to have a better selection. Look also at the Ferry Plaza market on Saturdays, where the **Monterey Fish Company** — Berkeley's premier fish market — maintains a stall.

Asian fish stores are generally of high quality. Look especially around the Japan Center, where groceries sell sliced fish for sushi. In Chinatown, don't be taken aback seeing people selecting live turtles and frogs; before being taken out of the store, the staff prepares them. In Chinatown, however, you basically have to know your fish, because few people speak English, and the staff is so busy handling crowds they wouldn't have time to explain, in any case.

- *Chinatown* — **New Sang Sang Market**: 1143 Stockton Street (tel: 433-0403). One of the best fish stores in Chinatown. Excellent selection, good prices, the freshest of the fresh.
- *Inner Richmond* — **Wing Hing Seafood Market**: 633 Clement Street (tel: 668-1666). Freshly cut and live fish to choose among in this authentic Asian fish mart.
- *Inner Richmond* — **Seafood Center**: 831 Clement, near 10th Avenue (tel: 752-3496). Extremely wide, high-quality selection.
- *Outer Sunset* — **Irving Seafood Market**: 2130 Irving Street (tel: 681-8369). Small but excellent fish selection.

227

- *Outer Sunset* — **Yum Yum Fish**: 2181 Irving Street (tel: 566-6433). Small Japanese market with a good variety, plus a chef cutting fresh sushi to take home or to eat in at the few tables.
- *Polk/Van Ness* — **Swan Oyster Depot**: 1517 Polk Street, near California (tel: 673-1101). A San Francisco tradition for 75 years. Fresh fish to take out, but regulars sit at the counter for delicious oysters, Crab Louie, chowder. Closes 5:30 pm; closed Sunday.
- *Potrero Hill* — **Nikko Fish**: 699 Illinois, at 3rd and 18th Streets (tel: 864-5261). Fresh fish in a tiny open-front shop. Closed Sunday.

# MEATS AND POULTRY

The better supermarkets listed above have excellent selections of ready-cut meats and some specially prepared items ready to take home and cook such as kabobs and marinated or stuffed meats. The selection at Whole Foods is impressive. But neighborhood butchers offer all of the above, plus personalized service and, often, home delivery. For holidays, place your order well in advance.

- *Bayshore* — **Polarica**: 107 Quint Street, near Third and Cesar Chavez (tel: 647-1300). Game and game birds, excellent chicken, imported lamb, wild mushrooms, berries, and smokehouse products.
- *Chinatown* — **New On Sang Poultry Co**: 1114 Grant Avenue (tel: 982-4694). Fresh fish and poultry, nicely displayed, plus prepared dishes to take out. Smaller shop at 617 Clement Street (tel: 752-4100).
- *Laurel Village* — **Bryan's Quality Meats**: 3473 California Street (tel: 752-3430). Respected grocer and butcher of exceptional quality. Fresh fish, artfully cut meats, prepared foods, salads. Parking in back. Closed Sunday.
- *Mission* — **Mission Market Meat Department**: 2590 Mission, at 22nd Street (tel: 282-1030). Excellent meats in a Latino

market building that also houses the Mission Market Fish and Poultry (tel: 282-3331).

- *Mission* — **Lucky Pork Store**: 2659 Mission, near 22nd Street (tel: 550-9016). A Chinese pork butcher popular with Latin Americans in the Mission district. All cuts, plus beef and goat.
- *North Beach* — **Little City**: 1400 Stockton, at Vallejo (tel: 986-2601). North Beach's premier butcher, with a good variety of high-quality, well-cut products.
- *Van Ness* — **Harris' Restaurant**: 2100 Van Ness (tel: 673-1888). Excellent steak house sells prime, aged meat at a retail counter during the dinner hours when the restaurant is open.

### Kosher Meat

Most supermarkets carry standard packaged kosher products, and all carry kosher for Passover items in the spring. Unfortunately, there are only two designated kosher meat outlets in the city. Ask at the Jewish Community Federation for *Resource*, a comprehensive guide to Jewish life in the Bay Area.

- *Outer Richmond* — **Israel Kosher Meat and Poultry**: 5621 Geary Boulevard (tel: 752-3064). Kosher meats, Empire poultry, frozen selections, deli department with sliced meats, plus packaged goods, kosher wine.
- *Outer Sunset* — **Tel Aviv Kosher Meats, Deli & Liquor**: 2495 Irving Street (tel: 661-7588). A small market in the Outer Sunset with kosher meats, frozen and packaged goods.

## COFFEE BEANS

Those same people who know exactly what kind of coffee they want in the coffeehouses also know exactly what kind of bean they want to grind at home or have the coffee roasters blend for them. Many supermarkets have their own selection of coffee beans and grinders, and **Peet's Coffee and Tea** and the **Spinelli Coffee Company** chains have several locations in the city. Try one of these specialty shops, especially those in North Beach.

- *Cole Valley* — **Bean There**: 201 Steiner Street (tel: 255-8855). Sip in or take out coffee and teas. Coffee is ground to order for your cup of coffee. Light meals.
- *Cow Hollow* — **Union Street Coffee Roastery**: 2191 Union Street (tel: 922-9559). Excellent coffee in this small roastery at the corner of Steiner Street.
- *North Beach* — **Graffeo Coffee Roasting Co**: 733 Columbus Avenue (tel: 986-2420). Since 1935, roasting dark and light Arabica beans. Offers decaffeinated Colombian, produced without chemicals. Also in San Rafael.
- *North Beach* — **Caffé Roma Coffee Roasting Company**: 526 Columbus Street (tel: 296-7662). Long-established North Beach coffee roaster.
- *North Beach* — **Caffe Trieste**: 609 Vallejo (tel: 982-2605). Next to the famous North Beach coffeehouse, this is a long-established coffee roaster, with its rich aromas wafting down the street.
- *Outer Sunset* — **House of Coffee**: 1618 Noriega Street (tel: 681-9363). Middle Eastern shop with good ground beans for Turkish coffee. Closed Sunday.

# EATING OUT AT HOME

After all this, do you still not feel like cooking or even going out? Then pick up a catalogue at street-side boxes from **Waiters on Wheels** (tel: 252-1470; www.waitersonwheels.com). Fine restaurants of all categories and price ranges display facsimiles of their menus for order by telephone. Pay a small surcharge and tip the driver, and you can have hot, ready-cooked meals from the best restaurants delivered to your door. Solely on the Internet, try **food.com** (www.food.com).

However, many restaurants themselves — especially just about every Asian restaurant, including the sushi bars — have takeout. If you do have the energy just to pick up a ready-cooked meal, try one of these shops or restaurants that offer takeout of their specialties. As already noted, the better supermarkets also have extensive counters with prepared dishes, ready to reheat.

- *Bernal Heights* — **Hungarian Sausage Factory**: 419 Cortland Avenue (tel: 648-2847). Sausages, hams, sauerkraut, stuffed cabbage, all take home or eat in. Evenings only; closed Monday.
- *Chinatown* — **Janmae Guey**: 1222 Stockton Street, near Broadway (tel: 433-3981). Delicious Chinese barbequed duck, chicken, pork ribs, and noodles to take out or to eat in. Inexpensive.
- *Embarcadero* — **MacArthur Park**: 607 Front Street (takeout tel: 781-5560). Restaurant known especially for its barbequed ribs and chicken; has an extensive counter for full-meal takeout.
- *Marina* — **Lucca**: 2120 Chestnut Street (tel: 921-7873). Exceptional Italian delicatessen selling pastas, sauces, cheese, frittatas, focaccia, salads, imported packaged products. Delicious sandwiches, freshly cut.
- *North Beach* — **Florence Ravioli Factory**: 1412 Stockton Street, near Columbus (tel: 421-6170). Popular Italian deli, with imported products, cheeses, prosciutto, and homemade ravioli.
- *North Beach* — **GiraPolli**: 659 Union Street (tel: 434-4472). Among the best of the rotisserie chicken in San Francisco. Comes with potatoes, vegetable, and a roll. Extremely difficult to park. Dinner only.

# Chapter Fourteen

# WATERING HOLES

## THE FRUIT OF THE VINE

California produces more than 90 percent of the wine made in the United States. The majority comes from the inland Central Valley, but the best comes from Northern California where the climate and soil are ideal. The cool breezes along the coastal strip of land that stretches from Mendocino in the north to Santa Barbara in the south encourage some of the most complex Chardonnays in the world, and some of the rich, red Pinot Noirs also prefer the foggy coasts. The vines that prefer the hot inland valleys produce the popular Merlot and the Sauvignon Blancs that range from the crisp to the creamy rich.

What people call the "wine country" comprises the Sonoma Valley, with its varying climates, and the Napa Valley, with its warm summer days and cool nights, so welcoming to the vines of the excellent, bold Cabernet Sauvignons, the ever-popular Chardonnay, and Zinfandel, a California favorite. But northern California offers much more. Just a bit farther north, the Alexander Valley and the land up toward Mendocino are also conducive to vines. Vineyards and wineries dot the map in the East Bay — in the Livermore Valley and Tri Valley, for example, heading up to the Sierra foothills toward Amador and El Dorado counties. And to the south, the Monterey, Salinas, and Carmel Valleys are all rich with vines.

Wine has been produced in the nearby valleys since the early 1800s, when Spanish priests first planted grapes for sacramental wines. In the late 1850s the Hungarian immigrant Agoston Haraszthy started producing and selling wine in Sonoma, at what is now the famous Buena Vista Winery. Just a few years later, Charles Krug brought German grapes into the Napa Valley; it is he who is credited with bringing grapes into the area although a few decades earlier Charles Yount had already planted vines for his family's use, near what is now Yountville.

Now, wine production is one of the area's most important industries, reaching ever more into new tastes and territories. The appreciation of the populace has kept up with the expansion, encouraging California winemakers to become among the most innovative in the world, willing to experiment with flavors and textures, with richer, fruitier combinations. If the French chateau methods were once the basic model for winemaking, California vintners — increasingly taking into consideration the area's climate and soil — are now adding a southern Mediterranean influence.

## Exploring Wine Country

In the Napa and Sonoma valleys there are hundreds of wineries — both large with many brands, and "boutiques" that make just a few types of wine under one brand name. Napa alone has more than 150 wineries, many of which flank the bisecting Highway

29. Almost all wineries have tasting rooms, with opportunities not just to taste the wines, but to learn about the grapes, the wine-making process, and the differences that give the wines their own particular essence. Some of the wineries also have picnic tables and gift shops, and some offer full meals to show off the range of their wines. The tourist offices below should have detailed information about wineries in their areas.

- **Napa Valley Visitors Bureau**: 1310 Napa Town Center, off First Street, Napa (tel: 707/226-7459; www.napavalley.com)
- **Sonoma Valley Visitors Bureau**: 453 First Street East, Sonoma (tel: 707/996-1090; www.sonomavalley.com)

You can also enjoy an afternoon's ride on the **Napa Valley Wine Train**, which provides a formal meal and wine tastings while touring the area; it leaves from central Napa (tel: 800/427-4124).

The **Blue & Gold Fleet** offers a one-day Wine Country tour from San Francisco, starting with a catamaran ride across the bay (info tel: 773-1188; reservations tel: 705-5555). Also in the city, **Napa Valley Winery Exchange**, at 415 Taylor Street, specializes in California wines. The proprietor will discuss them with you, find wines to fit your taste, and can advise on places to visit in the wine country (tel: 771-2887); closed Sunday.

The longer you are in California, the more you can appreciate its wines. The more you learn about them, the more you will be able to distinguish each nuance and overtone in their wide range of tastes, colors, and textures. To begin, consider one of the wine appreciation seminars at the continuing education establishments in San Francisco mentioned in Chapter Seven, haunt the wine shops that have tastings on weekends, and make periodic ventures to the areas that produce different grapes. Look in the newspapers for tours, special wine-related outings, and wine festivals. For a handy reference, buy *A Companion to California Wine: An Encyclopedia of Wine and Winemaking from the Mission Period to the Present*, a detailed and well-presented description of the history, geography, grapes, and wineries of California. *Food and Wine Magazine's* annual *Official Wine Guide* has a section on California wines, and it is both basic and detailed in its descriptions.

Don't forget, though, that the whole point of drinking wine is to enjoy it. No matter the current popularity of certain wines, the superior attitude of certain wine snobs, and even the authoritative stance of shop proprietors—everybody has different tastes, so if you don't like a wine, it's not for you.

## Trying Wines

In restaurants, wine is sold by the glass and by the bottle (generally 750 ml), and sometimes by the half-bottle. Depending on how much you drink, it can make economic sense to order a bottle of wine for two people, as there are four 6 oz. servings in a bottle, and the cost is perhaps 20 percent less than four single glasses.

Waiters in just about any restaurant are knowledgeable about the wines of that restaurant and will be glad to discuss the wine appropriate for your meal and for your taste. Some restaurants will allow you a small taste of a wine before you order a glass, and most will also allow you to exchange it for another if you do not like it. It is very rare for a wine to be sent back because it has "turned" and isn't good. Many restaurants have a "house wine," and these are often produced from famous wineries but labeled with the name of the restaurant.

The price of a bottle of wine in a restaurant is increasing, as establishments try to turn a larger profit any place they can. Generally, the price should be about double what the establishment paid for the bottle, but some restaurants are now charging triple. Once you have learned about wines and their prices, you can determine which varietals and vintages are worth the price.

Many bars hold special tastings from particular wineries (as do the wine shops mentioned below). Some offer "flights," samplings of similar wines, often in half-glass sizes. You can also try the wine bars, although in San Francisco, where interesting wines are so easily available in just about any eating establishment, there are fewer bars devoted solely to wines than in other cities.

- *Financial District* — **London Wine Bar**: 415 Sansome Street (tel: 788-4811)
- *Hayes Valley* — **Hayes and Vine**: 377 Hayes Street (tel: 626-5301)
- *Union Square* — **First Crush**: 101 Cyril Magnin (tel: 982-7874)

## PURCHASING WINE

Prices run the gamut from the very cheap to the astronomical. The type of wine, the vineyard, the number of bottles produced, and the particular year the grapes were harvested all contribute to how a wine is priced. California wines have become popular worldwide and some recent harvests have been small, so the price of the better wines has increased. In general, the better the wine, the higher the cost. But good, drinkable wines are available at reasonable prices, often at under $10 per bottle, so it is not necessary to spend a fortune on wine. It all just takes know-how: knowing where and when to shop for wines, reading advertisements for sales, buying enough to create a cellar of wines to drink at future dates, and paying attention not only to the offerings of major wineries, but experimenting with "boutique" wineries that produce small amounts of good wines.

Shops have sales on particular items, and when they do, think about stocking your cellar. All the discount groceries mentioned in Chapter Thirteen sell well-known labels at good prices, plus interesting imported wines, not just from France or Italy, but from Chile and Australia as well; if you have found a wine you like, go back immediately and buy more, for inventory runs out quickly and that particular wine may not turn up again. Supermarkets sell a variety of wines, but these are not necessarily the best buys. Many of the wine shops have tastings of the wines they are currently featuring, and surprisingly, these are usually affordable.

- *Bayshore* — **Beverages & More**: 201 Bayshore Boulevard (tel: 648-1233). A large selection of wines and spirits, both domestic and imported. Good prices. Other stores in the area (info tel: 888/772-3866).
- *Cow Hollow* — **PlumpJack Wines**: 3201 Fillmore Street, near Union (tel: 346-9870). Popular neighborhood shop, offering more than one hundred California and Italian wines at reasonable prices.
- *North Beach* — **Coit Liquor**: 585 Columbus Avenue (tel: 986-4036). Small shop but extensive selection of domestic, French, and Italian wines. Good prices and knowledgeable personnel.
- *Polk/Van Ness* — **The Jug Shop**: 1567 Pacific Avenue, at Polk (tel: 885-2922). Large liquor shop with excellent prices, an extensive collection of wines and beers.
- *SOMA* — **Wine Club**: 953 Harrison Street (tel: 512-9086). Excellent prices on a large selection of domestic and imported wines; tastings, books, accessories. Entrance and parking on side, along Oak Grove Street.

## The Wine Label

Labels say it all, front and back. The front carries specific information that is required by the U.S. Bureau of Alcohol, Tobacco and Firearms. The brand name of the wine is often most prominent, as wineries strive for customer recognition and loyalty. For small companies this may be the name of the winery itself; large companies may have several brand names. The type of wine is generally specified by the variety of grape, such as Pinot Noir, and these varietals must contain at least 75 percent of the named grape. Some lesser wines may use a semi-generic name such as Burgundy or even an overall name such as "red table wine," and some blends may bear the name *Meritage*. Nearby will be the "appellation of origin," indicating where the grapes were grown. Appellation is increasingly noticed by consumers, focusing on the soil and the site as much as the winemaker.

At the bottom, the name of the winery that bottled the wine usually appears. Although the winery may be in Napa, it doesn't mean the grapes are from there (that's the appellation of origin): if the label says "produced by," it means that at least 75 percent of the wine was made by the bottler; if it says "cellared by," or "vinted by," the wine was probably purchased from a different winery. The percentage of alcohol appears on the front label along with the date, known as the "vintage year," that the grapes were picked.

The back of the label often describes the wine in detail, and sometimes says which food it best accompanies. It also contains the required warnings about alcohol and health.

## BREW PUBS

Beer appreciation is growing among San Franciscans. The city does not lack for pubs that offer a wide selection of draft and bottled domestic and imported beers and ales, plus interesting selections from regional micro-breweries. Taking on the character of the neighborhood they serve, pubs offer various kinds of entertainment, including large television screens for sports viewing. But it is the brew-pub—saloons that handcraft their own recipes for beers and ales on the premises—that offer the most innovative selections of brews. Some offer standard pub fare, some are elegant restaurants in themselves, and all provide a convivial atmosphere.

The micro-brewery trend may well have started here in San Francisco, when in 1965 the decision was made to preserve the bankrupt **Anchor Brewing Company**, at 1705 Mariposa Street. Now it is San Francisco's local pride, brewing the famous Anchor Steam Beer; the factory does not have a pub, but does give tours and tastings (tel: 863-8350).

- *Fisherman's Wharf*—**Steelhead Brewing Company**: 353 Jefferson Street, in Anchorage Plaza (tel: 775-1795). Good micro-brewery from this west coast chain. Gourmet pizza, pasta, burgers, and seafood.

238

- *Haight* — **Magnolia**: 1398 Haight Street, at Masonic (tel: 864-7468). A brew pub in the heart of the Haight, serving lunch, dinner, and weekend brunch.
- *Marina* — **Faultline Brewing Company**: 2001 Chestnut Street (tel: 922-7397). Good beers and a homemade root beer, pub food, and imaginative upscale entrees.
- *North Beach* — **San Francisco Brewing Company**: 155 Columbus Avenue, at Pacific (tel: 434-3344). Domestic and imported beers, plus those brewed on the premises. Tastings, good food, and live music most evenings.
- *Ocean Beach* — **Beach Chalet**: 1000 The Great Highway at John F. Kennedy Drive (tel: 386-8439). Fabulous views of the beach, an eclectic menu, plus sampler of beers brewed on the premises.
- *Pacific Heights* — **The B Spot**: 2301 Fillmore Street, at Clay (tel: 614-1111). Three handcrafted beers and upscale pub food.
- *Potrero Hill* — **Potrero Brewing Company**: 535 Florida Street (tel: 552-1967). Outdoor dining, pool tables, full bar, housemade beers and ales.
- *SOMA* — **Thirsty Bear**: 661 Howard Street (tel: 974-0905). Brewery and restaurant serving Spanish food.
- *South Embarcadero* — **Gordon Biersch**: 2 Harrison Street, at the Embarcadero (tel: 243-8246). German beers, extensive menu, plus pizza and snacks. Crowds often spill out onto the street.
- *Union Square* — **E & O Trading**: 314 Sutter (tel: 693-0303). Southeast Asian restaurant and brewery.

# THE BAR

Bars come in many shapes and forms: the romantic bar with a spectacular view atop a tall hotel, the loud sports bar with television screens in every corner, the neighborhood bar where you can spend a comfortable evening chatting with your friends. Most restaurants have a bar in front, and these can seat people waiting for their table, diners without a reservation, or those just wanting to stop by for a drink. Some bars open by lunchtime, some in the late afternoon, and restaurant bars are generally open during the restaurant's business hours. Restaurant and other bars usually offer inexpensive cocktails, beers, and snacks in the early evening, during an often loosely defined "happy hour," to a regular clientele that gathers after work. Some bars have theme nights, others have live music; some are known for their particularly delicious concoctions (especially nowadays the martini and the cosmopolitan) — experimentation is what San Francisco is about. Whatever your choice, you'll find it somewhere in the city. No bar may serve alcoholic beverages between 2:00 am and 6:00 am, and most take their last call around 1:45 am.

Bars such as **The Cliff House, Top of the Mark** in the Mark Hopkins Hotel, **Harry Denton's Starlight Room** at the Sir Francis Drake, or **The Equinox** at the top of the Grand Hyatt have spectacular views and are fun to go to from time to time but are often crowded with tourists. Some bars, a few of which are listed below, also have great views, are directly on the waterfront, and have outdoor tables during good weather.

A host of Irish bars such as **The Plough and the Stars, The Front Room, Lefty O'Doul's, Pat O'Shea's Mad Hatter,** and **Martin Macks Bar** in the Haight offer Irish beers in addition to a full bar and decent bar food, dart competitions, and live music, and they celebrate all Ireland's holidays in grand style. Otherwise, here are few of the greats:

- *Cow Hollow* — **Perry's**: 1944 Union Street (tel: 922-9022). One of the original singles bars, this remains a lively place to gather, with good pub food and a friendly atmosphere.
- *Embarcadero* — **Bix**: 56 Gold Street, between Sansome and Montgomery (tel: 433-6300). Jazz piano, supper-club menu, great bar in an Art Deco ambience, splendid martinis. Often rated as San Francisco's best bar.

- *Embarcadero* — **Pier 23**: Pier 23 (tel: 362-5125). Right on the water, this bar is great all day long. Tables outside, live music in the evenings, a popular weekend brunch.
- *Mission* — **Blondie's Bar and No Grill**: 540 Valencia Street (tel: 864-2419). No ambience, no grill, nothing but what some people say are the best drinks in town, especially the oversized, delicious martini.
- *Mission* — **Dalva**: 3121 16th Street, at Albion (tel: 252-7740). A DJ spins music for a lively crowd in this bar that is rated among the best in the city.
- *North Beach* — **Tosca**: 242 Columbus Avenue (tel: 986-9651). Almost a landmark for everyone who comes to San Francisco and a loyal clientele of locals. The jukebox plays only opera. Try its brandy-laced cappuccino.
- *North Beach* — **BlueBar**: 501 Broadway (tel: 981-2230). Downstairs from the popular Black Cat restaurant, this beautiful, comfortable bar schedules jazz, performance art, poetry performances, and short plays.
- *South Embarcadero* — **The Ramp**: 855 China Basin, off Third Street (tel: 621-2378). Right on the water amid the working piers, with an outdoor bar and tables.
- *South Embarcadero* — **Mission Rock**: 817 China Basin Street, near Mariposa (tel: 626-5355). Great deck for sunning, listening to music. Inexpensive drinks and good food.
- *Union Square* — **Red Room**: 827 Sutter, in the Commodore Hotel (tel: 346-7666). Also a city favorite, this bar is glamorous in its all-red decor. Crowded by the fashionable.
- *Union Square* — **The Redwood Room**: Clift Hotel, 495 Geary (tel: 775-4700). Not to be confused with the Red Room, this is one of the city's classiest bars, good for a drink before or after the theater.

241

# DRINKING AGE

In California, you must be 21 years of age in order to purchase or consume alcohol. Even if you are a young-looking 35-year-old, you may be "carded," that is, asked to show your identification. Take it as a compliment. As discussed in Chapter Ten, do not drink alcohol and drive; San Francisco's police are tough on drivers who have been drinking.

# CHAPTER FIFTEEN

# THE SPORTING LIFE

## ALL YEAR 'ROUND

The Bay Area's moderate climate allows outdoor activity on just about any day of the year, from sailing on the Bay, to jogging along its shores, to bicycling on hilly trails, to playing tennis and rollerblading—almost anything that can be done outdoors. Access to outdoor sports, in fact, is a main draw for people moving to the Bay Area. San Francisco itself has more than 120 parks (many with miles of hiking trails), over 70 playgrounds, five golf courses, 100 tennis courts, nine swimming pools, almost six miles of ocean beach, several lakes, fishing piers, fly-casting pools, and a marina with a small craft harbor. Private facilities throughout the city offer gyms with aerobics programs, yoga, and martial arts. The

Bay Area also has famous national baseball and football teams. What more could one want?

# RESOURCES

The daily newspapers report results of the previous day's important sporting events and announce the events of that day and those in the near future. For articles of seasonal interest and extensive ads for shops, gyms, resorts, vitamins, and more, look for *City Sports*, a tabloid handout found in sports shops and health clubs (10 issues annually). Other free sport-specific tabloids such as *Inside Tennis* or *Hockey and Skating* can be found in shops and fitness clubs.

# SPECTATOR SPORTS

San Franciscans are avid sports spectators. Seats for the major games are often sold out long in advance, but the city's sports bars provide large-screen TVs for viewing of just about any match shown on cable or satellite. Tickets for all sporting events are available from the box office or from BASS (tels: 478-2277; 510/762-2277). The San Francisco Giants have several stores in San Francisco, where you can get information on games, get tickets, and buy souvenirs.

### Baseball

The San Francisco team, **The San Francisco Giants**, belongs to the National League (ticket office tel: 800/442-6873). After many years of torturing fans at windy, cold Candlestick Park, the team plays in the new Pacific Bell Park in sunny, warm China Basin. Seating 41,000 people, this park may be reached by bus, train, streetcar, and ferry. It is within walking distance of the Financial District.

The Oakland team, **The Oakland Athletics (The A's)**, belongs to the American League (ticket office tel: 510/638-0500). It plays at the Oakland Coliseum, at Interstate 880 and Hegenberger Road. The BART Colosseum Station is close by.

## Football

Overlapping the summer baseball season, the football season begins in late August. The **San Francisco 49ers ("The Niners")** is the home team (ticket office tel: 656-4900). And in Oakland, the team is **The Oakland Raiders** (tickets through BASS). Both are among the top teams in their respective "conferences," the rivalry between them (and their fans) is fierce, and fans are as partial to their football teams as they are to their baseball teams. The Raiders play in the Coliseum, and the Niners play at 3Com Park (formerly named Candlestick). Season ticket-holders account for most of the Niners seats, but tickets to the Raiders can sometimes be had.

## Soccer

What the rest of the world calls football, Americans call soccer. Since the 1994 World Cup and the 1999 victory by the American women's team, soccer is gaining popularity in the United States. The Bay Area professional team **The San Jose Earthquakes** plays at Spartan Stadium at San Jose State University (ticket office tel: 408/985-4625). International soccer matches can be seen on the Spanish-language channels, selectively on the cable sports channels of ESPN and ESPN2 (plus regular "highlights of the week" programs), but only rarely on the national networks.

## Basketball

The Bay Area team is the **Golden State Warriors**, which generally plays in the Oakland Coliseum Arena (ticket office tel: 510/986-2200). The season runs from November through April. Tickets are available at the box office or from BASS/Ticketmaster (tels: 421-8497, 421-2700).

## Horse Racing

The two race tracks in the Bay Area alternate their schedules, so that racing takes place almost the entire year. **Golden Gate Fields** is in Albany, on Gilman Street (off Interstate 80); races are held from January to the end of June (tel: 510/559-7300). **Bay Meadows** in San Mateo (off US 101, Hillsdale Exit) has thorough-bred and quarter horse tracks, and its season runs from August through January (tel: 650/574-7223).

# WALKING

There's little to say about walking in San Francisco except that everyone does it. Walking is a favorite sport, and here in this moderate climate, many people walk 365 days a year. People walk to work whenever they can, wearing business suits and walking shoes (to be changed to dress shoes at work). For exercise, people walk up and down the hills, slowly or quickly, singly or in groups, along the Embarcadero, in the parks, at Crissy Field, along the 3½-mile Golden Gate Promenade, across the Golden Gate Bridge. The best walking is where the views are breathtaking: the trails in the Presidio and Golden Gate Park certainly qualify, and Strybing Arboretum in Golden Gate Park is exceptional. So is Ocean Beach, even when the fog and wind are fierce.

# RUNNING

Run anywhere you want in San Francisco, on city streets, up and down the hills, in the parks, along the waterfront. Joggers of all speeds run through the city streets before work and at lunchtime, and drivers are used to weaving around them. On weekends, runners prefer jogging where there is one of the city's famous views—all the places mentioned above, for walking. In the parks, women should stay on well-traveled paths, run during daylight hours, and perhaps run with a friend.

The **Dolphin South End Runners** is the largest running club in the area (infotel: 978-0837). The club sponsors friendly runs and competitive races, workouts and social events. There's a small membership fee and usually an entry fee for each race.

# ENJOYING NATURE

You can appreciate the beautiful natural resources of the area without even leaving the city, by walking in **Golden Gate Park**, the **Presidio**, and along the shoreline at **Crissy Field**—but the entire Bay Area is a wealth of opportunities that can take many pleasant years to explore. For a description of the outdoor activities available, there's no book better than Peggy Wayburn's *Adventuring in the Bay Area*, which offers a region-by-region coverage of the nine Bay Area counties in terms of access, outings, weather, travel tips, natural history, and wildlife. An important reference to keep on your shelf. Also check the sports sections of the daily papers for their reports on "the outdoors."

**Sierra Club**, an environmental association, puts on a year-round schedule of hikes, backpacking trips, and other activities, plus social events. Contact the Bay Chapter office at 2530 San Pablo Avenue, Berkeley (tel: 510/848-0800), or its bookshop at 6014 College Avenue, Oakland (tel: 510/658-7470). For trail guides and environmental information, visit the Sierra Club Bookstore at 85 2nd Street (tel: 977-5600); closed Sunday. The **Golden Gate Audubon Society**, at 2530 San Pablo Avenue in Berkeley, hosts field trips, birdwatching walks, workshops, etc (tel: 510/843-2222).

To get involved in the parks, join **Friends of Recreation & Parks**, whose members enjoy the parks together, and who help parks by volunteering, sponsoring events, and raising money (tel: 750-5105; group walks info tel: 263-0991).

In addition to the natural areas described below, **McLaren Park**, **Glen Canyon Park**, **Bernal Park**, and others also have hiking trails. Consider especially the 100 acre Crissy Field, which is devoted to ecology and free recreation, and coastal areas such as **Golden Gate Promenade**, **Ocean Beach**, and the **Esplanade**, or the **Ridge Trail**, which stretches from Lake Merced to Golden Gate Park, and which will eventually circle the entire bay.

247

**Golden Gate Park**, dating from about 1865, is one of the country's major urban parks. Reclaimed from sand dunes and landscaped over about 25 years, the park now comprises some 1,017 diverse acres, offering respite and outdoor activities to hundreds of thousands of people each year. Its museums and concerts provide cultural and educational opportunities as well. The park begins at the Panhandle, between Oak and Fell Streets, which is lined by some of the oldest trees in the city. With rolling hills, fragrant forests, and seemingly endless variety, the park continues for some three miles out to the sandy beaches at the edge of the continent.

East of the 19th Avenue bisect, the park is the most civilized. Here are tennis courts, playgrounds, museums, the California Academy of Sciences, and the exquisite Strybing Arboretum and Botanical Gardens, as well as Stow Lake, the largest in the park. West of 19th Avenue, where the fog may hover for days, are the activities that take more space: golf, doggie runs and training, riding, soccer, polo, fly-casting, and model boat sailing. Especially beloved are the buffalos in the large paddock on John F. Kennedy Drive, at about 39th Avenue. Throughout the park there are hiking trails and bicycle paths, forested groves, and lawns and meadows for picnics or games of Frisbee, and there isn't a foggy or rainy day of the year that they're not enjoyed.

**The Presidio:** Larger than Golden Gate Park (almost twice as large as New York's Central Park), the Presidio's 1,410 acres were from 1776 a strategically placed military garrison. In 1994, however, the United States Army finally vacated this stunningly beautiful area that has been called "the jewel of the Pacific," turning it over to the Golden Gate National Recreation Area for an urban park. Fortunately it is now managed by the National Park Service, and is protected from development. The fragrant forests, unspoiled beaches, and coastal bluffs are open to the public, including many miles of paved roads and hiking trails, plus a golf course, bowling alley, and tennis courts for more structured recreation.

**Golden Gate National Recreation Area (GGNRA)**: The GGNRA spans some 115 miles over a three-county area and is the largest urban national park in the world, encompassing parts of San Francisco itself as well as the wilder reaches outside the city. It includes the Presidio and the beaches mentioned below, Fort Mason and Fort Funston, and the Marin Headlands directly across the Golden Gate Bridge (which is also part of the GGNRA).

# FARTHER AFIELD

Living in San Francisco means that within twenty minutes you can be walking the trails of the Marin Headlands in the GGNRA, or strolling among the spectacular redwood trees at Muir Woods. Just a few more minutes and you can be hiking the trails of Mt. Tamalpais, the highest mountain in the area. In fact, there are 43 state parks in the Bay Area, including the popular whale-watching spot **Sonoma Coast State Beach**, with ten miles of shoreline. Within three hours you can be on snowy slopes of the Sierra Nevada for a weekend of skiing or in a raft paddling down some of the fastest rivers in the west. For a day's outing, try these areas within easy reach from the city:

- *On the Bay* — **Angel Island**: A State Park, once the port of entry for Asian immigrants. With spectacular views and many miles of trails for hiking and bicycling, the 750 acre Angel Island is popular for camping and picnics. Daily ferries from Tiburon during the summer, weekends during the winter. Bikes are allowed and may be rented near the ferry and on the island. This is one of the first places the fog hits, so bring sweaters.
- *On the Ocean* — **Whale Watching**: During gray whales' migration season (December to May) the **Oceanic Society** leads whale-watching trips, plus cruises to the **Farallones National Wildlife Refuge**, a 950 square mile sanctuary off the coast that is a haven for marine mammals and sea birds (reservations tel: 474-3385). Dress warmly and bring binoculars.

249

- *Marin* — **Muir Woods National Monument**: Five hundred and sixty acres of towering redwoods (some 200 years old and 250 feet tall), six miles of footpaths, both hilly and flat, and beautiful light, filtering through the leafy bowers. Off Route 101, at Mill Valley exit, or off Route 1, Panoramic Highway.
- *Marin* — **Mt. Tamalpais State Park**: Fifty miles of hiking trails from the top of the mountain down to the ocean, campsites, horse trails, and exquisite views in this 6,300 acre park just a half-hour from downtown. Biking allowed on the fire roads. Mill Valley to Route 1, the Panoramic Highway.
- *East Bay* — **Tilden Regional Park**: Extremely popular East Bay park, its mountainous trails run past charming lakes, through a variety of nature areas.
- *East Bay* — **Mount Diablo State Park**: Challenging uphill (and then downhill) hikes with wonderful views in all directions.
- *Peninsula* — **San Bruno Mountain State Park**: One of the wildest of the parks in the area, with a 1,314-foot summit, 12 miles of trails, picnic tables, beautiful spring wildflowers on about 1,600 acres. At Brisbane. From Highway 101, take Sierra Point exit to Lagoon Road.
- *Peninsula* — **San Pedro Valley Park**: See charming Brooks Falls with their 175-foot drop; continue on to McNeil State Park and Montara Montain, with its gorgeous views of the coast. Off Linda Mar Boulevard in Pacifica.

# BICYCLING

For sports cycling, the entire Bay Area has excellent trails on an extremely varied terrain, from mountainous to flat, and often with outstanding views. In the city, bikers head for Golden Gate Park, along the Great Highway, the Golden Gate Promenade, and around Lake Merced. There's a bicycle path on the Golden Gate Bridge, leading to some of Marin's most outstanding trails. For a complete resource, buy one of the guides to bicycling in the Bay Area; most rate the rides from gentle to challenging: try *Bay Area*

*Bike Rides* by Ray Hosler, or *Cycling the San Francisco Bay Area: 30 Rides to Historical and Scenic Places* by Carole O'Hare. For day rental in Golden Gate Park and nearby, try the stand at Stow Lake or one of the bike shops on Stanyan Street.

- *Cow Hollow*—**City Cycle**: 3001 Steiner Street (tel: 346-2242). Bicycles for the serious cyclist.
- *Fisherman's Wharf*—**Blazing Saddles**: 1095 Columbus Avenue and at Pier 41 (tel: 202-8888). Bikes come equipped with computers of tour routes of the Marin Headlands, down to Muir Woods, and up to Mt. Tamalpais.
- *Fisherman's Wharf*—**Adventure Bicycle Company**: 968 Columbus Avenue (tel: 771-8735). Tour suggestions detailed and displayed inside. Bikes, trailers for kids, etc.
- *Golden Gate Park*—**Surrey Bikes & Blades**: At Stow Lake (tel: 668-6699). Closed Wednesdays and in inclement weather.
- *Golden Gate Park*—**Golden Gate Park Bike and Skate**: 3038 Fulton, at 6th Avenue (tel: 668-1117). Bikes and inline skates for rent.
- *Haight*—**Avenue Cyclery**: 756 Stanyan Street (tel: 387-3155). Sales of upscale bicycling equipment, plus rentals for those who want to pedal in the park. Excellent repair shop.
- *Haight*—**American Cyclery**: 510 Frederick Street (tel: 664-4545) and 858 Stanyan (tel: 876-4545). Across from each other, two locations for this long-established, well-stocked shop.
- *Mission*—**Valencia Cyclery**: 1077 Valencia, at 22nd Street (tel: 550-6600; repair and parts shop tel: 550-6601). Large selection of equipment and accessories.

## INLINE SKATING

For **inline skating**, many people take their rollerblades to Golden Gate Park, where a rollerblade hockey game can often be found near the tennis courts. The Marina Green or the Embarcadero are also popular for skaters. But people skate just about anyplace in the city, and sometimes you can find an inline game on the city's playgrounds. For indoor hockey in San Francisco, try **Bladium** at 1050 3rd Street, China Basin, which sponsors tournaments, leagues, and youth programs (tel: 442- 5060). In Oakland, try the **Sport Arena** at 210 Hegenberger Loop (tel: 510/562-9499). Look for the free *Hockey and Skating* tabloid that can be found in skate shops. Skate rentals can be found near Stow Lake in Golden Gate Park, on the park's periphery, and in various other locations around the city; see *Skates* in the Yellow Pages.

- *Fisherman's Wharf*—**New World Sports**: 1365 Columbus Avenue, at Beach (tel: 776-7801)
- *Haight*—**Skates on Haight**: 1818 Haight Street (tel: 752-8375)
- *Sunset*—**Skate Pro**: 3401 Irving (tel: 752-8776)

# MULTI-SPORT FITNESS CLUBS

Urban San Francisco offers several extensive multi-sport fitness clubs, almost country clubs within the city. In addition to their standard facilities, most offer scheduled athletic events, tournaments, and social gatherings. Expect to pay an initiation fee, plus monthly dues.

- *City-wide*—**Embarcadero YMCA**: 169 Steuart Street, near Mission (tel: 957-9622). Popular facility with aerobics, yoga, and dance classes, Olympic-size pool, and racquetball/squash and basketball courts. The YMCA in the Presidio, at Lincoln and Funston Streets, also has an extensive fitness facility and pool (tel: 447-9622). The "Y" at 220 Golden Gate Avenue, close to the Civic Center, is similarly equipped (tel: 885-0460).
- *Embarcadero*—**Golden Gateway Tennis and Swim Club**: 370 Drumm Street (tel: 616-8800). Two outdoor swimming pools, nine tennis courts, a fitness center, aerobics classes, tournaments and special events—all in the heart of the city.
- *Masonic*—**Koret USF Health & Recreation Center**: Turk and Parker Streets (tel: 422-6820). Part of the University of San

Francisco, this facility with swimming pool, gym, and racquet-ball courts is open to non-students until 2:00 pm daily and all day weekends. Pay by the session or buy a pass for 15 sessions.

- *SOMA* — **San Francisco Tennis Club**: 645 5th Street (tel: 777-9000). An upscale club including indoor and outdoor tennis courts, a fitness facility, aerobics classes, sauna and hot tub, restaurant. In addition to the monthly dues, there is a court fee for using the indoor courts.
- *Telegraph Hill* — **San Francisco Bay Club**: 150 Greenwich Street (tel: 433-2200). Tennis, racquetball and squash, swimming pool, aerobics, sun deck, events and activities.

# GYMS

In addition to the more extensive multi-sport clubs above, every neighborhood has its storefront gym, some just with workout machines, some more extensively equipped, offering aerobics classes, jacuzzi, and steam baths. You'll see these small clubs as you walk around your neighborhood; monthly dues are generally reasonable, and some clubs allow per-use payment. The downtown district has several chains of fitness clubs that open early and stay open late, and these, obviously, are most crowded before and after work, and at lunchtime. Facilities at these clubs vary; some have swimming pools and some do not, but they are all generally well-equipped for the activities they offer. These usually have short-term as well as regular membership, and if you belong to one, you may use the others in the chain.

- **Club One Fitness**: Locations in the Financial District, and others around the Bay Area.
- **24-Hour Fitness**: Seven locations throughout the city. Dozens of others throughout the Bay Area.
- **Pinnacle Fitness**: Six locations, two with indoor swimming pools.

253

# TENNIS

More than 130 free public tennis courts dot the city's parks, and they are "first-come first-served." For the *Guide to Public Tennis Courts* ask at the **San Francisco Recreation and Parks Department** at McLaren Lodge, Fell and Stanyan Streets, in Golden Gate Park, or call the Tennis Department (tel: 753-7100). Golden Gate Park has 21 courts, which must be reserved in advance, and which cost a small fee (tel: 753-7001). The city also offers an extensive program of free tennis lessons. Below are some popular public courts; see also Multi-sport Fitness Clubs above.

- *Noe Valley* — **Dolores Park**: 18th Street and Dolores. Six courts. Daytime only.
- *Marina* — **Moscone Recreation Center**: Chestnut and Buchanan Streets. Four lighted courts.
- *Excelsior* — **McLaren Park**: Mansell Drive, near University Street. Six courts.
- *North Beach* — **North Beach Playground**: Lombard and Mason Streets. Three lighted courts.

# SWIMMING

Yes, San Francisco is on the ocean, but swimming in the cold waters off the city's beaches can not only be chilling, it can definitely be risky: some of the most inviting-looking beaches have dangerous undertows and rip tides, so swimming, and wading — even in waters that appear calm — may be unsafe. It is best to sun yourself, jog, or walk along the beaches to enjoy the view, but to reserve your swimming for the city's pools. If you want a good swimming beach (despite the cold water) and pleasant amenities, go north to **Stinson Beach**, which on a good day is about 45 minutes from the city on the Panoramic Highway; on weekends, the lines of cars can seem endless.

If open water swimming in the Bay interests you, try the open water clubs: the **Dolphin Swim and Boat Club** is a group of hardy folk who swim in the Bay year round and row on the Bay and on Lake Merced. The clubhouse is at 502 Jefferson Street, at the foot of Hyde Street (tel: 441-9329). The Dolphins sponsor competitive swims and social events, announced in the quarterly newsletter. Meetings are the third Wednesday of the month. Try also the **South End Rowing Club**, next door at 500 Jefferson (tel: 776-7372).

- **Baker Beach**: In the Presidio. Popular for picnics, fishing and sunbathing (in various states of undress).
- **Aquatic Park**: Just beyond Ghirardelli Square at the foot of Van Ness, this is downtown's nearest swimming beach. Good sandy beach, but don't expect the water to be warm.
- **Land's End Beach**: Near Geary Boulevard and the Great Highway. Down a steep trail, a small picturesque beach popular with the gay crowd. Clothing optional. Swimming prohibited.
- **Ocean Beach**: Along the Great Highway. Always popular 4-mile strip of sand. Great for jogging, strolling, sunbathing. Often dangerous for swimming.
- **China Beach**: in Seacliff at 28th Avenue, off El Camino del Mar (tel: 558-3706). Down a steep trail to a swimming beach, protected from the tides. Swim in the summer months when a lifeguard is on duty. Call ahead to inquire about conditions, for weather changes quickly in San Francisco.

The best bet is to try a swimming pool. The multi-sport fitness clubs listed above have pools, and "Park and Rec" maintains eight municipal public pools. A full list, including opening hours for each pool, is available at McLaren Lodge, in Golden Gate Park. Prices are reasonable, especially if you buy a series. Swim lessons are also available.

- *Japantown* — **Hamilton Recreational Center**: Geary Boulevard at Steiner (tel: 292-2001)
- *Mission* — **Garfield Pool**: Harrison and 26th Streets (tel: 695-5001)

255

- *Mission* — **Mission Pool**: 19th Street at Valencia (tel: 695-5002)
- *North Beach* — **North Beach Pool**: Lombard Street at Mason (tel: 274-0200)
- *Panhandle* — **Angelo Rossi**: Arguello Boulevard at Anza (tel: 666-7014)
- *Parkside* — **Sava Pool**: 19th Avenue and Wawona (tel: 753-7000)
- *Sunset* — **Balboa Park**: Ocean Avenue and San Jose (tel: 337-4701)
- *Visitacion Valley* — **Coffman Pool**: Visitacion Avenue at Hahn (tel: 337-4702)

## Other Water Sports

- *Sailing*: The opportunity to go sailing just about any time of the year is a distinct benefit of the San Francisco life. Opening Day on the Bay in May can be an awesome sight, and events over the Bay such as fireworks or the aerial displays of the Blue Angels see thousands of boats perched in the water waiting for the show. For people without boats, it's sometimes possible to sign on as crew. Try the **Saint Francis Yacht Club** (tel: 563-6363), or the **Golden Gate Yacht Club** (tel: 346-2628), both membership clubs located in The Marina, or one of the boat clubs toward the south at Pier 54. For sailing lessons, one of the best in the area is the **Cal Sailing Club**, at University Street at the Marina, in Berkeley (tel: 510/287-5905).
- *Surfing*: Surfing in wet suits is popular, but despite the surfers who brave the currents, remember that the undertows off Ocean Beach are dangerous. Beginners often surf at Pacifica's Linda Mar Beach, and experts go down to Half Moon Bay. Windsurfers tend to use Lake Merced and the more challenging area at Crissy Field, past the Marina. **San Francisco School of Windsurfing** offers courses in windsurfing on Lake Merced (tel: 753-3235); and **Boardsports**, which also has rentals of various types of water sports equipment, gives lessons near Alameda (tel: 929-7873).

Photo: San Francisco Convention & Visitors Bureau

*Fishing off a municipal pier.*

- *Rowing*—**Lake Merced Boathouse**: Rent a rowboat, canoe, or pedal boat, at Harding Road and Skyline Boulevard. **Stow Lake Boathouse**—Rent a rowboat or pedal boat in Golden Gate Park. Picnic on the island of Strawberry Hill. See also the swim and boat clubs mentioned above.
- *Fishing*—The city's municipal piers: at the end of Van Ness or at the end of Broadway—permit fishing in the heart of the city, and people occasionally reel in flounder, sand dabs, cod, bass, perch, or crabs. Unfortunately, cleanup programs to eliminate toxic substances and other contaminants in the Bay have been only partially successful. As of 1999 the California Office of Environmental Hazard Assessment suggests that adults should eat Bay fish no more than twice each month, and that striped bass more than 35 inches long not be consumed.

  Fortunately, people also fish from the banks or a boat on the 350 acre Lake Merced, which has been stocked with trout, rock cod, catfish and bass. Golden Gate Park has several fly-casting pools by the Anglers Lodge, just west of the Polo Fields.

## GOLF

It may be surprising that there are five golf courses in a city as small as San Francisco. Some courses are nine-hole only, compact and full of twists and turns. Golf is a year-round sport, despite the winter rains and the summer fog, but San Franciscans are hardy, and swathed in sweaters and jackets, they wait patiently for their tee-off time. There are a few private membership clubs in the city, and many clubs around the Bay Area are open to the public. In the East Bay, **Tilden Park Golf Course** in Berkeley is particularly popular (tel: 510/848-7373), as is **Chuck Corica Golf Complex** in Alameda (tel: 510/522-4321). For a complete listing of the clubs in the Bay Area, purchase *The Golf Road Map* at golf shops (see Chapter Sixteen); see also the Yellow Pages for extensive listings.

For a covered practice range, putting green, and golf lessons in the heart of the city, try **Mission Bay Golf Center**, at 1200 6th

Street, off Fourth and Channel (tel: 431-7888). Although membership is not required, joining allows discounts on lessons and on buckets of balls, plus discounted play at the city's golf courses. The center hosts tournaments and social events.

- **Gleneagle's Golf Course**: In McLaren Park, at Sunnydale Avenue and Hahn Street (tel: 587-2425). A hilly nine-hole course, with wonderful views.
- **Golden Gate Park Golf Course**: 47th Avenue between Fulton and John F. Kennedy Drive (tel: 751-8987). Compact nine-hole course.
- **Harding Golf Course**: In Harding Park, at 99 Harding Road near Skyline Boulevard (tel: 664-4690). Both nine and eighteen challenging holes in a forested setting. Driving range.
- **Presidio Golf Course**: 300 Finley Road, at Arguello, in the Presidio (tel: 415-4653). Eighteen holes, practice center, Arnold Palmer Golf Academy.
- **Lincoln Park Golf Course**: In Lincoln Park, at 34th Avenue and Clement Street (tel: 221-9911). Eighteen difficult holes on beautiful terrain with spectaclar views. Practice area, putting green, etc.

# SKIING

Some of the best skiing in the country takes place on the ski slopes of the Sierra Nevada, only three hours from San Francisco. In the winter, daily weather updates report the snow level and depth of snow pack of the major ski areas of the region: **Lake Tahoe**, **Incline**, **Alpine Meadows**, **Yosemite**, and **Bear Valley**. Be prepared to carry tire chains in your car and from time to time to be stuck in the mountains until the roads are cleared of snow. Sunday night traffic off the mountains can be slow. For highway conditions, call the California Department of Transportation's 24-hour automated information line; you will need to enter the number of the highway you are inquiring about (tel: 800/427-7623).

The **San Francisco Ski Club** (tel: 337-9333) is a club for single skiers and snowboarders, which also offers white-water rafting, bicycling outings and other events year-round. Sporting goods shops sell ski wear in the winter, some shops rent it, and most have information on ski areas: try these below:

- *Berkeley* — **REI Coop**: 1338 San Pablo Avenue, Berkeley (tel: 510/527-4140)
- *San Rafael* — **Swiss Ski Sports**: 821 E. Francisco Boulevard (tel: 721-2401)
- *San Francisco* — **Soma Sports**: 689 3rd Street (tel: 777-2165)

# OTHER SPORTS

- *Basketball* — You can probably pick up a basketball game in the Golden Gate panhandle, Dolores Park, at some of the city's playgrounds, the Moscone Recreation Center in the Marina, or the Potrero Hill Recreation Center.
- *Bowling* — **Japantown Bowl**: 1790 Post Street, at Webster (tel: 921-6200). Large bowling complex with 40 lanes, a cafe, sports TV. Inquire about joining a league. **Presidio National Park Bowling**: Building 93, between Moraga and Montgomery Streets (tel: 561-2695). Yerba Buena Bowling Center: Metreon, 750 Folsom Street (tel: 777-3727). A San Francisco experience!
- *Dance* — **Academy of Ballet**: 2121 Market Street (tel: 552-1166). For all ages. Classes for toning and stretching, through classical ballet moves. **Renaissance Ballroom**: 285 Ellis Street (tel: 474-0920). Learn the cha cha or the waltz; most social dances are taught here. **Recreation and Parks Department Dance**: 50 Scott Street in the Harvey Milk Center (tel: 554-9523). Dance lessons in a variety of steps: square dancing, jazz, tap, etc. **Jewish Community Center**: 3200 California Street (tel: 292-1221). Dance lessons for all ages. Ballet, modern, jazz, swing, hip-hop, etc. See *Dancing* in the Yellow Pages and *Dance* in Chapter Seventeen.

*Practicing tai chi in Washington Square.*

- *Billiards* — **Chalkers Billiard Club**: 101 Spear Street, in Rincon Center (tel: 512-0450). Especially popular with the lunchtime office crowd; evening happy hour. **The Great Entertainer**: 975 Bryant Street (tel: 861- 8833). Pool and billiard tables, snooker, shuffleboard, ping-pong, darts, video arcade, plus bar and restaurant. Open until 2:00 am weekdays, 3:00 am Saturday. **Hollywood Billiards**: 61 Golden Gate Avenue (tel: 252-9643). More than thirty antique pool tables, snooker and billiards. Open from 3:00 pm until 4:00 am on weekdays and 6:00 am on weekends. Happy hours weekdays 4:30–7:00 pm.

- *Horseback riding* — **Golden Gate Park Stables**: John F. Kennedy Jr. Drive and 36th Avenue (tel: 668-7360). Guided rides through the park and along the oceanfront, plus pony rides for children. Instruction available.

- *Ice-skating* — **Yerba Buena Gardens** sports a year-round, covered ice-skating rink. **Justin Herman Plaza**, at California Street and the Embarcadero, erects a small rink in the winter.

261

- *Martial Arts and Yoga* — As would be expected, San Francisco has many Asian exercise establishments. For any one of a dozen types of martial arts *dojos*, see the Yellow Pages under *Martial Arts Instruction*. Health clubs offer yoga classes for all levels of ability, and there are small studios in just about every neighborhood that specialize in a variety of yoga techniques and instruction. See *Yoga Instruction* in the Yellow Pages.
- *Rock Climbing* — **Mission Cliffs Rock Climbing Center**: 2295 Harrison, at 19th Street (tel: 550-0515). Indoor rock climbing on about 14,000 square feet of climbing terrain.

# SPAS

What could be better after a long week at work than a relaxing couple of hours at a spa? Most health clubs have sauna and steam baths, and some offer massage; massage and beauty treatments are also available at some downtown salons. But locals are particularly fond of the **Kabuki Hot Springs** in the Japan Center, at 1750 Geary Boulevard, at Fillmore (info tel: 922-6000). Kabuki offers a full range of *shiatsu* massages, body treatments and Japanese baths. Try also:

- *Marina* — **Heaven Wellness Center**: 2215 Chestnut Street (tel: 749-6414). Salon and day spa offers hair services, plus massage and facials, steam, acupuncture, nutritional counseling and yoga classes.
- *Mission* — **Osento Baths**: 955 Valencia Street (tel: 282-6333). Gathering place for women. Peaceful bath house, with saunas, outdoor deck, massage.
- *Noe Valley* — **Elisa's Health Spa**: 4028A 24th Street (tel: 821-6727). Outdoor/indoor hot tubs, steam baths and sauna. Massage, skin peels, herbal body wraps.
- *Van Ness* — **The Hot Tubs**: 2200 Van Ness Avenue (tel: 441-8827). Hot tubs and saunas, shiatsu and Swedish massage. Also in Berkeley.

- *Union Square* — **Elizabeth Arden Red Door Salon & Spa**: 126 Post Street (tel: 989-4888). Luxurious spa. Hair and body treatments, cosmetics, makeovers, facials, aromatherapy massage, thermal wraps.
- *Union Square* — **77 Maiden Lane Salon & Spa**: 77 Maiden Lane (tel: 391-7777). Elegant downtown spa. Hair and makeup services, manicure, pedicure, hot mud treatments, and massage.

## AND LAST... ABOUT DOGS

Brisk dog walking is good exercise and an excellent way to meet neighbors. While dogs are not allowed in most parks (signs are generally posted at entrances), some parks have areas designated "off leash" where dogs may run freely, and some neighborhood parks have dog runs. Golden Gate Park has several off-leash areas and Ocean Beach is off-leash until Stairway 21. Dolores Park between the Mission and Noe Valley is a dog and owner gathering place. Call "Park and Rec" for its brochure *Dog Running Areas in City Parks*.

Note that the city's "pooper-scooper" law requires that dog litter be picked up and disposed of properly, whether you are walking your dog in a park or on the street. People actually do obey the law, and the city is basically litter-free as a result. Carry a plastic bag with you and look for the nearest trash receptacle.

Photo: Eleanor Burke

PLEASE BE COURTEOUS, CLEAN-UP AFTER YOUR PET FMLP.

# Chapter Sixteen

# SHOPPING AT YOUR DOOR

## ALL DAY, EVERY DAY

As small and compact as it is, San Francisco's stores sell everything you need for your home somewhere within the city's confines. Nothing is hard to find: consulting the Yellow Pages and understanding the commercial character of the different districts should allow you to make your way comfortably onto the shopping scene without trouble — and without much wait, for you can shop seven days a week, if the fancy strikes you.

Almost all stores are open by 10:00 am. Although service and repair shops are generally closed on Sunday, all large stores and chain stores are open on Sundays, and in fact, this is a popular shopping day. Sunday hours, however, may be shorter than on weekdays, so it is best to call ahead to check. Department stores may stay open until 9:00 pm and some of the national chains — **Tower Records**, **Virgin Megastore** — even later. Small shops generally close around dinnertime, although specialty boutiques and bookshops in areas where the evening is lively often stay open late. As mentioned in Chapter Thirteen, supermarket complexes open early and stay open late every day, and they often have hardware, pharmacy, stationery, and even a few clothing items — hosiery or underwear — you might want on a Sunday. Shops listed here are all open on Sunday, unless noted.

# WHERE TO SHOP

A description of the city's shopping districts must begin directly on Union Square, where large multi-department shops rule the scene, selling goods from the utilitarian to the upscale and elegant. Macy's is the only true department store, stocking household goods, furniture, and linens, as well as clothing and accessories, and it has decent merchandise at good prices. **Saks Fifth Avenue** and **Neiman Marcus** are the most fashionable of the clothing chains. But the streets that surround Union Square house smaller, upmarket shops, and both local boutiques and branches of national chains. **Gump's**, the most elegant and prestigious of old San Francisco shops, has entrances on both Post and Maiden Lane. Just across Market Street, is **Nordstrom's**, a multi-story fashion mart atop the large City Centre Mall.

It would be your lucky day if you found a parking space around Union Square, so do not count on it. Most parking meters in this area are reserved during the day for commercial vehicles unloading their wares (so why trucks insist on double parking and blocking the streets remains a mystery). Other meters may be for a half-hour only and cost as much as 25 cents for 10 minutes. Fortunately, three city-run parking lots are located in the area (see Chapter Ten), and nearby Market Street offers public transportation to most parts of the city.

*Union Square, the city's major theater and shopping district.*

Although the department stores have their attractions, San Franciscans in general are partial to the districts for everyday shopping. Each neighborhood has its commercial character, and you will come to know what type of items and prices you will find on Union Street (high) as opposed to those you will find on Haight (low). On Union, for example (if you can find a parking space), starting at about Gough, you'll find lively upscale and interesting clothing and jewelry boutiques intermingled with crowded trendy restaurants and cafes, bars and nightspots. The same holds true on Chestnut Street and on Upper Fillmore, from about Washington to California, which includes some elegant resale shops. The Sacramento and Presidio intersection has artsy shops of all sorts, but also a large selection of children's items, reflecting its neighborhood's ambience (also true of Noe Valley). North Beach has fewer clothing shops than coffeehouses, but Chestnut and Union Streets are only a short drive away, and the four-building Embarcadero Center a short walk.

Some areas are known for a particular focus: art galleries downtown and around the Civic Center, antique shops on Jackson and on Sacramento near Presidio, modern furniture below Potrero Hill, appliances South of Market or in the Mission. South of Market also sees the huge discount chains — **Costco, Office Max, Bed, Bath and Beyond** — and small factory clothing outlets: some are so popular that tour buses from the suburbs bring people in on Saturdays for a day of discount shopping.

Check also commercial corridors such as Geary Boulevard, Lombard Street, and 19th Avenue. These arteries and their side streets all have stores and local services, and in these areas parking may well be easier. The malls and some large shops and chains, of course, have parking lots for their customers.

Nationwide stores in all merchandise categories are increasingly present in the city. These shops — **Borders** and **CompUSA**, for example — offer good prices and an extensive selection. But citizens' groups are fighting to exclude these megastores from their districts, trying to preserve both the character of the neighborhoods and the small independent merchant. As rents continue to rise in the city, forcing the small business out, they may have less success than at present. The above notwithstanding, chains and local businesses combine to make all shopping options available, and you should have no trouble finding what you want.

## PRICES AND PAYING

The few stores and services mentioned below have been selected as representative examples of the types of shops in San Francisco that give good quality for the price—whatever the price. That does not mean that you won't find a bargain elsewhere, for you certainly will. Nor does it mean that a particular discount store will be inexpensive, but it certainly will offer a steep discount from the retail price and be worth the money for that particular item. People do not bargain on prices, as a rule, but if merchandise is damaged and you still want to buy it, you may be given a discount.

Except for some small shops, stores accept the major credit cards. Some will also take a personal check on a California bank (a few will take out-of-state checks) when you produce photo identification. It is illegal for a shop to ask that a credit card be used as identification. Stores do not charge extra for using a credit card, but a few will offer a discount for cash.

Ask about the store's refund policy. The large stores and chains generally make refunds with no questions asked if the merchandise is brought back within a reasonable length of time — a week or so—and will also exchange ill-fitting goods for a larger or smaller size, or even a different color. Some stores will exchange for other merchandise only. Stores are not required to make refunds, and each store sets its own policy. If there is an unusual policy, such as "all sales final," a notice is often displayed; this sign is also often displayed during a sale. If you have doubts, ask in advance.

The sales tax in San Francisco is 8.5 percent; in outlying areas it may be somewhat less. This is not a value added tax, and foreign visitors do not receive a refund upon leaving the United States. There are duty free shops in the Union Square area.

## SHOPPING CENTERS

Small shopping malls that cater to locals—with markets, repair shops, pharmacies—cluster in the different neighborhoods. The larger malls are generally anchored by a large clothing store such as Macy's, surrounded by dozens of smaller specialty stores. **Stonestown Galleria** is the largest and most varied shopping mall in the city, rivaling those in the suburbs which sprawl across many acres; downtown, **City Centre** has some interesting shops, and, as mentioned above, it is anchored at the top by Nordstrom's.

Otherwise, for the best range of shops, think about the enormous suburban shopping malls that are close to the city, but which do require transportation by car.

A few minutes south of the city, try **Serramonte Center** and **Westlake Shopping Center** in Daly City, **Tanforan Park** in San Bruno, and, just a little bit farther, **Hillsdale Shopping Center** in San Mateo. Farther south, in Palo Alto, it's worth an afternoon just to explore the extremely upmarket **Stanford Shopping Center**, off Highway 280. About 15 minutes north of the city, at Corte Madera, two major shopping malls — **Town and Country** and **The Village** — flank the 101 Freeway. Nearby in the East Bay, try the **South Shore Center** in Alameda or the **Pacific East Mall** in Albany. In Oakland, **Jack London Square** offers shopping and restaurants on the edge of the bay. More extensive malls are farther east at Walnut Creek and Pleasanton, several anchored by large department stores; in Concord look for **The Willows** and **Sun Valley**.

In addition to the malls within the city listed below, **The Cannery**, **Pier 39**, **The Anchorage**, and **Ghirardelli Square**, although primarily tourist destinations, do hold some interesting and offbeat shops. And the **Canton Bazaar** and **China Trade Center** on the tourist path in Chinatown offer imported goods such as clothing, jewelry, some Oriental furniture, and table linens.

- *Downtown* — **San Francisco Centre**: 855 Market at 5th Street. A vertical shopping mall of small shops, anchored by the upscale Nordstrom clothing retailer.

- *Downtown* — **Crocker Galleria**: 50 Sutter Street, near Montgomery. Multi-story mall of elegant boutiques and little eateries; cafe-style tables and chairs under the skylight give the feeling of eating outdoors in any season.

- *Embarcadero* — **Embarcadero Center**: Battery and Sacramento Streets. A three-level shopping, dining, and cinema complex, spread across four buildings connected by walkways. Parking garage.

- *Pacific/Presidio Heights* — **Laurel Village**: 3500 California Street, past Presidio. Excellent local mall, with upscale supermarts, wine store, kitchenware store, children's clothing and toy stores, bookstore, cafes, etc. Metered parking in front and free in rear.
- *Sunset* — **Stonestown Galleria**: 19th Avenue at Winston Drive. Almost a city in itself, Stonestown contains a supermarket, dozens of shops, Nordstrom's and Macy's department stores, a multiplex cinema, a medical building, and small restaurants. Parking.
- *Wharf* — **Northpoint Centre**: 250 Bay Street, between Powell and Mason. Neighborhood convenience mall with Safeway, Walgreens, Blockbuster Video, Radio Shack, General Nutrition, and a few small shops. Parking.

# CLOTHING

Shops throughout the city offer clothing of all styles, quality, and prices. Those near Union Square may sport designer labels and the highest prices, but even the outlying districts sell interesting clothes at prices that match the quality and design. Shopping is almost a game for many San Franciscans, however, who tend to brag about how little they paid for an item of clothing or an accessory. That one can shop adequately and inexpensively is not only owing to the frequent sales of those department stores and boutiques, but to the presence in the city and the entire Bay Area of a wide selection of designer discount shops, factory outlet stores, and nationwide discount clothing chains. These offer out-of-season clothes, discontinued styles, and overstocks. It isn't likely that you would find any damaged or inferior merchandise, but of course the quality reflects each manufacturer's approach.

Within the city, the South of Market area abounds with small discount shops, plus the family clothing chain **Burlington Coat Factory**, at 899 Howard Street (tel: 495-7234), and other inexpensive chains such as **Marshall's**, **Mervyn's**, and **Ross**.

Discount houses, of course, usually stock what happens to come in and may not replace an item once it is sold out. Sales assistance in the larger shops may not be as personal as in smaller stores, but customer service is generally good. And, although many have been in their locations for years, bargain shops may come and go. Call in advance to be certain the shop is still there and to ascertain its hours. For a complete guide, look for the often updated *Bargain Hunting in the Bay Area* by Sally Socolich. The shops directly below, which are well-established, are just a few examples of the range of merchandise available. For well-priced appliances, furniture, and household items, see below.

- *Family clothing* — **Esprit Factory Outlet**: 499 Illinois, at 16th Street (tel: 957-2540). Well-known designer selling casual clothes and shoes for the family. Sales make the prices even better.

- *Men's clothing* — **California Big and Tall**: 625 Howard Street (tel: 495-4484). Clothes for large and tall men. Closed Sunday and Monday.

- *Men's shirts* — **Van Heusen Factory Store**: 601 Mission Street (tel: 243-0750). Van Heusen shirts for men, casual sportswear for men and women.

- *Women's clothing* — **Georgiou Factory Outlet**: 925 Bryant Street (tel: 554-0150). Past season's designs and overstocks from this well-known chain of contemporary women's clothes. Good prices and a "club" card for extra discounts. Closed Sunday. Other shops in outlying areas.

- *Women's clothing* — **Loehmann's**: 222 Sutter Street (tel: 982-3215). Outpost of New York store selling designer clothes at excellent prices. Also in Westlake Mall in Daly City.

- *Bedclothes* — **Warm Things**: 3063 Fillmore Street, near Union (tel: 931-1660). Factory-direct prices on goose down comforters, shams, covers, robes, slippers, and down vests. Stores in other areas.

271

- *Jewelry* — **Cresalia Jewelers**: 111 Sutter Street (tel: 781-7371). Large shop with a wide selection of jewelry and watches, silver, and table accessories at excellent prices.
- *Luggage* — **Luggage Center**: 828 Mission Street (tel: 543-3771). Discounts on a variety of brand name luggage and accessories. Repairs. Closed Sunday. Also in Berkeley and Burlingame.
- *Music* — **Tower Outlet**: 660 3rd Street, near Townsend (tel: 957-9660). Overstocks and returns from the Tower Records chain. CDs, videos, cassettes, books. A changing but always interesting selection.
- *Perfumes* — **Perfumania**: 333 Jefferson Street (tel: 931-0815). Brand name perfumes for men and women at good prices. Special sales.
- *Sports gear* — **North Face Outlet**: 1325 Howard Street (tel: 626-6444). Huge warehouse of outdoor equipment: tents, clothing, sleeping bags, etc.

### Beyond the City

Factory outlet malls offer good prices because the stores are run by the companies themselves, thereby bypassing the wholesaler and retailer whose prices must reflect their own profits. Several outlet malls are within an hour's drive of the city in all directions (except West, of course). Famous designers such as Liz Claiborne, Jones of New York, Donna Karan, and Tommy Hilfiger have stores in several of the malls offering out of season clothes and overstocks, and sometimes returns from other shops; clothing is generally of the same quality as found in retail stores.

Some of the malls have so many stores and are so spread out they have free shuttle buses. All are open on Sunday and have ample parking, but are crowded on weekends and before holidays.

- *Napa County* — **Napa Premium Outlets**: One of the newest and most popular, with about 50 stores. At Highway 29 and First Street in Napa.

- *Napa County*—**St Helena Premium Outlets**: Small upscale outlet mall. On Highway 29, just north of St. Helena.
- *Sonoma County*—**Petaluma Village Outlets**: About 50 stores of all types. Take 101 north; exit at old Redwood Highway.
- *South*—**Outlets at Gilroy**: Almost 200 factory stores, famous clothing labels, housewares, books, etc. Take Highway 101 south to the Leavesley exit. Shuttle bus between three different areas of shops.
- *South*—**Great Mall of the Bay Area**: Almost two hundred shops and several large anchor stores. At Milpitas, off Highways 680 and 880, at the Montague Expressway and Capitol Avenue.
- *Northeast*—**Factory Stores at Vacaville**: 321 Nut Tree Road, Vacaville. More than 125 stores with a convenient shuttle bus.

## Children's Clothing and Equipment

Department stores, shopping centers, and some discount shops carry good quality children's clothing and furniture, and both the **Gap Kids** and **Gymboree** chains have several outlets. The most varied shops tend to be in family neighborhoods, especially in Presidio Heights and Noe Valley. For advertisements for children's shops and services (as well as articles of interest and schedules of child-oriented events), pick up *Bay Area Parent* or *Parents' Press*, which are free monthly tabloids. You can find them most often in children's shops.

- *Laurel Village*—**Junior Boot Shop**: 3555 California Street (tel: 751-5444). Longtime children's shoe shop.
- *Noe Valley*—**Little Bean Sprouts**: 3961A 24th Street (tel: 550-1668). Neighborhood shop with clothes and accessories for young children.
- *Noe Valley*—**Small Frys**: 4066 24th Street (tel: 648-3954). Comfortable, affordable clothing for children, newborn to size 7. Famous brands.

273

- *Noe Valley* — **Peek.a.bootique**: 1306 Castro Street (tel: 641-6192). New and used clothes, equipment, playthings for the smaller set.
- *Presidio Heights* — **Tuffy's Hopscotch**: 3307 Sacramento Street (tel: 440-7599). Good selection of children's shoes.
- *Presidio Heights* — **Jonathan Kaye**: 3615 Sacramento Street (tel: 922-3233). Children's furniture, clothes, knickknacks.
- *Presidio Heights* — **Kindersport**: 3566 Sacramento Street (tel: 563-7778). Junior ski and sports outfitters. Good selection.
- *Presidio Heights* — **Dottie Dolittle**: 3680 Sacramento Street (tel: 563-3244). Upscale, classic children's clothing for play or dress from infants to girls size 14.

## ... And Their Toys

The internationally known **Toys 'R' Us** has several locations in the city and suburbs, and **F.A.O. Schwarz** at 48 Stockton Street is an outpost of the elegant New York shop (tel: 394-8700). Local toy shops, however, are often learning-centered:

- *Laurel Village* — **Hearth Song**: 3505 California Street (tel: 379-9900). Thousands of toys, dolls, games, books and gifts. Also in East Bay.
- *Noe Valley* — **The Ark**: 3845 24th Street (tel: 821-1257). Well-stocked neighborhood toy shop.
- *Downtown* — **Jeffrey's Toys**: 7 3rd Street (tel: 243-8697). Excellent selection in a well-established toy shop.
- *West Portal/Cow Hollow* — **Ambassador Toys**: 186 W. Portal Avenue (tel: 759-8697). Handcrafted toys, and dolls from around the world, plus a good selection of books and games. Also at 1981 Union (tel: 345-8697).
- *Laurel Village* — **Imaginarium**: 3535 California Street (tel: 387-9885). Educational, imaginative toys, "where bright futures begin."

## Sports Clothing and Gear

Most of the pro shops at sports clubs have clothing items and equipment, but these may be more expensive than the large chain stores or small shops dedicated to the sport you are interested in. Sporting tabloids carry ads for sporting goods, and the sports section of daily newspapers announce sales as well. For sporting gear, also try the **REI Coop** at 1338 San Pablo Avenue, in Berkeley (tel: 510/527-4140); and see the North Face, above.

- **Big 5**: Sporting equipment and clothing chain with several stores in the area; in San Francisco, at Lakeshore Plaza, 1533 Sloat Boulevard (tel: 681-4593).

- *Financial District* — **Don Sherwood Golf and Tennis World**: 320 Grant Avenue (tel: 989-5000). Long-established shop selling equipment, clothing, footwear. Also in Walnut Creek and San Jose.

- *Financial District* — **Tennis & Squash Shop of San Francisco**: 424 Clay Street (tel: 956-5666). A large selection of tennis and squash racquets and accessories. Stringing available.

- *Marina* — **MetroSport**: 2198 Filbert Street, at Fillmore (tel: 923-6453). Dedicated to the runner, selling footware, apparel and accessories. Also in Palo Alto and Cupertino.

- *Russian Hill* — **Lombardi Sports**: 1600 Jackson Street, at Polk (tel: 771-0600). Huge sporting goods shop selling equipment and clothes at good prices.

- *SOMA* — **Soma Sports**: 689 3rd Street, at Townsend (tel: 777-2165). Everything for the skier, and other sports as well.

- *Union Square* — **Copeland's Sports**: 901 Market Street (tel: 495-0928; golf tel: 512-7272). Large store with sporting equipment, athletic shoes, active wear, and a large golf selection. Good prices. Also at Stonestown Galleria (tel: 566-5521; golf tel: 566-5544).

- *Union Square* — **McCaffery's Golf Shop**: 80 Sutter Street, at Montgomery (tel: 989-4653). Golf equipment at good prices.

275

# SETTING UP HOUSE

Kitchens and bathrooms in rental houses and apartments come fully equipped with appliances and cupboards, but you may need some smaller appliances, lamps, carpets, or housewares. Three suburban department stores offer reasonable prices on high-quality appliances and are only a short drive from the city center.

- **Sears**: Tanforan Mall, San Bruno (info tel: 650/553-8800)
- **JC Penney**: Westlake Shopping Center, Westlake (info tel: 650/756-3000)

Shops below also offer good prices and an extensive selection. Look, too, for some of the major chains such as **Home Depot**, which is at 2 Colma Boulevard, in Colma (tel: 650/755-9600), or at Costco, described in Chapter Thirteen, which also has kitchen appliances and houseware.

- *Bayshore*—**Goodman Lumber**: 445 Bayshore, between Alemany and Cesar Chavez (tel: 285-2800). Enormous store selling appliances, garden furniture, fixtures, hardware, tools, and housewares. Good prices.
- *Bayshore*—**Peer Light**: 301 Toland Street, near Cesar Chavez (tel: 543-8883). Electrical and lighting supplies, chandeliers, wall lamps, some table lamps. Good prices. Closed Sunday.
- *Civic Center*—**Circuit City**: 1200 Van Ness (tel: 441-1300). Home appliances, televisions, computers and printers, videos, music systems.
- *Mission*—**A&M Carpets**: 98 12th Street, at South Van Ness (tel: 863-1410). Wide variety of carpets on rolls, reproductions of Oriental rugs, discontinued smaller rugs, berbers, all at good prices. Closed Sunday.
- *Mission*—**Cherin's**: 727 Valencia Street (tel: 864-2111). Long-established shop selling kitchen equipment, washers and dryers, built-in appliances. Low prices. Closed Sunday.
- *Richmond*—**Lamps Plus**: 4700 Geary Boulevard (tel: 386-0933).

A vast assortment of lamps and electrical fixtures, at factory-direct prices. Other shops in Bay Area.

- *South of Market* — **House of Louie**: 1045 Bryant, at 9th Street (tel: 621-7100). Excellent prices on all kinds of home appliances, from kitchen and bathroom equipment to televisions, mattresses, and some furniture.

- *South of Market* — **City Lights**: 1585 Folsom, at 12th Street (tel: 863-2020). An extensive selection of lighting fixtures, lamps, bulbs, ceiling fans. Closed Sunday.

- *Sunset* — **ABC Appliances**: 2048 Taraval, at 31st Avenue (tel: 564-8166). Good prices on large appliances, kitchen and bathroom equipment. Open Sunday 10:00 am–2:00 pm.

For kitchen items, try Macy's, hardware stores such as **Cole Hardware** at any of its three locations, or a houseware specialty shop. The **Williams-Sonoma** chain sells expensive, elegant kitchen and diningware, gadgets, and cookbooks; the downtown shop is at 150 Post Street (tel: 362-6904), and there are several others in the city and suburbs. **Crate and Barrel**, the inexpensive homeware chain, also has addresses throughout the area; the San Francisco shop is at 125 Grant Avenue (tel: 986-4000).

- *Bayshore* — **Heritage House**: 2190 Palou Avenue (tel: 285-1331). Brand names on china, glasses, flatware. Good prices. Bridal registry. Closed Sunday.

- *Castro* — **Cliff's Variety**: 479 Castro, near 18th Street (tel: 431-5365). Housewares, hardware, gadgets, knickknacks in a large, friendly store.

- *Chinatown* — **Ginn Wall Hardware**: 1016 Grant Avenue (tel: 982-6307). Large shop selling hardware, plus woks, steam baskets, kitchen implements and everything else you'd want for Chinese cooking.

- *Cow Hollow* — **Fredericksen's Hardware**: 3029 Fillmore Street, near Union (tel: 292-2950). Much more than a hardware store,

Fredericksen's well-stocked shelves hold a good selection of kitchen implements and housewares.

- *Fisherman's Wharf* — **Cost Plus Imports**: 2552 Taylor Street (tel: 928-6200). Inexpensive, colorful housewares, some furniture, baskets of all shapes and sizes, and a packaged gourmet food and wine section.

- *Presidio Heights* — **Forrest Jones**: 3274 Sacramento Street, near Presidio (tel: 567-2483). Packed floor to ceiling with lamps, housewares, gadgets, baskets — wonderful to browse through.

- *South of Market* — **Bed, Bath and Beyond**: 555 9th Street (tel: 252-0490). Brand-names of bed and bath, kitchen equipment, housewares. Also in Oakland.

- *Union Square* — **Sur La Table**: 77 Maiden Lane (tel: 732-7900). Interesting kitchen implements you might not find elsewhere — for people who take cooking seriously. Cookbooks, dishware. Closed Sunday.

## Furniture

Furniture stores run the gamut from tiny expensive boutiques to large showrooms in nearby suburbs, to discount clearance centers. Some of the smallest shops are the most interesting, and these often advertise in the Sunday *Examiner Magazine*. Several shops with eclectic collections are focused just below Potrero Hill. National furniture chains have showrooms outside the city center: **Levitz** is off Highway 101 in south San Francisco, **Ethan Allen** is off Highway 101, at the Tiburon exit, and **Breuners** and **Thomasville** have several outlets. **Scandinavian Designs** has outlets in the East, North and South Bay. Check also the three suburban department stores listed above. Within the city, Macy's has an extensive furniture showroom. Look also in the Yellow Pages.

- **Copenhagen**: 1835 Van Ness Avenue (tel: 775-4000). This "house of Danish furniture" has several levels of contemporary furnishings for the home and office.

- **Noriega Furniture**: 1455 Taraval, at 25th Avenue (tel: 564-4110). Upscale furniture outlet with downscale prices. Excellent designer pieces, lamps, wall decorations. What they don't have can be ordered. Open until 9:00 pm Thursday; closed Sunday.
- **Tiempo Interiors**: 383 Rhode Island, at 17th Street (tel: 626-3888). Interesting modern furniture and lighting. Also in San Rafael.

If you are confident of your ability to detect imperfections, or if you are willing to take a color someone else ordered and then returned, or a discontinued style, try a clearance center.

- **Sears Outlet Store**: 1936 West Avenue 140th, San Leandro (tel: 510/895-0546). Major appliances and furniture. One of a kind, out of carton, discontinued, used, scratched and dented merchandise.
- **Macy's Furniture Clearance Center**: 1208 Whipple Road, Union City, about 1 mile east of Highway 880 (tel: 510/441-8833). Enormous depot for canceled orders, floor samples, returned, damaged or slightly soiled merchandise, surplus inventory, etc. Call for days and times.
- **Busvan**: 900 Battery Street (tel: 981-1405). Funky but agreeable shop of basic, bargain furniture, new and used. Look hard and you'll find bargains. Also at 244 Clement, near 4th Avenue (tel: 752-5353).
- **Furniture Express Outlet**: 667 Folsom Street (tel: 495-2848). Scandinavian and contemporary furniture, some unpainted wooden items. Good prices.

## Furniture Rental
If you are staying short-term or renting temporarily, you might try renting furniture. Both companies below offer high-quality, attractive furniture and appliances.

- **Cort Furniture Rental**: 447 Battery Street (tel: 982-1077).

Other locations, plus some furniture clearance centers in the suburbs.

- **Brook Furniture Rental**: 500 Washington Street, at Sansome (tel: 956-6008; fax: 956-9390)

### House Plants

Flower stands dot the street corners of the city in every season of the year, and flowers and plants can be had at supermarkets and even some hardware stores. Large garden stores can be found in towns throughout the Bay Area. Also take a look at the bustling Flower Market at Sixth and Brannan Streets: some of the wholesalers sell their plants and flowers to retail customers, plus accessories and holiday decorations. The Flower Market is open weekdays from 2:00 am to 2:00 pm.

- **Plant Warehouse**: 1461 Pine Street, near Polk (tel: 885-1515). Good for house plants. Also at 3237 Pierce Street (tel: 345-1597).
- **Red Desert**: 1632 Market Street (tel: 552-2800). Cactus and succulents.
- **Plant'It Earth**: 2215 Market Street, at Sanchez (tel: 626-5082). House plants, orchids, grow light systems, organic soils and foods.
- **Sloat Garden Center**: 2700 Sloat Street (tel: 566-4415). Indoor and outdoor plants, soil, tools, etc.

## FILLING YOUR BOOKCASE

Major chains—**Borders, B. Dalton, Walden Books**—offer books at excellent prices, sometimes at a discount with a membership card. But do not neglect the independent bookshops, each with its own character and approach, and all struggling to survive in a market increasingly infiltrated by the chains. Many shops have authors' events. Used book shops—**Green Apple, Acorn**, and **Carroll's**—offer bargains and some great finds.

The annual **San Francisco Book Festival** is held each fall at Fort Mason. The San Francisco Public Library maintains a full schedule of literary events: readings, slide presentations, exhibits, etc. In addition, The Friends of the San Francisco Public Library sponsor a season of prestigious literary events and readings each year; inquire at the library.

North of the city in Corte Madera, **Book Passage** at 51 Tamal Vista Boulevard (tel: 927-0960) is a well-known shop with an extensive travel collection, a cafe, and a regular schedule of author appearances. In Berkeley, **Cody's Books**, at 2454 Telegraph Avenue, is the place to find everything and everybody (tel: 510/ 845-7852). And south in Menlo Park, try the wonderful **Kepler's Books and Magazines** at 1010 El Camino Real (tel: 650/324-4321).

- *Castro* — **A Different Light Bookstore**: 489 Castro Street (tel: 431-0891). Center for gay and lesbian books, periodicals.
- *Civic Center* — **McDonald's Bookshop**: 48 Turk Street, at Market (tel: 673-2235). Since 1926, this large shop has been selling used books and periodicals — in all categories and languages. Closed Sunday.
- *Civic Center* — **A Clean Well Lighted Place for Books**: 601 Van Ness Avenue (tel: 441-6670). Extensive collection. Readings and authors' events.
- *Downtown* — **Alexander Book Co**: 50 2nd Street (tel: 495-2992). Excellent collection, plus an informative newsletter. Readings at lunchtime. Closed Sunday.
- *Downtown* — **Stacey's**: 581 Market Street (tel: 421-4687). Popular, well-stocked, multi-level bookshop.
- *Japantown* — **Marcus Book Store**: 1712 Fillmore Street (tel: 346-4222). Books, greeting cards, games, and posters of interest to the African American community. Also in Oakland.
- *Hayes Valley* — **Get Lost Travel Books**: 1825 Market Street (tel: 437-0529). Travel books, maps, and travel gear.

- *Mission* — **Modern Times**: 888 Valencia, at 20th Street (tel: 282-9246). Left-wing periodicals, general interest books, books for gays and lesbians, multicultural books for children, and some books in Spanish.
- *North Beach* — **City Lights**: 261 Columbus Avenue, at Broadway (tel: 362-8193). Owned by Lawrence Ferlinghetti, poet laureate of San Francisco. Open until midnight.

## Foreign Language Bookstores

- *Chinese* — **Eastwind Books & Arts**: 1435 Stockton Street (tel: 772-5888). Extensive selection of Chinese-language books for adults and children. English-language section upstairs.
- *Chinese* — **China Books and Periodicals**: 2929 24th Street, between Alabama and Florida (tel: 282-2994). Chinese and American books about all facets of China.
- *Chinese* — **New China Books**: 642 Pacific Avenue (tel: 956-0752). General store and Chinese cultural center, with current periodicals, books, videos, and compact discs.
- *European* — **European Book Company**: 925 Larkin Street, near Geary (tel: 474-0626). French, German and Spanish books. Current foreign newspapers and magazines. Closed Sunday.
- *European* — **Café de la Presse**: 352 Grant Avenue at Bush (tel: 398-2680). French, Italian, and German newspapers, periodicals and books, and a cafe that is good for a leisurely cup of coffee.
- *Italian* — **A. Cavalli Italian Bookstore**: 1441 Stockton Street (tel: 421-4219). Italian books, periodicals, a few housewares and knickknacks, guidebooks to Italy, etc. Closed Sunday.
- *Japanese* — **Kinokuniya Bookstore**: 1581 Webster Street, in the Japan Center (tel: 567-7625). Major selection of books and current periodicals in Japanese, some in English.
- *Korean* — **Korean Book Center**: 5633 Geary Boulevard, near 20th Avenue (tel: 221-4250). Books in Korean, newspapers and magazines, cassettes, CDS, and gifts. Closed Sunday.

- *Spanish* — **Iaconi Books**: 970 Tennessee Street (tel: 821-1216). Excellent selection for children, young adults, and adults. Open weekdays.

## Computers

Computers shops are everywhere. General electronics shops such as the **Good Guys** and **Circuit City** stock computers, as do the large office supply chains — **Office Depot**, **Office Max**, and **Staples**. The nationwide chains have excellent prices on both Apple and IBM-compatible products. Although local shops may have a smaller inventory, they can often order what you want and in general offer more personal service. See the Yellow Pages under *Computer Dealers* for addresses. For up-to-date information on technology and advertisements for computers and accessories, look for the free tabloids *Computer Currents* or *Micro Times*, both of which can be found in news boxes on city streets.

- **CompUSA**: 760 Market Street (tels: 800/266-7872, 391-9778). Large selection of hardware and software. Also at Tanforan Shopping Center in San Bruno.
- **ComputerWare**: 343 Sansome Street (tel: 362-3010). A dedicated Mac resource, selling hardware, software, peripherals and accessories.

# Chapter Seventeen

# THE ENTERTAINMENT SCENE

## THE CITY THAT KNOWS HOW

From world-class opera, ballet, and symphony, to live theater, to American and international films, to rock concerts that draw thousands, to topless bars that draw mostly tourists, and to cabaret, dance and comedy clubs, San Francisco has something for everyone. Restaurants offer jazz, jazz clubs serve food, art galleries and museums serve wine and canapés at their exhibit openings, bookstores host readings by famous authors, and in general, you can find something interesting to do just about any time of day. In this city that celebrates its love of the outdoors, you'll also find lively neighborhood street fairs, outdoor concerts and theater, opera in the parks, and spectacular events on the Bay. And it seems as though there's always a parade or a race somewhere in the city on any given Sunday.

Each district has its own entertainment approach, and this reflects the mood of the area. North Beach, for instance, is known for its coffeehouses and topless bars, Nob Hill for its plush piano bars, and SOMA for its offbeat nightspots and dance clubs. The Castro, of course, is known for its gay hangouts, although gay-friendly bars can be found throughout the city. And the Mission, while remaining distinctly Latino, is beginning to reflect its new popularity with the cyberspace set.

Think also of options in nearby cities, for they are usually less than a half-hour away and often reachable by BART. The **Oakland Ballet**, for example, and the **Berkeley Symphony** both draw major performers on the classical music scene. **Ashkenaz** in Berkeley features Caribbean music, and in Oakland, **Yoshi's** currently performs the best jazz in the area (and offers good sushi as well). The popular **Pacific Film Archives**, also in Berkeley, screens everything from classics to cult favorites.

For outdoor events, pay attention to the weather of the particular area. Sunday afternoon concerts at Stern Grove, for example, may be foggy and windy, even as eastern portions of the city may bask in the sun. Be prepared to bring a jacket to any outdoor event, plus groundsheets for the damp grass.

San Francisco is an "early city," as people who work in the Financial District go to work before dawn. Most people eat dinner before their evening's entertainment, and afterwards head for home. Some clubs remain open after 2:00 am, not serving alcohol, and although the younger set might head to **The Endup** or to 24-hour **Sparky's** for a hamburger, most San Franciscans just go home.

## INFINITE RESOURCES

The daily newspapers list that day's (and upcoming) events in their Arts/Datebook sections. On Friday, along with weekend listings, most of the reviews of films and other works that are opening appear; opera and concert reviews generally appear a day or two after the opening. On Sunday, when the San Francisco newspapers issue one combined paper, the *Pink Section* lists the events for the week to come. The free weekly tabloids, *The Bay Guardian* (www.sfbg.com) and *SF Weekly* (www.sfweekly.com), announce all the major events as well, and also more of the small offbeat and eclectic happenings. Advertisements for events project well into the future, sometimes several months. The publications below list and review events.

- *San Francisco*: monthly magazine listing events, public TV, and radio schedules
- *San Francisco Arts Monthly*: extensive calendar of arts and cultural events each month
- *East Bay Express*: an extensive free weekly tabloid covering events in the East Bay
- *Icon*: lesbian monthly, publishing articles and reviews, and listing some events
- *Pacific Sun:* covering events in Marin County
- *Poetry Flash*: a Berkeley publication, lists current literary events
- *Bay Area Reporter*: gay newspaper, listing and reviewing current events
- *San Francisco Bay Times*: gay and lesbian newspaper that lists and reviews events

You can also search on the Internet; as of this writing, these were the most popular sites:

- www.citysearch7.com
- www.sfstation.com
- www.digitalcity.com/sanfrancisco
- www.bayinsider.com
- www.sfgate.com

# GETTING TICKETS

Tickets to the most popular events—classical concerts, theater, rock concerts, and sporting events—are snapped up quickly, so, although it's cheaper to buy them at the box office, it is often best to order them through a ticket agency, despite the service charge. Order well in advance. Phone orders are accepted with a credit card number, and tickets can be delivered, mailed, or held at "will-call" at the box office. You may also order tickets on the Internet, from **www.tickets.com**.

- **BASS Tickets**: Tickets for concerts, theater, sporting events, and just about anything else, throughout the Bay Area (tels: 478-2277, 776-1999, 510/762-2277). BASS has outlets at **Tower Records** at Bay and Columbus Streets and **Wherehouse Music** at 165 Kearny.
- **City Box Office**: 153 Kearny Street, at Sutter (tel: 392-4400). Open weekdays and Saturday until 4:00 pm.
- **Tix Bay Area**: A small booth nestled on the sidewalk on the east side of Union Square, along Stockton Street (tel: 433-7827). Half-price tickets for day-of-performance theater and musical events. Cash only. Open 11:00 am–6:00pm Tuesday–Thursday, until 7:00 pm weekends. Closed Sunday and Monday.
- **Mr. Ticket**: 2065 Van Ness Avenue (tel: 292-7238). Tickets for sports, concerts, theater, and all arena events.
- **Ticketmaster**: Phone orders for all tickets (tels: 421-8497, 421-2700).

In addition to Tix above, there are other opportunities for reduced-price or even free tickets. If you volunteer at a theater, for example, you can see the show for free. Students with valid identification can often get reduced-price tickets. Some smaller theaters also offer reduced-price tickets an hour before a performance starts, and a very few allow you to pay what you can at the door.

# MUSEUMS

To learn about the city's museums, consult a tourist guidebook, for such guides offer the most extensive information about the collections in each museum. Also stop by the **San Francisco Visitors' Center** (see Calendar below). Many museums host traveling exhibits, and these may require ticket purchase in advance. The newspapers list these special exhibitions. Most museums have one day a month when admission is free.

If you are interested in volunteering your expertise at one of the city's many museums, libraries, or cultural institutions, call the San Francisco Volunteer Center, or the Volunteer Centers of the Bay Area, both mentioned in Chapter Nine.

- **Business Art Council**: 235 Montgomery Street (tel: 352-8832). Coordinates volunteers to use their professional expertise in museums, theaters, and other arts-related non-profits.
- **Contemporary Extension**: 151 3rd Street (tel: 357-4086). Member-run organization for the young professional who wants to expand knowledge and take an active role in supporting the **Museum of Modern Art (MOMA)**.
- **Friends of the San Francisco Public Library** (tel: 557-4256). Friends volunteer at the library, help operate the several bookshops, and support the library in other ways.

To get the most out of cultural activities, you might attend "preview" seminars and lectures focusing on upcoming performances and exhibits. Universities offer courses on the season's opera selections, and these are often listed in the opera program. In addition, the **Junior League of San Francisco** sponsors each year a series of free preview lectures concerning that evening's performance either at ACT (American Conservatory Theater) or the San Francisco Ballet. Lectures are given by the play's director or by people connected with the ballet. Call for a schedule (tel: 775-4100).

# THEATER

As you would imagine, San Francisco's theater scene is wildly diverse, from Shakespeare in the Park to experimental efforts in tiny, offbeat venues, and to Broadway musicals that stay around for years. Some theaters offer readings of new works, which of course vary in style and quality. Look for *Callboard*, which is available at Tix and sometimes in bookstores.

Generally, live theater is performed Tuesday–Sunday, and Mondays are "dark." On Sundays, there are matinees at the important theaters, except at "Berkeley Rep," described below. Some touring companies come through with short runs, and their schedules may be different. Note that most theaters use volunteers in some capacity or other, often as ushers. If this interests you, call the theaters directly for information.

- **ACT (American Conservatory Theater)**, at 415 Geary Street, is the city's major local theater company (tel: 749-2228). Pronounced "ay-cee-tee," not "act", ACT offers both classics and new works, and features visiting artists along with the local cast. Generally the annual repertory performs eight plays, from fall through spring. Subscriptions and single performance tickets are available.
- **Berkeley Repertory Theatre**, at 2025 Addison Street, near the Berkeley BART station, is the East Bay's premier theater company, and many San Franciscans subscribe as well as to ACT (tel: 510/845-4700). "Berkeley Rep" performs both classic and contemporary works. The season is fall to spring, with special summer performances.

Three theaters — **The Curran, Golden Gate**, and **The Orpheum** — are known for "best of Broadway" plays and musicals that have either played in New York or are heading there. They also host some local performances. Tickets may be had from the joint ticket office (info tel: 551-2000; telephone orders tel: 512-7770) or from BASS. **Marines Memorial Theater** also hosts

Broadway musicals and some local productions (tel: 771-6900).

**Fort Mason**, the former military installation turned cultural center, with its three theaters, presents innovative drama, new music, unconventional plays, children's entertainment, imaginative dance, and more. Look for performances at the **Bayfront Theater** (tel: 392-4400), the **Cowell Theater** (tel: 441-3400), and the **Magic Theater** (tel: 441-8822). The **Young Performer Theater** highlights aspiring actors (tel: 346-5550).

**Beach Blanket Babylon**, at 678 Beach Blanket Babylon Boulevard (Green Street), is a rather zany musical spoof of pop culture (and local celebrities) which has been running for 25 years, changing its content to fit the times (tel: 421-4222). There are also a few theater festivals; check newspapers for dates.

- June — **In the Street Festival**: Street festival in the Tenderloin celebrates street theater and performance art.
- September — **California Shakespeare Festival**: Golden Gate Park and other venues around the Bay Area. Bring a sweater.
- September — **Fringe Festival**: Ten days of just about anything you can imagine, with local and visiting performers and companies. In various venues around the city.
- September–October — **Solo Mio Festival**: Held at theaters at Fort Mason, this festival features one-person shows.
- July–September — **Mime Troupe in the Park**: First show held at Dolores Park and other city parks.

# CLASSICAL MUSIC

**The San Francisco Symphony** holds its concerts at Louise M. Davies Symphony Hall, at Van Ness Avenue, at Grove (ticket office tel: 864-6000; ticket fax: 554-0108). The regular season runs from September to June, with special events year-round. Long-time subscribers retain the best seats from year to year, but as the building dates only from 1982 (upgraded in 1992), the acoustics throughout the hall are very good. Occasionally tickets become available at the last minute, and some inexpensive Center Terrace seats (to the rear of the stage) are sold two hours before performances. The Symphony issues an annual schedule that details all ticket options, including dates for the open rehearsals, which take place on Wednesday mornings, about once a month; tickets cost $15 and there is no reserved seating. If you are interested in the symphony, consider joining the groups below:

- **San Francisco Symphony Volunteer Council**: Davies Symphony Hall (tel: 552-8000). Volunteer behind the scenes at the gift shop, in the office, with the Concerts for Kids Program, and more. **Symphonix** is the young professionals group. It offers meetings, musical programs, social events, discounts on dinner and concerts.

**San Francisco Opera** draws international stars for its lavish productions, which are staged at the War Memorial Opera House: 301 Van Ness Avenue (tel: 864-3330). The season usually begins in mid-September. Subscribers renew their seats from year to year, but single tickets can be had, and occasionally people stand outside at performance time trying to sell single tickets for that evening's performance or others in the future. Tickets can cost up to $145 for a box seat, yet cheaper alternatives exist and standing room is available. The box office is at 199 Grove Street. If you are interested in becoming involved in the opera, consider joining these groups:

- **San Francisco Opera Guild Volunteer Program**: 301 Van Ness Avenue (tel: 565-6433). Volunteer throughout the opera world: in the gift shop, administrative offices, costume shop, or in other ways behind the scenes. **Bravo!** is a young professionals' group that participates in a variety of events related to the opera: receptions, benefits, etc (tel: 565-3285).

**San Francisco Ballet**, the oldest ballet company in America, performs new works and classical ballet. Its regular season takes place at the Opera House, after the opera season closes, generally from February until June (tel: 865-2000). Special events include the ballet's annual performances of Tchaikovsky's *Nutcracker Suite* at Christmas. Subscriptions may be customized to only the performances you choose. Although tickets go quickly, sometimes there are single tickets available, and students with identification may buy discounted tickets on the afternoon of the performance.

- **Encore!** 455 Franklin Street (tel: 553-4634). Young professionals attend social and educational events, get discounted tickets to the ballet, etc.

San Francisco is also known for its locally based dance troupes. Look for performances of the **ODC Theater** and the **Margaret Jenkins Dance Company**, which performs at Yerba Buena and tours worldwide. **Smuin Ballets** performs at Fort Mason's Cowell Theater.

## And More …

Performing groups have their own seasons and specialties. **San Francisco Performances**, a major presenter of chamber music, has a fall-spring schedule. **The Women's Philharmonic** and students of the **San Francisco Conservatory of Music** have regular concerts. Look also for performances of San Francisco's own **Kronos Quartet**, which for more than 25 years has performed 20th century music from Bela Bartok to Duke Ellington.

Gay men might also want to audition or volunteer for the **San Francisco Gay Men's Chorus**: 400 Castro Street (tel: 863-4472). The chorus presents three major concerts each year, plus outreach concerts for community groups. Auditions for singers are held twice yearly; inquire at the SFGMC office. Volunteers are always needed to keep track of wardrobe, ticket sales, production, etc.

- **Stern Grove Midsummer Music Festival**: 44 Page Street, Suite 600 (tel: 252-6252). Eleven free outdoor concerts in a lovely eucalyptus stand at Stern Grove, off 19th Avenue and Sloat. Popular with all San Franciscans—from the counter-culture to the highly cultured. Be prepared for fog. Offerings range from classical to blues, from ballet to jazz. For children there's a nice playground, and for golfers, a putting green.

- **Midsummer Mozart Festival** held in Davies Hall and in Berkeley, at the Congregational Church (tel: 954-0850)
- **Classical Philharmonic**: 1155 East 14th Street, Suite 215 (tel: 989-6873, 510/352-3945, 925/484-9783). Varied repertoire for the chamber symphony performed December–May in San Francisco, Pleasanton, and Castro Valley.
- **Sunday Concerts in the Park**: Band shell in front of the California Academy of Sciences. Every Sunday in the summer, the Golden Gate Park Band gives a free concert at 1:00 pm. Great for a picnic.
- **Noontime Concerts**: International touring musicians play half-hour classical music programs on Tuesday and Thursday at 12:30 pm at Old Saint Mary's Cathedral at 600 California Street, and Wednesday at 12:30 pm at St. Patrick's Church, at 756 Mission.
- **Old First Concerts** are held year-round on Friday evenings and Sunday afternoons at the Old First Church, at 1751 Sacramento Street (tel: 864-3330). From jazz and world music to chamber and choral, this series is inexpensive and extremely popular.

# DINNER WITH MUSIC

Dozens of restaurants play live music, and conversely dozens of live music venues serve good food. Newspapers usually have advertisements not only for supper clubs, but for popular brunch restaurants—**Pier 23** or **Scott's Embarcadero**, for example—that also have live music. Don't forget the East Bay, where **Yoshi's** serves the hottest jazz and coolest sushi. A few other suggestions:

293

- **Biscuits and Blues**: 401 Mason Street, at Geary (tel: 292-2583). Blues club serving Southern food — biscuits, shrimp, catfish, chicken, and corn fritters — and live music every night. Closed Monday and Tuesday.
- **Bix**: 56 Gold Street, between Sansome and Montgomery (tel: 433-6300). Excellent menu, cool piano and jazz.
- **Black Cat**: 501 Broadway, at Kearny (tel: 981-2233). Lunch, dinner and jazz until 2:00 nightly.
- **Bruno's**: 2389 Mission Street (tel: 648-7701). Old Italian restaurant reborn by adding live music and a dance floor. Closed Sunday.
- **Café Claude**: 7 Claude Lane, off Bush at Kearny (tel: 392-3505). French food in a casual atmosphere. Live jazz evenings except Wednesday and Sunday.
- **Enrico's**: 504 Broadway (tel: 982-6223). Sidewalk cafe in North Beach serving good food and live jazz.
- **Piaf's**: 1686 Market Street (tel: 864-3700). French cuisine and a lively cabaret performance.

## ROCK CONCERTS

When touring rock groups and performers come to the area, they perform at large concert halls and arenas. Events are publicized well in advance and tickets sell quickly, so check ticket agencies as soon as you see the ad for a concert that appeals to you. On the Internet, try www.sfbayconcerts.com or the **Be-At-Line** after 2:00 pm for up-to-the-minute information (tel: 626-4087).

- **The Fillmore**: 1805 Geary Boulevard
- **Bill Graham Civic Auditorium**: 99 Grove Street
- **The Warfield**: 982 Market Street
- **Great American Music Hall**: 859 O'Farrell Street

Most concert sites around the Bay Area are accessible by public transportation, and most have extensive parking facilities.

- **Concord Pavillion**: 200 Kirker Pass Road, Concord
- **Oakland Coliseum**: Hegenberger Road and I-880, Oakland
- **Cow Palace**: Geneva Avenue and Santos Street, Daly City
- **Shoreline Amphitheater**: 1 Amphitheater Parkway, Mountain View
- **Zellerbach Hall**: University of California, Berkeley
- **Greek Theater**: Outdoors at the University of California, Berkeley

To hear music at the clubs in the city, check the listings above or *SF Weekly* or the *Bay Guardian*, both of which publish lists of venues. Many of the best rock clubs — **Slim's**, **Maritime Hall**, **Bottom of the Hill**, **Chameleon**, and **Paradise Lounge** — are South of Market. **Bimbo's**, which presents live jazz and blues, is in North Beach, on Columbus. Most of the clubs charge admission, ranging from $3 to $40, and a few require the purchase of two drinks. Not all take credit cards.

# BLUES

The weekend-long **San Francisco Blues Festival** takes place late in September on the Great Meadow at Fort Mason. In addition to Biscuit and Blues and Pier 23 mentioned above, blues clubs such as **Blues Stop** and **Boom Boom Room** are extremely popular.

# JAZZ

Jazz can be found just about anywhere, at any time, especially South of Market or in the Mission. Elsewhere, check the clubs such as **Bimbo's**, **Elbo Room**, **Storyville**, **Hotel Utah**, and **El Rio**, mentioned below. **Rasselas**, near staid Pacific Heights, swings until 1:30 am. Don't neglect jazz in the East Bay, however — **Yoshi's**, mentioned above, and **Kimball's East**, in Emeryville. In addition, jazz festivals play an important part of the musical year.

- July — **San Francisco Summer Jazz Festival**: Free noontime concerts

- July — **Fillmore Street Fair**: Jazz and All that Art on Fillmore
- Mid-September — **San Francisco Jazz Festival**: Two weeks of jazz, in venues around the city

# DANCE

From salsa to swing, you can find dance opportunities in dozens of venues around the city, whether live to a band, with a disc jockey, or in places where there's just a jukebox and an empty space in front of it. When you check out dance clubs, find out hours of opening and cover charges.

- **1015 Folsom** (recorded information tel: 431-1200). Three rooms of loud danceable music, often voted the best dance spot in the city.
- **Broadway Studios**: 435 Broadway (tel: 291-0333). Dance or take dance lessons. Three bars, large wooden ballroom-style dance floors.
- **Café du Nord**: 2170 Market Street (tel: 296-8696). Old speakeasy now offering salsa, swing, cabaret, and theme nights.
- **DNA Lounge**: 374 11th Street (tel: 626-1409). Trendy locale, cutting-edge live music, DJ spinners on Fridays.
- **Metronome Ballroom**: 1830 17th Street (tel: 252-9000). Dance lessons and general dancing in a real ballroom below Potrero Hill.
- **Roccapulco**: 3140 Mission Street, near Cesar Chavez (tel: 648-6611). Salsa is the beat in this two-story club, performed by visiting international groups.
- **Six**: 60 6th Street (tel: 863-1221). Not a great neighborhood, but a great dance venue. Two levels, a comfortable lounge, and always interesting music.
- **Sound Factory**: 525 Harrison, at 1st Street (tel: 339-8686). In a warehouse-type space, a variety of music type and a party atmosphere.

# FILMS

Films play a major part in the entertainment life of San Franciscans: first-run American movies, major foreign films, independent art films, and revivals of some of those that have been overlooked or almost forgotten. Almost all the newly released films can be found in different venues at different times, making it convenient to see one where and when you want. At the most popular films, however, lines can be long, so be prepared to go early and to wait. Often there are two lines: the "ticket holders" line for people who have already bought their tickets, and the line for those waiting to purchase them.

Most of the major movie theaters are multi-screen. The largest (so far) is the **Sony Metreon** at Yerba Buena Gardens, with 15 screens, a giant IMAX screen, eight restaurants, theme and game areas, and retail stores. **AMC Van Ness** has 10 screens; the **AMC Kabuki-8** has eight. Even some of the oldest cinemas have split their space to allow two screens. In a very few—**Opera Plaza** and the **Lumiere**—some of the screening rooms (and screens) are quite small, so there, too, if you think a film will be crowded, go early to get a seat.

New films open on Friday. Film schedules are printed in every daily newspaper, and on Friday there are film reviews. The *San Francisco Chronicle* prints pictures of a little man in a chair next to each review: if he's shown dozing, you might want to skip the picture, but if he's shown applauding wildly or jumping out of his chair, you can expect the film to be a success. San Franciscans often talk about movie reviews in terms of the "little man." The free weekly newspapers—*The Bay Guardian* and *SF Weekly*—also review films according to their newspapers' slants, as do the gay newspapers, *The Bay Area Reporter* and the *Bay Times*.

## Interesting and Unusual

Some cinemas are known for their particular mix. **The Castro** hosts revivals and many of the film festivals during the year.

297

The extensive Landmark chain—**Bridge, Clay, Embarcadero, Lumiere**, and **Opera Plaza**—shows the best of the foreign films, as well as first-run American movies. (At Opera Plaza, you can often find films that were at other theaters for a while; catch them here before they disappear altogether.) And some small "cult" moviehouses—**Roxie** and **Red Vic**—show unusual foreign films, "art" films, and other independent films that might not be commercial enough to hit the bigger houses.

Films are also sometimes screened at museums such as the **Museum of Modern Art** or at the **Yerba Buena Gardens Center for the Arts**, generally in conjunction with a current exhibit. Yerba Buena also shows the avant-garde and experimental films of the **San Francisco Cinematheque** on Thursday nights; on Sundays their films are shown at the **San Francisco Art Institute** on Chestnut Street.

## Foreign Films

Foreign films are shown with subtitles, not dubbed. In addition to the cinemas (including the World Theater on Broadway, which shows films in English and Chinese), check the foreign language institutes, which schedule regular showings of films, which may or may not have subtitles: **Goethe Institute, Alliance Française,** and the **Istituto Italiano di Cultura.** A new phenomenon, **Foreign Cinema** at 2534 Mission, near 21st Street, is a French bistro that shows foreign movie classics on a large white wall overlooking the dining area (tel: 648-7600). Reserve in advance; closed Monday.

## Prices and Bargains

Most theaters offer a "bargain matinee" for the first performance of the day. The Landmark chain offers a multi-ticket discount coupon, and AMC theaters have a card that offers a free film after 20 visits. A regular seat currently costs $7–8 for adults. Seniors are allowed discounts at any showing. AMC theaters consider people 55 and over to be seniors, but at other theaters people are considered seniors at either 62 or 65.

You can buy tickets in advance for major shows. AMC theaters have a ticket machine in the lobbies. Otherwise, you can either go to the box office and purchase your ticket for a screening later that day or you can call **Movie Phone** and order tickets to films and festivals by credit card (tel: 777-3456). There is a $1 surcharge on each ticket.

## Film Festivals

Almost every month there are film festivals, some lasting one week and others two weeks. Some draw the entire city to major movie houses, some are revivals shown in smaller venues. Look for festivals that celebrate local film and video makers, of which there are many. Films to be shown have their dates and venues announced well in advance, and often they are screened in more than one theater around the Bay Area. Film festivals are eagerly awaited, so buy your tickets well in advance.

Outside the city, the October **Mill Valley Film Festival** shows dozens of independent and international films, in addition to hosting a "videofest" of interactive media programs. Other well-regarded festivals in the area are the **Bay Area Women's Film Festival** in Berkeley in March and the **Black Filmworks Festival** in Oakland in September.

- Mid-March — **Asian-American Film Festival**, at the Kabuki and Castro theaters
- Mid-April — **San Francisco International Film Festival**: Two weeks of films, held mainly at the Kabuki, and also at other venues
- Sometime in April — **Italian Film Festival**: Various venues around the city
- Late in June — **International Lesbian and Gay Film Festival**, coinciding with Gay Pride celebration. Generally at the Castro, Victoria and Roxie theaters.

- Sometime in July—**San Francisco Jewish Film Festival**: International films with a Jewish theme, generally at the Castro, in Berkeley, and in Mill Valley.
- Sometime in September—**Festival Cine Latino**, usually held at the Victoria and at Yerba Buena Gardens.
- Mid-November—**American Indian Film Festival**, held at the Palace of Fine Arts Theater.
- Sometime in November—The **Film Arts Festival of Independent Cinema** shows works from Bay Area filmmakers. At several venues, including the Castro and the Roxie, plus the Main Library and Asian Art Museum.

## COMEDY CLUBS

In addition to the several comedy clubs, each August San Francisco hosts a **Comedy Celebration Day**, which takes place in Sharon Meadow of Golden Gate Park.

- **Cobb's Comedy Club**: 2801 Leavenworth Street, in the Cannery (tel: 928-4320)
- **The Punch Line**: 444 Battery Street, at Washington (tel: 397-7573)

## GAY AND LESBIAN RESOURCES

For a comprehensive look at gay and lesbian San Francisco, visit A Different Light Bookshop or Modern Times (see Chapter Sixteen), or **Bernal Books,** the well-stocked general bookstore for the Bernal Heights community, at 401 Cortland Avenue (tel: 550-0293). Look for a gay/lesbian guidebook, such as *Fodor's Gay Guide to San Francisco and the Bay Area* by Andrew Collins. Some others, such as *Time Out: San Francisco*, have sections on gay- and lesbian-friendly venues.

To find out what's going on currently, refer to the daily newspapers and the well-known publications listed at the beginning of this chapter; look also for *Frontiers, Creampuff, Odyssey,* and *Q San*

*Francisco*, all of which have news, articles, ads, and information about events. In addition to the general websites also listed above, you can search gay-specific sites for information (www.webcastro. com; www.qsanfrancisco.com).

- **Pacific Center** acts as a resource for gay/lesbian information throughout the entire Bay Area (tel: 510/548-8283). Open 4–10 pm weekdays, and 11 am–5 pm Saturdays.
- **James C. Hormel Gay and Lesbian Center**, at the San Francisco Main Public Library (tel: 557-4566). Books, periodicals and articles of interest for the gay/lesbian life.
- **Women's Building**: 3543 18th Street (tel: 431-1180). Community center offering meeting space to several lesbian and feminist groups, plus hosting its own events, meetings and seminars for women. Free publications are generally found in the lobby.
- **Lesbian/Gay/Bisexual/Transgender Community Center**: 1800 Market Street. Not yet open as of this writing, the center is planned as the community's central information point.
- **Lesbian & Gay Historial Society of Northern California**: 973 Market Street (tel: 777-5455). Historical archives.
- **Eureka Valley-Harvey Milk Library**: 3555 16th Street (tel: 554-9445). This branch of the Public Library has a good collection of gay/lesbian materials, including the current local and national gay newspapers.

## For the Men ...

In terms of gay venues, there are hundreds of gyms, bars, shops, and restaurants that are either completely gay or gay-friendly. Although the Castro now seems to be permanently the heart of the community, the Polk Gulch area is becoming popular once again (**Tango Tango**, **The Giraffe**, and **1100 Polk Club**). In 1999, the *San Francisco Chronicle's* "Readers' Choice Poll" rated **The Cafe** at 2367 Market Street and the nearby **Café Flore** at 2298 Market as the city's best gay hangouts. The *Bay Guardian* rated **The Stud** at 399 9th Street as the best gay bar.

### For the Women …

Although two women together have always been accepted more readily than two men together, since the feminist movement of the seventies, lesbians have felt more at home in Berkeley and in Oakland. Currently, the lesbian presence in San Francisco is increasing, especially in the Inner Mission and Bernal Heights. In recent *Chronicle* and *Bay Guardian* surveys, **The Lexington Club** at 3464 19th Street, between Mission and Valencia, was rated as the "best lesbian hangout." **The Cafe** was rated second, and the **Wild Side West** at 424 Cortland Avenue, in Bernal Heights, was rated third. **El Rio**, at 3158 Mission Street, is popular for dancing to live music with a distinctly Latin rhythm; it sports a mixed clientele. The bookshops with lesbian sections and the gay/lesbian tabloids should have some information about what's currently hot; watch also for information on events, especially in the *Icon* and *Bay Times*; *Girlfriends* is issued monthly. You can also access www.qsanfrancisco.com.

# CALENDAR OF NATIONAL HOLIDAYS AND LOCAL EVENTS

An international city, San Francisco celebrates the festivals of many countries. Some festival dates may vary from year to year, depending on the calendar. As for local events, do not forget that San Franciscans love to party, and that tourists expect—and get—a lively scene. You can find a parade, race, or walk in honor of a charitable cause almost every weekend of the year. Look for each neighborhood's weekend street fair, for each one reflects the ambience of that district. It would be impossible to list them all here, but some of the major events are listed below, and the film and theater festivals above. Look also in the daily newspapers, the *Bay Guardian* and the *SF Weekly* for festivals and fairs in towns throughout the Bay Area, especially the county fairs in summer. And, you can get cultural event information from the Visitors' Information Center on the lower level of Hallidie Plaza, at Market Street and Powell, or if you have the patience to sit through a long recorded message, by phone (tel: 391-2000; 24-hour recorded info tel: 391-2001; www.sfvisitor.org).

Many national holidays are celebrated on Monday, no matter the actual date they commemorate, in order to give workers a long weekend break. On national holidays, all government offices are closed, including the Post Office, but except for Christmas and Easter, the largest stores and supermarkets may be open for at least part of the day. Banks are closed on national holidays but by law may not be closed more than three days in a row, and on any day cash can be had from the ubiquitous ATM machines. National holidays are printed in boldface type.

### January
- **1: New Year's Day**
- **Third Monday: Martin Luther King Jr Day**. In honor of the civil rights leader slain in 1968.
- Late month or early February: Tet Festival. Near the Civic Center. Multicultural event, with Asian, Latino and African American groups celebrating Vietnamese New Year.

### February
- **Third Monday: President's Day**
- Dates vary: Chinese New Year. A long parade, marching bands, dragons, and lots of firecrackers.
- San Francisco Ballet season begins.

### March
- Sunday closest to March 17: St. Patrick's Day Parade. All the Irish bars celebrate well into the night.
- Late month: Tulip Festival at the tourist attraction Pier 39.

### *April*

- Mid-month: Cherry Blossom Festival at the Japan Center. Parade, arts and crafts, tea ceremonies, performances, all held on two successive weekends.
- Baseball season begins: Opening games for San Francisco Giants and Oakland A's.

### *May*

- 5: Cinco de Mayo: Latin American festival and parade at the Civic Center and at 24th and Mission.
- Third Sunday: Bay to Breakers Race. A San Francisco "happening," drawing 100,000 runners, would-be runners, people in outrageous costumes, people in no costumes at all. A 12 km course from the Bay to the Ocean.
- Opening day on the Bay: Official sailing season begins, although people sail all year, weather permitting.
- Odd-numbered years only: Black and White Ball. The whole city comes to this charity benefit held in various venues. Wear only black or white, dance, and listen to the music.
- **Last Monday: Memorial Day**
- Memorial Day Weekend: Carnaval. Lively festival in the Mission district.

### *June*

- First weekend: Union Street Festival. Extremely upscale arts and crafts fair, plus entertainment, food, etc.
- Second weekend: Haight Street Fair. Typically Haight, but with excellent food stalls of all sorts.
- Fourth Sunday: Lesbian, Gay, Bisexual, Transgender Pride Celebration. Second largest annual event in the State (after the Rose Bowl Parade), with 200 floats, people strolling alone or as couples, celebration until all hours.
- Dates vary: San Francisco Ethnic Dance Festival. Dozens of ethnic dance troupes and soloists perform at the Palace of Fine Arts.

- All summer: Stern Grove Midsummer Music Festival. Free Sunday concerts in Stern Grove.
- June and July: Midsummer Mozart Festival, held at Davies Hall and in Berkeley.

## July
- **4: Independence Day**
- Midmonth: San Francisco Marathon. Twenty-six mile course from Golden Gate Park to the Civic Center.
- Dates vary: *Nihonmachi* Street Fair in Japantown. Entertainment, food, crafts.

## August
- Date varies: Football season begins. San Francisco 49ers opening game.

## September
- **First Monday: Labor Day**
- Labor Day Weekend: A La Carte, à la Park — Sharon Meadow, Golden Gate Park. Huge food fair, with offerings from some of San Francisco's popular restaurants. Tastings of California's best wines, as well.
- Latino Summer Fiesta: 24th Street and Mission; formerly celebrating Mexican Independence Day, it's now a general patriotic Latino festival. Crafts, booths, food, entertainment.
- Mid-month: San Francisco Jazz Festival.
- September–October: San Francisco Shakespeare Festival. Free Shakespeare plays outdoors at Liberty Tree Meadow in Golden Gate Park. Dress warmly.
- San Francisco Opera and Symphony season begins; also Opera in Golden Gate Park on the first Sunday of the season.
- Third weekend: San Francisco Blues Festival at the Great Meadow at Fort Mason.
- San Francisco Fair: Check date by calling 391-200.
- End of month: Folsom Street Fair. Certainly one of the city's

more colorful and eccentric neighborhood fairs. Can draw more than 100,000 people.

### October

- Early in month: Blessing of the Animals at St. Boniface Church, near the Civic Center. On the Feast Day of St. Francis of Assisi, the patron saint of animals, the annual pet-blessing event.
- Early in month: Immigrant Pride Day. Since 1995, a three-fold event celebrating Immigrant Pride Day, Dia de la Raza, and Indigenous People's Day, at 24th Street, from Mission Street to Bryant.
- First Sunday in October: Castro Street Fair. Gay and lesbian festival, drawing all of San Francisco.
- **Second Monday: Columbus Day**. Celebrates the Italian heritage in San Francisco. Parade on Columbus Avenue, festivities, a fair at Fisherman's Wharf, and a blessing of the fishing fleet. Usually the U.S. Navy comes to town for Fleet Week, and The Blue Angels, precision Navy flyers, take to the skies over San Francisco.
- Closest to full moon: Chinese Moon Festival, annual harvest event in Chinatown.
- Mid-month: Open Studios. Artists all over town open their studios to the public.
- Toward the end of the month. San Francisco Book Festival. San Francisco Bay Area Book Council sponsors a major independent bookseller event at Fort Mason. Books on display and some at bargain prices, book signings, readings, etc.
- 31: Halloween. Celebrated around the Civic Center, but also in the Castro, with outrageous costumes. This is one of the major events of the year.

### November

- 2: *Dia de los Muertos*: Mexican fiesta, exhibits, and lively parade to honor the dead. In the Mission.

- **11: Veterans Day**. Parade along Market Street to the Ferry Building.
- **Fourth Thursday: Thanksgiving Day**
- Late in month: Run to the Far Side. Walk or run, dressed in a costume depicting your favorite cartoon character from Gary Larson's *Far Side* cartoons. Benefit for the California Academy of Sciences.

### December

- Dates vary: Christmas Tree and Chanukah Menorah lighting in various venues around the city—Union Square, Ghirardelli Square, Fell and Stanyan Streets.
- Mid-month: Sing-it-yourself-Messiah, at Louise M. Davies Symphony Hall. The San Francisco Conservatory of Music gives people the chance to sing Handel's *Messiah*.
- Mid-month: Nutcracker Suite performed by San Francisco Ballet.
- **25: Christmas Day**

# THE AUTHOR

Frances Gendlin has held leadership positions in magazine and book publishing. She was editor and publisher of *Sierra*, the magazine of the Sierra Club, a worldwide environmental organization, and was the association's director of public affairs. As executive director of the Association of American University Presses, she represented the 100-member publishing houses to the public and fostered scholarly publishing interests. In 1997, she wrote *Rome At Your Door* (also published as *Living & Working Abroad: Rome*), a widely read guide to living in that city. In 1998, using the same format, she wrote *Paris At Your Door* (*Living & Working Abroad: Paris*).

While she was growing up, her family moved several times to different areas of the United States, each with its own characteristics and culture, climate, and cuisine. This has led her to appreciate many new cultures, to wonder about their differences and similarities to her own, and to try and understand them. All her life she has enjoyed travel and new adventures, meeting interesting people and making new friends.

After having lived in San Francisco for twenty years, Frances Gendlin now has moved to New York. She owns a freelance editorial business. She evaluates manuscripts and guides, helps writers with their projects, and teaches English and business writing to foreign professionals, both in the United States and abroad. Thanks to the advent of the modem and fax, she can work virtually anywhere in the world. She has thus been able to arrange her professional life to accommodate her love of travel. Currently, she spends part of each year in Rome and Paris.

# INDEX